Office of Government Commerce

Service Operation

London: TSO

Published by TSO (The Stationery Office) and available from:

Online
www.tsoshop.co.uk

Mail, Telephone, Fax & E-mail
TSO
PO Box 29, Norwich, NR3 1GN
Telephone orders/General enquiries: 0870 600 5522
Fax orders: 0870 600 5533
E-mail: customer.services@tso.co.uk
Textphone 0870 240 3701

TSO Shops
123 Kingsway, London, WC2B 6PQ
020 7242 6393 Fax 020 7242 6394
16 Arthur Street, Belfast BT1 4GD
028 9023 8451 Fax 028 9023 5401
71 Lothian Road, Edinburgh EH3 9AZ
0870 606 5566 Fax 0870 606 5588

TSO@Blackwell and other Accredited Agents

Published for the Office of Government Commerce under licence from the Controller of Her Majesty's Stationery Office.

First published 2007

ISBN 978 0 11 331046 3

Printed in the United Kingdom for The Stationery Office

Contents

List of figures

All diagrams in this publication are intended to provide an illustration of ITIL Service Management Practice concepts and guidance. They have been artistically rendered to visually reinforce key concepts and are not intended to meet a formal method or standard of technical drawing. The ITIL Service Management Practices Integrated Service Model conforms to technical drawing standards and should be referred to for complete details. Please see www.best-management-practice.com/itil for details.

List of tables

OGC's foreword

Since its creation, ITIL has grown to become the most widely accepted approach to IT service management in the world. However, along with this success comes the responsibility to ensure that the guidance keeps pace with a changing global business environment. Service management requirements are inevitably shaped by the development of technology, revised business models and increasing customer expectations. Our latest version of ITIL has been created in response to these developments.

This is one of the five core publications describing the IT service management practices that make up ITIL. They are the result of a two-year project to review and update the guidance. The number of service management professionals around the world who have helped to develop the content of these publications is impressive. Their experience and knowledge have contributed to the content to bring you a consistent set of high-quality guidance. This is supported by the ongoing development of a comprehensive qualifications scheme, along with accredited training and consultancy.

Whether you are part of a global company, a government department or a small business, ITIL gives you access to world-class service management expertise. Essentially, it puts IT services where they belong – at the heart of successful business operations.

Peter Fanning

Acting Chief Executive

Office of Government Commerce

Chief Architect's foreword

ITIL Service Management Practice guidance is structured around the Service Lifecycle. Common across the lifecycle is the overall practice itself, which relies on processes, functions, activities, organizational models and measurement, which together allow IT Service Management (ITSM) to integrate with the business processes, provide measurable value and evolve the ITSM industry forward in our pursuit of service excellence.

Nowhere else in the ITIL Service Lifecycle does the effect of how we perform as service providers touch the customers as intimately as Service Operations. This is where the strategy, design, transition and improvements are delivered and supported on a day-to-day basis.

The Service Operation publication brings Service Management to life for the business, and the accountability for the performance of the services, the people who create them and the technology that enables them are monitored, controlled and delivered in this stage of the Service Lifecycle.

This publication will help guide us all to achieve service excellence and to see the value of ITSM in a broad, business-focused view of it. Whether you are new to the practice of ITIL or a seasoned practitioner, the guidance in this publication will expand your vision and knowledge of how to be the best-of-breed service provider through implementation of Service Operation.

There is a saying that hindsight is 20/20. The guidance in *Service Operation* is distilled from over 20 years of experience in ITSM by world experts, business people and ITSM practitioners and the lessons learned by them about what service excellence really is and how to achieve it.

Anyone involved in operating services will benefit from the guidance in the following pages of this publication. *Service Operation* offers the best advice and guidance from around the world and a path to what is possible in your future.

Sharon Taylor

Chief Architect, ITIL Service Management Practices

Preface

This publication encompasses and supersedes the operational aspects of the ITIL Service Support and Service Delivery publications and also covers most of the scope of ICT infrastructure Management. It also incorporates operational aspects from the Planning to Implement, Application Management, Software Asset Management and Security Management publications.

The basic principles of best practice IT service management encompassed within earlier versions of ITIL remain unchanged. Common sense remains common sense!

However, the technologies, tools and relationships have changed significantly, even in the relatively short time since the latest version of ITIL was completed. Whilst this publication re-uses and updates relevant material from the earlier versions where appropriate, it also includes many new concepts and industry practices to give complete coverage of best-practice guidance for today's Service Operation in a single volume, for today's business and technological environment.

Contact information

Full details of the range of material published under the ITIL banner can be found at www.best-management-practice.com/itil

For further information on qualifications and training accreditation, please visit www.itil-officialsite.com. Alternatively, please contact:

APMG Service Desk
Sword House
Totteridge Road
High Wycombe
Buckinghamshire
HP13 6DG

Tel: +44 (0) 1494 452450
E-mail: servicedesk@apmg.co.uk

Acknowledgements

Chief Architect and authors

Sharon Taylor (Aspect Group Inc)	Chief Architect
David Cannon (HP)	Author
David Wheeldon (HP)	Author

ITIL authoring team

The ITIL authoring team contributed to this guide through commenting on content and alignment across the set. So thanks are also due to the other ITIL authors, specifically Jeroen Bronkhorst (HP), Gary Case (Pink Elephant), Ashley Hannah (HP), Majid Iqbal (Carnegie Mellon University), Shirley Lacy (ConnectSphere), Vernon Lloyd (Fox IT), Ivor Macfarlane (Guillemot Rock), Michael Nieves (Accenture), Stuart Rance (HP), Colin Rudd (ITEMS) and George Spalding (Pink Elephant).

Mentors

Christian Nissen and Paul Wilkinson.

Further contributions

A number of people generously contributed their time and expertise to this Service Operation publication. Jim Clinch, as OGC Project Manager, is grateful for the support provided by HP to the authoring team on the development of this publication and particularly the contribution of Peter Doherty and Robert Stroud, and for the support of Jenny Dugmore, Convenor of Working Group ISO/IEC 20000, Janine Eves, Carol Hulm, Aidan Lawes and Michiel van der Voort.

The authors would also like to thank Stuart Rance and Ashley Hanna of Hewlett-Packard, Christian F Nissen (ITILLIGENCE), Maria Vase (Itilligence), Eu Jin Ho (UBS), Jan Bjerregaard, (Sun Microsystems), Jan Øberg (ØBERG Partners), Lars Zobbe Mortensen (Zobbe Consult & Zoftware), Mette Nielsen (Carlsberg IT), Michael Imhoff (IBM), Niels Berner (Novo Nordisk), Nina Schertiger (HP), Signe-Marie Hernes Bjerke (DNV), Steen Sverker Nilsson (Westergaard CSM), Ulf Myrberg (BiTa), Russell Jukes, Debbi Jancaitis, Sheldon Parmer, Ramon Alanis, Tim Benson and Nenen Ong of Hewlett-Packard IT, Jaye Thompson, Dee Seymour, Andranik Ziyalyan, Young Chang, Lauren Abernethy, April McCowan, Becky Wershbale, Rob Garman, Scott McPherson, Sandra Breading, Rick Streeter, Leon Gantt, Charlotte Devine, Greg Algorri, Mary Fischer, Bill Thayer and Diana Osberg of The Walt Disney Company's Enterprise IT, Dennis Deane and John Sowerby of DHL, Richard Fahey and Chris Hughes of HP Global Delivery Application Services, Cindi Locker and Dhiraj Gupta of Progressive Casualty Insurance Company, Peter Doherty and Robert Stroud from Computer Associates and Paul Tillston from Hewlett-Packard, Brian Jakubec, Vernon Blakes, Angela Chin, Colin Lovell, Ken Hamilton, Rose Lariviere, Jenny McPhee, Tom Nielsen, Roc Paez, Lloyd Robinson, Paul Wilmot, Jeanette Smith and Ken Wendle of Hewlett-Packard.

In order to develop ITIL Service Management Practices to reflect current best practice and produce publications of lasting value, OGC consulted widely with different stakeholders throughout the world at every stage in the process. OGC would also like to thank the following individuals and their organisations for their contributions to refreshing the ITIL guidance:

The ITIL Advisory Group

Pippa Bass, OGC; Tony Betts, Independent; Signe-Marie Hernes Bjerke, Det Norske Veritas; Alison Cartlidge, Xansa; Diane Colbeck, DIYmonde Solutions Inc; Ivor Evans, DIYmonde Solutions Inc; Karen Ferris, ProActive; Malcolm Fry, FRY-Consultants; John Gibert, Independent; Colin Hamilton, RENARD Consulting Ltd; Lex Hendriks, EXIN; Carol Hulm, British Computer Society-ISEB; Tony Jenkins, DOMAINetc; Phil Montanaro, EDS; Alan Nance, ITPreneurs; Christian Nissen, Itilligence; Don Page, Marval Group; Bill Powell, IBM; Sergio Rubinato Filho, CA; James Siminoski, SOScorp; Robert E. Stroud, CA; Jan van Bon, Inform-IT; Ken Wendle, HP; Paul Wilkinson, Getronics PinkRoccade; Takashi Yagi, Hitachi.

Reviewers

Jorge Acevedo, Computec S.A; Valerie Arraj, InteQ; Colin Ashcroft, City of London; Martijn Bakker, Getronics PinkRoccade; Jeff Bartrop, BT & Customer Service Direct; John Bennett, Centram Ltd; Niels Berner, Novo Nordisk; Ian Bevan, Fox IT; Signe-Marie Hernes Bjerke, DNV; Jan Bjerregaard, Sun Microsystems; Enrico Boverino, CA; Stephen Bull, Sierra Systems; Bradley Busch, InTotality; Howard Carpenter, IBM; Diane Colbeck, DIYmonde Solutions Inc; Nicole Conboy, Nicole Conboy & Associates; Sharon Dale, aQuip International; Sandra Daly, Dawling Consultancy; Michael Donahue, IBM; Paul Donald, Lucid IT; Juan Antonio Fernandez, Quint Wellington Redrood; Juan

Jose Figueiras, Globant; Rae Garrett, Pink Elephant; Klaus Goedel, HP; Detlef Gross, Automation Consulting Group GmbH; Matthias Hall, University of Dundee; Lex Hendriks, EXIN; Jabe Hickey, IBM; Kevin Hite, Microsoft; Eu Jin Ho, UBS; Michael Imhoff, IBM; Scott Jaegar, Plexant; Tony Jenkins, DOMAINetc; Tony Kelman-Smith, HP; Peter Koepp, Independent; Joanne Kopcho, Capgemini America; Debbie Langenfield, IBM; Sarah Lascelles, Interserve Project Services Ltd; Peter Loos, Accenture Services GmbH; Emmanuel Marchand, Advens; Jesus Martin, Ibermatica SA; Phil Montanaro, EDS; Luis Moran, Independent; Lars Zobbe Mortensen, Zobbe Consult & Zoftware; Ron Morton, HP; Darren Murtagh, Retravision; Ulf Myrberg, BiTa; Mette Nielsen, Carlsberg IT; Steen Sverker Nilsson, Westergaard CSM; Jan Øberg, ØBERG Partners; Eddy Peters, CTG; Poul Mols Poulsen, Coop Norden IT; Bill D Powell, IBM; Roger Purdie, The Art of Service; Padmini Ramamurthy, Satyam Computer Services Ltd; Frances Scarff, OGC; Nina Schertiger, HP; Markus Schiemer, Unisys; Barbara Schiesser, Swiss ICT; Klaus Seidel, Microsoft; Gilbert Silva, Techbiz Informatica Ltd; Joseph Stephen, Department of Transportation, US Government; Michala Sterling, Mid Sussex District Council; Rohan Thuraisingham, Friends Provident Management Services Ltd; Matthew Tolman, Sandvik; Jan van Bon, Inform-IT; Maria Vase, ITILLIGENCE; Christoph Wettstein, CLAVIS klw AG; Andi Wijaya, IBM; Aaron Wolfe, Pink Elephant; Takashi Yagi, Hitachi; YoungHoon Youn, IBM.

Introduction

1

1 Introduction

This publication provides best-practice advice and guidance on all aspects of managing the day-to-day operation of an organization's information technology (IT) services. It covers issues relating to the people, processes, infrastructure technology and relationships necessary to ensure the high-quality, cost-effective provision of IT service necessary to meet business needs.

The advent of new technology and the now blurred lines between the traditional technology silos of hardware, networks, telephony and software applications management mean that an updated approach to managing service operations is needed. Organizations are increasingly likely to consider different ways of providing their IT at optimum cost and flexibility, with the introduction of utility IT, pay-per-use IT Services, virtual IT provision, dynamic capacity and Adaptive Enterprise computing, as well as task-sourcing and outsourcing options.

These alternatives have led to a myriad of IT business relationships, both internally and externally, that have increased in complexity as much as the technologies being managed have. Business dependency on these complex relationships is increasingly critical to survival and prosperity.

1.1 OVERVIEW

Service Operation is the phase in the ITSM Lifecycle that is responsible for 'business-as-usual' activities.

Service Operation can be viewed as the 'factory' of IT. This implies a closer focus on the day-to-day activities and infrastructure that are used to deliver services. However, this publication is based on the understanding that the overriding purpose of Service Operation is to deliver and support services. Management of the infrastructure and the operational activities must always support this purpose.

Well planned and implemented processes will be to no avail if the day-to-day operation of those processes is not properly conducted, controlled and managed. Nor will service improvements be possible if day-to-day activities to monitor performance, assess metrics and gather data are not systematically conducted during Service Operation.

Service Operation staff should have in place processes and support tools to allow them to have an overall view of Service Operation and delivery (rather than just the separate components, such as hardware, software applications and networks, that make up the end-to-end service from a business perspective) and to detect any threats or failures to service quality.

As services may be provided, in whole or in part, by one or more partner/supplier organizations, the Service Operation view of end-to-end service must be extended to encompass external aspects of service provision – and where necessary shared or interfacing processes and tools are needed to manage cross-organizational workflows.

Service Operation is neither an organizational unit nor a single process – but it does include several functions and many processes and activities, which are described in Chapters 4, 5 and 6.

1.2 CONTEXT

1.2.1 Service Management

IT is a commonly used term that changes meaning with context. From the first perspective, IT systems, applications and infrastructure are components or sub-assemblies of a larger product. They enable or are embedded in processes and services. From the second perspective, IT is an organization with its own set of capabilities and resources. IT organizations can be of various types such as business functions, shared services units and enterprise-level core units.

From the third perspective, IT is a category of services utilized by business. They are typically IT applications and infrastructure that are packaged and offered as services by internal IT organizations or external service providers. IT costs are treated as business expenses. From the fourth perspective, IT is a category of business assets that provide a stream of benefits for their owners, including, but not limited to, revenue, income and profit. IT costs are treated as investments.

1.2.2 Good practice in the public domain

Organizations operate in dynamic environments with the need to learn and adapt. There is a need to improve performance while managing trade-offs. Under similar pressure, customers seek advantage from service providers. They pursue sourcing strategies that best serve their own business interest. In many countries, government agencies and non-profit-making enterprises have a similar propensity to outsource for the sake of

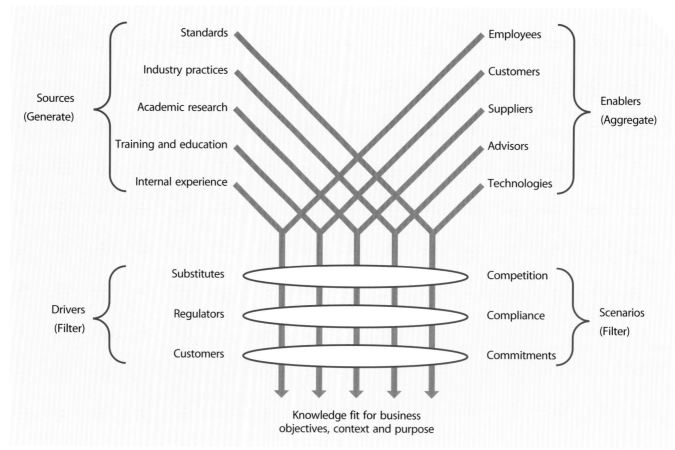

Figure 1.1 Source of Service Management Practice

operational effectiveness. This puts additional pressure on service providers to maintain a competitive advantage with regard to the alternatives that customers may have. The increase in outsourcing has particularly exposed internal service providers to unusual competition.

To cope with the pressure, organizations benchmark themselves against peers and seek to close gaps in capabilities. One way to close such gaps is the adoption of good practices across the industry. There are several sources for good practices, including public frameworks, standards and the proprietary knowledge of organizations and individuals (see Figure 1.1).

Public frameworks and standards are attractive when compared with proprietary knowledge:

■ Proprietary knowledge is deeply embedded in organizations and therefore difficult to adopt, replicate or transfer, even with the cooperation of the owners. Such knowledge is often in the form of tacit knowledge which is inextricable and poorly documented.

■ Proprietary knowledge is customized for the local context and specific business needs, to the point of being idiosyncratic. Unless the recipients of such

knowledge have matching circumstances, the knowledge may not be as effective in use.

■ Owners of proprietary knowledge expect to be rewarded for their long-term investments. They may make such knowledge available only under commercial terms, through purchases and licensing agreements.

■ Publicly available frameworks and standards such as ITIL, Control Objectives for IT (COBIT), CMMI, eSCM-SP, PRINCE2, ISO 9000, ISO 20000 and ISO 27001 are validated across a diverse set of environments and situations rather than the limited experience of a single organization. They are subject to broad review across multiple organizations and disciplines. They are vetted by diverse sets of partners, suppliers and competitors.

■ The knowledge of public frameworks is more likely to be widely distributed among a large community of professionals through publicly available training and certification. It is easier for organizations to acquire such knowledge through the labour market.

Ignoring public frameworks and standards can needlessly place an organization at a disadvantage. Organizations should cultivate their own proprietary knowledge on top

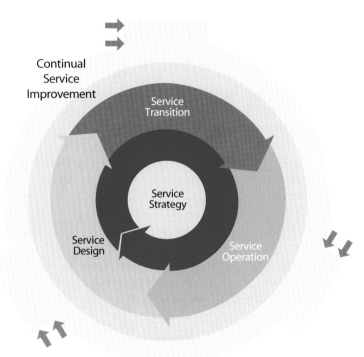

Figure 1.2 ITIL Core

of a body of knowledge based on public frameworks and standards. Collaboration and coordination across organizations are easier on the basis of shared practices and standards.

1.2.3 ITIL and good practice in Service Management

The context of this publication is the ITIL Framework as a source of good practice in Service Management. ITIL is used by organizations worldwide to establish and improve capabilities in Service Management. ISO/IEC 20000 provides a formal and universal standard for organizations seeking to have their Service Management capabilities audited and certified. While ISO/IEC 20000 is a standard to be achieved and maintained, ITIL offers a body of knowledge useful for achieving the standard.

The ITIL Library has the following components:

- **ITIL Core**: best-practice guidance applicable to all types of organizations that provide services to a business
- **ITIL Complementary Guidance**: a complementary set of publications with guidance specific to industry sectors, organization types, operating models and technology architectures.

The ITIL Core consists of five publications (see Figure 1.2). Each provides the guidance necessary for an integrated approach as required by the ISO/IEC 20000 standard specification:

- Service Strategy
- Service Design
- Service Transition
- Service Operation
- Continual Service Improvement.

Each publication addresses capabilities having direct impact on a service provider's performance. The structure of the core is in the form of a lifecycle. It is iterative and multidimensional. It ensures that organizations are set up to leverage capabilities in one area for learning and improvements in others. The Core is expected to provide structure, stability and strength to Service Management capabilities, with durable principles, methods and tools. This serves to protect investments and provide the necessary basis for measurement, learning and improvement.

The guidance in ITIL can be adapted for changes of use in various business environments and organizational strategies. The Complementary Guidance provides flexibility to implement the Core in a diverse range of environments. Practitioners can select Complementary Guidance as needed to provide traction for the Core in a given business context, much as tyres are selected based on the type of automobile, purpose and road conditions. This is to increase the durability and portability of knowledge assets and to protect investments in Service Management capabilities.

1.2.3.1 Service Strategy

The Service Strategy volume provides guidance on how to design, develop and implement Service Management, not only as an organizational capability but also as a strategic asset. Guidance is provided on the principles underpinning the practice of Service Management which are useful for developing Service Management policies, guidelines and processes across the ITIL Service Lifecycle. Service Strategy guidance is useful in the context of Service Design, Service Transition, Service Operation and Continual Service Improvement. Topics covered in Service Strategy include the development of markets, internal and external, service assets, service catalogue and implementation of strategy through the Service Lifecycle. Financial Management, Service Portfolio Management, Organizational Development and Strategic Risks are among other major topics.

Organizations use the guidance to set objectives and expectations of performance towards serving customers and market spaces and to identify, select and prioritize opportunities. Service Strategy is about ensuring that organizations are in a position to handle the costs and risks associated with their service portfolios and are set up not just for operational effectiveness but for distinctive performance. Decisions made with regard to Service Strategy have far-reaching consequences, including those with delayed effect.

Organizations already practising ITIL use this volume to guide a strategic review of their ITIL-based Service Management capabilities and to improve the alignment between those capabilities and their business strategies. This volume of ITIL encourages readers to stop and think about why something is to be done before thinking of how. Answers to the first type of questions are closer to the customer's business. Service Strategy expands the scope of the ITIL Framework beyond the traditional audience of ITSM professionals.

1.2.3.2 Service Design

The Service Design volume provides guidance for the design and development of services and service management processes. It covers design principles and methods for converting strategic objectives into portfolios of services and service assets. The scope of Service Design is not limited to new services. It includes the changes and improvements necessary to increase or maintain value to customers over the lifecycle of services, the continuity of services, achievement of service levels and conformance to standards and regulations. It guides organizations on how to develop design capabilities for Service Management.

1.2.3.3 Service Transition

The Service Transition volume provides guidance for the development and improvement of capabilities for transitioning new and changed services into operations. This publication provides guidance on how the requirements of Service Strategy encoded in Service Design are effectively realized in Service Operations while controlling the risks of failure and disruption. The publication combines practices in Release Management, Programme Management and Risk Management and places them in the practical context of Service Management. It provides guidance on managing the complexity related to changes to services and Service Management processes, preventing undesired consequences while allowing for innovation. Guidance is provided on transferring the control of services between customers and service providers.

1.2.3.4 Service Operation

This volume embodies practices in the management of Service Operations. It includes guidance on achieving effectiveness and efficiency in the delivery and support of services so as to ensure value for the customer and the service provider. Strategic objectives are ultimately realized through Service Operations, therefore making it a critical capability. Guidance is provided on how to maintain stability in Service Operations, allowing for changes in design, scale, scope and service levels. Organizations are provided with detailed process guidelines, methods and tools for use in two major control perspectives: reactive and proactive. Managers and practitioners are provided with knowledge allowing them to make better decisions in areas such as managing the availability of services, controlling demand, optimizing capacity utilization, scheduling of operations and fixing problems. Guidance is provided on supporting operations through new models and architectures such as shared services, utility computing, web services and mobile commerce.

1.2.3.5 Continual Service Improvement

This volume provides instrumental guidance in creating and maintaining value for customers through better design, introduction and operation of services. It combines principles, practices and methods from Quality Management, Change Management and Capability Improvement. Organizations learn to realize incremental and large-scale improvements in service quality, operational efficiency and business continuity. Guidance is provided for linking improvement efforts and outcomes with Service Strategy, Service Design and Service Transition. A closed-loop feedback system, based on the

Plan, Do, Check, Act (PDCA) model specified in ISO/IEC 20000, is established and capable of receiving inputs for change from any planning perspective.

The day-to-day operational management of IT Services is significantly influenced by how well an organization's overall IT service strategy has been defined and how well the ITSM processes have been planned and implemented. This is the fourth publication in the ITIL Service Management Practices series and the other publications on Service Strategy, Service Design and Service Transition should be consulted for best practice guidance on these important stages prior to Service Operation.

Service Operation is extremely important, as it is on a day-to-day operational basis that events occur which can adversely impact service quality. The way in which an organization's IT infrastructure and its supporting ITSM processes are operated will have the most direct and immediate short-term bearing upon service quality.

1.3 PURPOSE

Service Operation is a critical phase of the ITSM lifecycle. Well-planned and well-implemented processes will be to no avail if the day-to-day operation of those processes is not properly conducted, controlled and managed. Nor will service improvements be possible if day-to-day activities to monitor performance, assess metrics and gather data are not systematically conducted during Service Operation.

Service Operation staff should have in place processes and support tools to allow them to have an overall view of Service Operation and delivery (rather than just the separate components, such as hardware, software applications and networks, that make up the end-to-end service from a business perspective) and to detect any threats or failures to service quality.

As services may be provided, in whole or in part, by one or more partner/supplier organizations, the Service Operation view of end-to-end service must be extended to encompass external aspects of service provision – and where necessary shared or interfacing processes and tools are needed to manage cross-organizational workflows.

1.4 USAGE

This publication should be used in conjunction with the other four publications that make up the ITIL Service Lifecycle.

Readers should be aware that the best-practice guidelines in this and other volumes are not intended to be prescriptive. Each organization is unique and must 'adapt

and adopt' the guidance for its own specific needs, environment and culture. This will involve taking into account the organization's size, skills/resources, culture, funding, priorities and existing ITSM maturity and modifying the guidance as appropriate to suit the organization's needs.

For organizations finding ITIL for the first time, some form of initial assessment to compare the organization's current processes and practices with those recommended by ITIL would be a very valuable starting point. These assessments are described in more detail in the ITIL Continual Service Improvement publication.

Where significant gaps exist, it may be necessary to address them in stages over a period of time to meet the organization's business priorities and keep pace with what the organization is able to absorb and afford.

1.5 CHAPTER OVERVIEW

Chapter 2 introduces the concept of Service Management as a practice. Here, Service Management is positioned as a strategic and professional component of any organization. This chapter also provides an overview of Service Operation as a critical component of the Service Management Practice.

The key principles of Service Operation are covered in Chapter 3 of this publication. These principles outline some of the basic concepts and principles on which the rest of the publication is based.

Chapter 4 covers the processes performed within Service Operation – most of the Service Operation processes are reactive because of the nature of the work being performed to maintain IT services in a robust, stable condition. This chapter also covers proactive processes to emphasize that the aim of Service Operation is stability – but not stagnation. Service Operation should be constantly looking at ways of doing things better and more cost-effectively, and the proactive processes have an important role to play here.

Chapter 5 covers a number of Common Service Operation activities, which are groups of activities and procedures performed by Service Operation Functions. These specialized, and often technical, activities are not processes in the true sense of the word, but they are all vital for the ability to deliver quality IT services at optimal cost.

Chapter 6 covers the organizational aspects of Service Operation – the individuals or groups who carry out Service Operation processes or activities – and includes some guidance on Service Operation organization structures.

Chapter 7 describes the tools and technology that are used during Service Operation.

Chapter 8 covers some aspects of implementation that will need to be considered before the operational phase of the lifecycle becomes active.

Chapter 9 highlights the challenges, Critical Success Factors and risks faced during Service Operation, while the Afterword summarizes and concludes the publication.

ITIL does not stand alone in providing guidance to IT managers and the appendices outline some of the key supplementary frameworks, methodologies and approaches that are commonly used in conjunction with ITIL during Service Operation.

Service Management as a practice

2 Service Management as a practice

2.1 WHAT IS SERVICE MANAGEMENT?

Service Management is a set of specialized organizational capabilities for providing value to customers in the form of services. The capabilities take the form of functions and processes for managing services over a lifecycle, with specializations in strategy, design, transition, operation and continual improvement. The capabilities represent a service organization's capacity, competency and confidence for action. The act of transforming resources into valuable services is at the core of Service Management. Without these capabilities, a service organization is merely a bundle of resources that by itself has relatively low intrinsic value for customers.

> **Definition of Service Management**
>
> Service Management is a set of specialized organizational capabilities for providing value to customers in the form of services.

Organizational capabilities are shaped by the challenges they are expected to overcome. An example of this is how in the 1950s Toyota developed unique capabilities to overcome the challenge of smaller scale and financial capital compared to its American rivals. Toyota developed new capabilities in production engineering, operations management and managing suppliers to compensate for its inability to afford large inventories, make components, produce raw materials or own the companies that produced them. [Source: Magretta, Joan 2002. *What Management Is: How it works and why it's everyone's business*. The Free Press.] Service Management capabilities are similarly influenced by the following challenges that distinguish services from other systems of value-creation, such as manufacturing, mining and agriculture:

- Intangible nature of the output and intermediate products of service processes: Difficult to measure, control and validate (or prove).
- Demand is tightly coupled with the customer's assets: Users and other customer assets such as processes, applications, documents and transactions arrive with demand and stimulate service production.
- High level of contact for producers and consumers of services: Little or no buffer between the customer, the front-office and the back-office.

- The perishable nature of service output and service capacity: There is value for the customer from assurance on the continued supply of consistent quality. Providers need to secure a steady supply of demand from customers.

However, Service Management is more than just a set of capabilities. It is also a professional practice supported by an extensive body of knowledge, experience and skills. A global community of individuals and organizations in the public and private sectors fosters its growth and maturity. Formal schemes exist for the education, training and certification of practising organizations and individuals influence its quality. Industry best practices, academic research and formal standards contribute to its intellectual capital and draw from it.

The origins of Service Management are in traditional service businesses such as airlines, banks, hotels and phone companies. Its practice has grown with the adoption by IT organizations of a service-oriented approach to managing IT applications, infrastructure and processes. Solutions to business problems and support for business models, strategies and operations are increasingly in the form of services. The popularity of shared services and outsourcing has contributed to the increase in the number of organizations that are service providers, including internal organizational units. This in turn has strengthened the practice of Service Management and at the same time imposed greater challenges upon it.

2.2 WHAT ARE SERVICES?

2.2.1 The value proposition

> **Definition of service**
>
> A service is a means of delivering value to customers by facilitating outcomes customers want to achieve, without the ownership of specific costs and risks.

Services are a means of delivering value to customers by facilitating outcomes customers want to achieve, without the ownership of specific costs and risks. Services facilitate outcomes by enhancing the performance of associated tasks and reducing the effect of constraints. The result is an increase in the probability of desired outcomes.

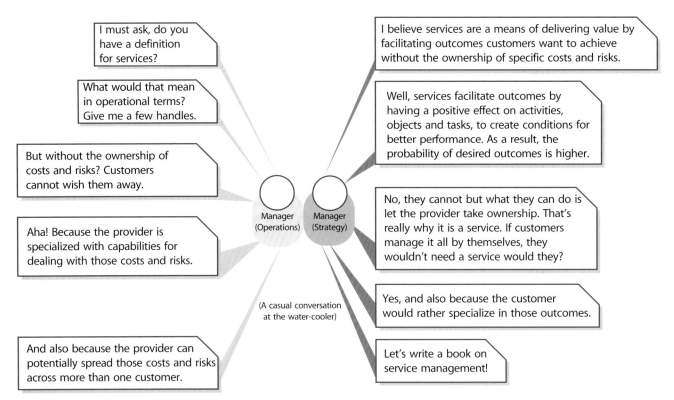

Figure 2.1 A conversation about the definition and meaning of services

2.3 FUNCTIONS AND PROCESSES ACROSS THE LIFECYCLE

2.3.1 Functions

Functions are units of organizations specialized to perform certain types of work and responsible for specific outcomes. They are self-contained, with capabilities and resources necessary for their performance and outcomes. Capabilities include work methods internal to the functions. Functions have their own body of knowledge, which accumulates from experience. They provide structure and stability to organizations.

Functions are a means of structuring organizations so as to implement the specialization principle. Functions typically define roles and the associated authority and responsibility for a specific performance and outcomes. Coordination between functions through shared processes is a common pattern in organization design. Functions tend to optimize their work methods locally, to focus on assigned outcomes. Poor coordination between functions, combined with an inward focus, leads to functional silos that hinder alignment and feedback critical to the success of the organization as a whole. Process models help avoid this problem with functional hierarchies by improving cross-functional coordination and control. Well-defined processes can improve productivity within and across functions.

2.3.2 Processes

Processes are examples of closed-loop systems because they provide change and transformation towards a goal and utilize feedback for self-reinforcing and self-corrective action (see Figure 2.2). It is important to consider the entire process or how one process fits into another.

Process definitions describe actions, dependencies and sequence. Processes have the following characteristics:

- **Measurable**: We are able to measure the process in a relevant manner. It is performance driven. Managers want to measure cost, quality and other variables, while practitioners are concerned with duration and productivity.
- **Specific results**: The reason a process exists is to deliver a specific result. This result must be individually identifiable and countable. While we can count changes, it is impossible to count how many Service Desks were completed.
- **Customers**: Every process delivers its primary results to a customer or stakeholder. They may be internal or external to the organization but the process must meet their expectations.
- **Responds to a specific event**: While a process may be ongoing or iterative, it should be traceable to a specific trigger.

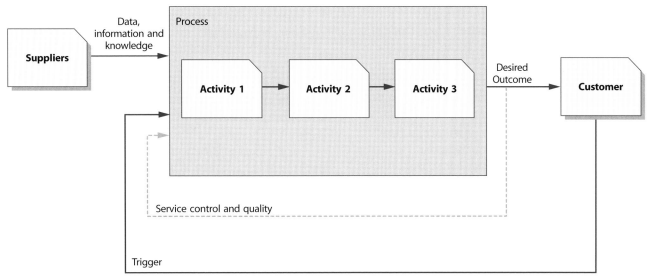

Figure 2.2 A basic process

Functions are often mistaken for processes. For example, there are misconceptions about Capacity Management being a Service Management process. First, Capacity Management is an organizational capability with specialized processes and work methods. Whether it is a function or a process depends entirely on organization design. It is a mistake to assume that Capacity Management can only be a process. It is possible to measure and control capacity and to determine whether it is adequate for a given purpose. Assuming that it is always a process, with discrete countable outcomes, can be an error.

2.3.3 Specialization and coordination across the lifecycle

Specialization and coordination are necessary in the lifecycle approach. Feedback and control between the functions and processes within and across the elements of the lifecycle make this possible. The dominant pattern in the lifecycle is the sequential progress starting from SS through SD-ST-SO and back to SS through CSI. However, that is not the only pattern of action. Every element of the lifecycle provides points for feedback and control.

The combination of multiple perspectives allows greater flexibility and control across environments and situations. The lifecycle approach mimics the reality of most organizations where effective management requires the use of multiple control perspectives. Those responsible for the design, development and improvement of processes for Service Management can adopt a process-based control perspective. Those responsible for managing agreements, contracts and services may be better served by a lifecycle-based control perspective with distinct phases. Both these control perspectives benefit from

systems thinking. Each control perspective can reveal patterns that may not be apparent from the other.

2.4 SERVICE OPERATION FUNDAMENTALS

2.4.1 Purpose/goal/objective

The purpose of Service Operation is to coordinate and carry out the activities and processes required to deliver and manage services at agreed levels to business users and customers. Service Operation is also responsible for the ongoing management of the technology that is used to deliver and support services.

Well-designed and well-implemented processes will be of little value if the day-to-day operation of those processes is not properly conducted, controlled and managed. Nor will service improvements be possible if day-to-day activities to monitor performance, assess metrics and gather data are not systematically conducted during Service Operation.

2.4.2 Scope

Service Operation includes the execution of all ongoing activities required to deliver and support services. The scope of Service Operation includes:

- **The services themselves**. Any activity that forms part of a service is included in Service Operation, whether it is performed by the Service Provider, an external supplier or the user or customer of that service
- **Service Management processes**. The ongoing management and execution of many Service Management processes are performed in Service Operation, even though a number of ITIL processes

(such as Change and Capacity Management) originate at the Service Design or Service Transition stage of the Service Lifecycle, they are in use continually in Service Operation. Some processes are not included specifically in Service Operation, such as Strategy Definition, the actual design process itself. These processes focus more on longer-term planning and improvement activities, which are outside the direct scope of Service Operation; however, Service Operation provides input and influences these regularly as part of the lifecycle of Service Management.

- **Technology**. All services require some form of technology to deliver them. Managing this technology is not a separate issue, but an integral part of the management of the services themselves. Therefore a large part of this publication is concerned with the management of the infrastructure used to deliver services.

- **People**. Regardless of what services, processes and technology are managed, they are all about people. It is people who drive the demand for the organization's services and products and it is people who decide how this will be done. Ultimately, it is people who manage the technology, processes and services. Failure to recognize this will result (and has resulted) in the failure of Service Management projects

2.4.3 Value to business

Each stage in the ITIL Service Lifecycle provides value to business. For example, service value is modelled in Service Strategy; the cost of the service is designed, predicted and validated in Service Design and Service Transition; and measures for optimization are identified in Continual Service Improvement. The operation of service is where these plans, designs and optimizations are executed and measured. From a customer viewpoint, Service Operation is where actual value is seen.

There is a down side to this, though:

- Once a service has been designed and tested, it is expected to run within the budgetary and Return on Investment targets established earlier in the lifecycle. In reality, however, very few organizations plan effectively for the costs of ongoing management of services. It is very easy to quantify the costs of a project, but very difficult to quantify what the service will cost after three years of operation.

- It is difficult to obtain funding during the operational phase, to fix design flaws or unforeseen requirements – since this was not part of the original value proposition. In many cases it is only after some time in operation that these problems surface. Most organizations do not have a formal mechanism to review operational services for design and value. This is left to Incident and Problem Management to resolve – as if it is purely an operational issue.

- It is difficult to obtain additional funding for tools or actions (including training) aimed at improving the efficiency of Service Operation. This is partly because they are not directly linked to the functionality of a specific service and partly because there is an expectation from the customer that these costs should have been built into the cost of the service from the beginning. Unfortunately, the rate of technology change is very high. Shortly after a solution has been deployed that will efficiently manage a set of services, new technology becomes available that can do it faster, cheaper and more effectively.

- Once a service has been operational for some time, it becomes part of the baseline of what the business expects from the IT services. Attempts to optimize the service or to use new tools to manage it more effectively are seen as successful only if the service has been very problematic in the past. In other words, some services are taken for granted and any action to optimize them is perceived as 'fixing services that are not broken'.

This publication suggests a number of processes, functions and measures which are aimed at addressing these areas.

2.4.4 Optimizing Service Operation performance

Service Operation is optimized in two ways:

- **Long-term incremental improvement**. This is based on evaluating the performance and output of all Service Operation processes, functions and outputs over time. The reports are analysed and a decision made about whether improvement is needed and, if so, how best to implement it through Service Design and Transition. Examples include the deployment of a new set of tools, changes to process designs, reconfiguration of the infrastructure, etc. This type of improvement is covered in detail in the Continual Service Improvement publication.

■ **Short-term ongoing improvement** of working practices within the Service Operation processes, functions and technology itself. These are generally smaller improvements that are implemented without any change to the fundamental nature of a process or technology. Examples include tuning, workload balancing, personnel redeployment and training, etc.

Although both of these are discussed in some detail within the scope of Service Operation, the Continual Service Improvement publication will provide a framework and alternatives within which improvement may be driven as part of the overall support of business objectives.

2.4.5 Processes within Service Operation

There are a number of key Service Operation processes that must link together to provide an effective overall IT support structure. The overall structure is briefly described here and then each of the processes is described in more detail in Chapter 4.

2.4.5.1 Event Management

Event Management monitors all events that occur throughout the IT infrastructure, to monitor normal operation and to detect and escalate exception conditions.

2.4.5.2 Incident and Problem Management

Incident Management concentrates on restoring unexpectedly degraded or disrupted services to users as quickly as possible, in order to minimize business impact.

Problem Management involves: root-cause analysis to determine and resolve the cause of incidents, proactive activities to detect and prevent future problems/incidents and a Known Error sub-process to allow quicker diagnosis and resolution if further incidents do occur.

2.4.5.3 Request Fulfilment

Request Fulfilment is the process for dealing with Service Requests – many of them actually smaller, lower-risk, changes – initially via the Service Desk, but using a separate process similar to that of Incident Management but with separate Request Fulfilment records/tables – where necessary linked to the Incident or Problem Record(s) that initiated the need for the request. To be a Service Request, it is normal for some prerequisites to be defined and met (e.g. needs to be proven, repeatable, pre-approved, proceduralized).

In order to resolve one or more incidents, problems or Known Errors, some form of change may be necessary. Smaller, often standard, changes can be handled through a Request Fulfilment process, but larger, higher-risk or infrequent changes must go through a formal Change Management process.

2.4.5.4 Access Management

Access Management is the process of granting authorized users the right to use a service, while restricting access to non-authorized users. It is based on being able accurately to identify authorized users and then manage their ability to access services as required during different stages of their Human Resources (HR) or contractual lifecycle. Access Management has also been called Identity or Rights Management in some organizations.

2.4.6 Functions within Service Operation

Processes alone will not result in effective Service Operation. A stable infrastructure and appropriately skilled people are needed as well. To achieve this, Service Operation relies on several groups of skilled people, all focused on using processes to match the capability of the infrastructure to the needs of the business.

These groups fall into four main functions, listed here and discussed in detail in Chapter 6.

2.4.6.1 Service Desk

The Service Desk is the primary point of contact for users when there is a service disruption, for Service Requests, or even for some categories of Request for Change. The Service Desk provides a point of communication to the users and a point of coordination for several IT groups and processes

2.4.6.2 Technical Management

Technical Management provides detailed technical skills and resources needed to support the ongoing operation of the IT Infrastructure. Technical Management also plays an important role in the design, testing, release and improvement of IT services. In small organizations, it is possible to manage this expertise in a single department, but larger organizations are typically split into a number of technically specialized departments.

2.4.6.3 IT Operations Management

IT Operations Management executes the daily operational activities needed to manage the IT Infrastructure. This is done according to the Performance Standards defined during Service Design. In some organizations this is a single, centralized department, while in others some activities and staff are centralized and some are provided by distributed or specialized departments. IT Operations Management has two functions that are unique and are generally formal organizational structures. These are:

■ IT Operations Control, which is generally staffed by shifts of operators and which ensures that routine operational tasks are carried out. IT Operations Control will also provide centralized monitoring and control activities, usually using an Operations Bridge or Network Operations Centre.

■ Facilities Management refers to the management of the physical IT environment, usually data centres or computer rooms. In many organizations Technical and Application Management are co-located with IT Operations in large data centres.

2.4.6.4 Application Management

Application Management is responsible for managing Applications throughout their lifecycle. The Application Management function supports and maintains operational applications and also plays an important role in the design, testing and improvement of applications that form part of IT services. Application Management is usually divided into departments based on the application portfolio of the organization, thus allowing easier specialization and more focused support.

2.4.6.5 Interfaces to other Service Management Lifecycle stages

There are several other processes that will be executed or supported during Service Operation, but which are driven during other phases of the Service Management Lifecycle. These will be discussed in the final part of Chapter 4 and include:

■ Change Management, which is a major process that should be closely linked to Configuration Management and Release Management. These topics are primarily covered in the Service Transition publication.

■ Capacity and Availability Management, which are covered in the Service Design publication.

■ Financial Management, which is covered in the Service Strategy publication.

■ Knowledge Management, which is covered in the Service Transition publication.

■ IT Service Continuity, which is covered in the Service Design publication.

■ Service Reporting and Measurement, which are covered in the Continual Service Improvement publication.

Service Operation
principles

3   Service Operation principles

When considering Service Operation it is tempting to focus only on managing day-to-day activities and technology as ends in themselves. However, Service Operation exists within a far greater context. As part of the Service Management Lifecycle, it is responsible for executing and performing processes that optimize the cost and quality of services. As part of the organization, it is responsible for enabling the business to meet its objectives. As part of the world of technology, it is responsible for the effective functioning of components that support services. The principles in this chapter are aimed at helping Service Operation practitioners to achieve a balance between all of these roles and to focus on effectively managing the day-to-day aspects while maintaining a perspective of the greater context.

3.1   FUNCTIONS, GROUPS, TEAMS, DEPARTMENTS AND DIVISIONS

The Service Operation publication uses several terms to refer to the way in which people are organized to execute processes or activities. There are several published definitions for each term and it is not the purpose of this publication to enter the debate about which definition is best. Please note that the following definitions are generic and not prescriptive. They are provided simply to define assumptions and to facilitate understanding of the material. The reader should adapt these principles to the organizational practices used in their own organization.

- **Function**: A function is a logical concept that refers to the people and automated measures that execute a defined process, an activity or a combination of processes or activities. In larger organizations, a function may be broken out and performed by several departments, teams and groups, or it may be embodied within a single organizational unit (e.g. Service Desk). In smaller organizations, one person or group can perform multiple functions – e.g. a Technical Management department could also incorporate the Service Desk function.
- **Group**: A group is a number of people who are similar in some way. In this publication, groups refer to people who perform similar activities – even though they may work on different technology or report into different organizational structures or even in different companies. Groups are usually not formal organization structures, but are very useful in defining common

processes across the organization – e.g. ensuring that all people who resolve incidents complete the Incident Record in the same way. In this publication the term 'group' does not refer to a group of companies that are owned by the same entity.
- **Team**: A team is a more formal type of group. These are people who work together to achieve a common objective, but not necessarily in the same organization structure. Team members can be co-located, or work in multiple different locations and operate virtually. Teams are useful for collaboration, or for dealing with a situation of a temporary or transitional nature. Examples of teams include project teams, application development teams (often consisting of people from several different business units) and incident or problem resolution teams.
- **Department**: Departments are formal organization structures which exist to perform a specific set of defined activities on an ongoing basis. Departments have a hierarchical reporting structure with managers who are usually responsible for the execution of the activities and also for day-to-day management of the staff in the department.
- **Division**: A division refers to a number of departments that have been grouped together, often by geography or product line. A division is normally self-contained and is able to plan and execute all activities in a supply chain.
- **Role**: A role refers to a set of connected behaviours or actions that are performed by a person, team or group in a specific context. For example, a Technical Management department can perform the role of Problem Management when diagnosing the root cause of incidents. This same department could also be expected to play several other roles at different times, e.g. it may assess the impact of changes (Change Management role), manage the performance of devices under their control (Capacity Management role), etc. The scope of their role and what triggers them to play that role are defined by the relevant process and agreed by their line manager.

3.2   ACHIEVING BALANCE IN SERVICE OPERATION

Service Operation is more than just the repetitive execution of a standard set of procedures or activities. All functions, processes and activities are designed to deliver a specified and agreed level of services, but they have to be delivered in an ever-changing environment.

This forms a conflict between maintaining the status quo and adapting to changes in the business and technological environments. One of Service Operation's key roles is therefore to deal with this conflict and to achieve a balance between conflicting sets of priorities.

This section of the publication highlights some of the key tensions and conflicts and identifies how IT organizations can recognize that they are suffering from an imbalance by tending more towards one extreme or the other. It also provides some high-level guidelines on how to resolve the conflict and thus move towards a best-practice approach. Every conflict therefore represents an opportunity for growth and improvement.

3.2.1 Internal IT view versus external business view

The most fundamental conflict in all phases of the ITSM Lifecycle is between the view of IT as a set of IT services (the external business view) and the view of IT as a set of technology components (internal IT view).

- The external view of IT is the way in which services are experienced by its users and customers. They do not always understand, nor do they care about, the details of what technology is used to manage those services. All they are concerned about is that the services are delivered as required and agreed.
- The internal view of IT is the way in which IT components and systems are managed to deliver the services. Since IT systems are complex and diverse, this often means that the technology is managed by several different teams or departments – each of which is focused on achieving good performance and availability of 'its' systems.

Both views are necessary when delivering services. The organization that focuses only on business requirements without thinking about how they are going to deliver will end up making promises that cannot be kept. The organization that focuses only on internal systems without thinking about what services they support will end up with expensive services that deliver little value.

The potential for role conflict between the external and internal views is the result of many variables, including the maturity of the organization, its management culture, its history, etc. This makes a balance difficult to achieve, and most organizations tend more towards one role than the other. Of course, no organization will be totally internally or externally focused, but will find itself in a position along a spectrum between the two. This is illustrated in Figure 3.1:

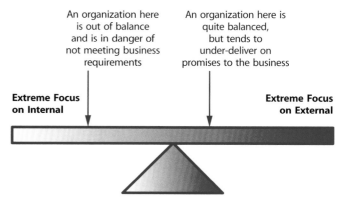

Figure 3.1 Achieving a balance between external and internal focus

Table 3.1 outlines some examples of the characteristics of positions at the extreme ends of the spectrum. The purpose of this table is to assist organizations in identifying to which extreme they are closer, not to identify real-life positions to which organizations should aspire.

Table 3.1 Examples of extreme internal and external focus

	Extreme internal focus	Extreme external focus
Primary focus	Performance and management of IT Infrastructure devices, systems and staff, with little regard to the end result on the IT service	Achieving high levels of IT service performance with little regard to how it is achieved
Metrics	■ Focus on technical performance without showing what this means for services ■ Internal metrics (e.g. network uptime) reported to the business instead of service performance metrics.	■ Focus on External Metrics without showing internal staff how these are derived or how they can be improved ■ Internal staff are expected to devise their own metrics to measure internal performance.
Customer/user experience	■ High consistency of delivery, but only delivers a percentage of what the business needs. ■ Uses a 'push' approach to delivery, i.e. prefers to have a standard set of services for all business units.	■ Poor consistency of delivery ■ 'IT consists of good people with good intentions, but cannot always execute' ■ Reactive mode of operation. ■ Uses a 'pull' approach to delivery, i.e. prefers to deliver customized services upon request
Operations strategy	■ Standard operations across the board ■ All new services need to fit into the current architecture and procedures.	■ Multiple delivery teams and multiple technologies ■ New technologies require new operations approaches and often new IT Operations teams.
Procedures and manual	Focus purely on how to manage the technology, not on how its performance relates to IT services	Focuses primarily on what needs to be done and when and less on how this should be achieved
Cost strategy	■ Cost reduction achieved purely through technology consolidation ■ Optimization of operational procedures and resources ■ Business impact of cost cutting often only understood later ■ Return on Investment calculations are focused purely on cost savings or 'payback periods'.	■ Budget allocated on the basis of which business unit is perceived to have the most need ■ Less articulate or vocal business units often have inferior services as there is not enough funding allocated to their services.
Training	Training is conducted as an apprenticeship, where new Operations staff have to learn the way things have to be done, not why	■ Training is conducted on a project-by-project basis ■ There are no standard training courses since operational procedures and technology are constantly changing.
Operations staff	■ Specialized staff, organized according to technical specialty ■ Staff work on the false assumption that good technical achievement is the same as good customer service.	■ Generalist staff, organized partly according to technical capability and partly according to their relationship with a business unit ■ Reliance on 'heroics', where staff go out of their way to resolve problems that could have been prevented by better internal processes.

This does not mean that the external focus is unimportant. The whole point of Service Management is to provide services that meet the objectives of the organization as a whole. It is critical to structure services around customers. At the same time, it is possible to compromise the quality of services by not thinking about how they will be delivered.

Building Service Operation with a balance between internal and external focus requires a long-term, dedicated approach reflected in all phases of the ITSM Service Lifecycle. This will require the following:

- An understanding of what services are used by the business and why.
- An understanding of the relative importance and impact of those services on the business.
- An understanding of how technology is used to provide IT services.
- Involvement of Service Operation in Continual Service Improvement projects that aim to identify ways of delivering more, increase service quality and lower cost.
- Procedures and manuals that outline the role of IT Operations in both the management of technology and the delivery of IT services.
- A clearly differentiated set of metrics to report to the business on the achievement of service objectives; and to report to IT managers on the efficiency and effectiveness of Service Operation.
- All IT Operations staff understand exactly how the performance of the technology affects the delivery of IT services and in turn how these affect the business and the business goals.
- A set of standard services delivered consistently to all Business Units and a set of non-standard (sometimes customized) services delivered to specific Business Units – together with a set of Standard Operating Procedures (SOPs) that can meet both sets of requirements.
- A cost strategy aimed at balancing the requirements of different business units with the cost savings available through optimization of existing technology or investment in new technology – and an understanding of the cost strategy by all involved IT resources.
- A value-based, rather than cost-based, Return on Investment strategy.
- Involvement of IT Operations staff in the Service Design and Service Transition phases of the ITSM Lifecycle.

- Input from and feedback to Continual Service Improvement to identify areas where there is an imbalance and the means to identify and enforce improvement.
- A clear communication and training plan for business. While many organizations are good at developing Communication Plans for projects, this often does not extend into their operational phase.

3.2.2 Stability versus responsiveness

No matter how good the functionality is of an IT service and no matter how well it has been designed, it will be worth far less if the service components are not available or if they perform inconsistently.

This means that Service Operation needs to ensure that the IT Infrastructure is stable and available as designed. At the same time, Service Operation needs to recognize that business and IT requirements change.

Some of these changes are evolutionary. For example, the functionality, performance and architecture of a platform may change over a number of years. Each change brings with it an opportunity to provide better levels of service to the business. In evolutionary changes, it is possible to plan how to respond to the change and thus maintain stability while responding to the changes.

Many changes, though, happen very quickly and sometimes under extreme pressure. For example, a Business Unit unexpectedly wins a contract that requires additional IT services, more capacity and faster response times. The ability to respond to this type of change without impacting other services is a significant challenge.

Many IT organizations are unable to achieve this balance and tend to focus on either the stability of the IT Infrastructure or the ability to respond to changes quickly.

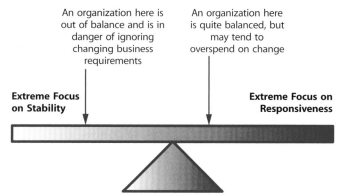

Figure 3.2 Achieving a balance between focus on stability and responsiveness

Table 3.2 Examples of extreme focus on stability and responsiveness

	Extreme focus on stability	Extreme focus on responsiveness
Primary focus	■ Technology ■ Developing and refining standard IT management techniques and processes.	■ Output to the business ■ Agrees to required changes before determining what it will take to deliver them.
Typical problems experienced	IT can demonstrate that it is complying with SOPs and Operational Level Agreements (OLAs), even when there is clear misalignment to business requirements	IT staff are not available to define or execute routine tasks because they are busy on projects for new services
Technology growth strategy	■ Growth strategy based on analysing existing demand on existing systems ■ New services are resisted and Business Units sometimes take ownership of 'their own' systems to get access to new services.	■ Technology purchased for each new business requirement ■ Using multiple technologies and solutions for similar solutions, to meet slightly different business needs.
Technology used to deliver IT services	Existing or standard technology to be used; services must be adjusted to work within existing parameters	Over-provisioning. No attempt is made to model the new service on the existing infrastructure. New, dedicated technology is purchased for each new project
Capacity Management	■ Forecasts based on projections of current workloads ■ System performance is maintained at consistent levels through tuning and demand management, not by workload forecasting and management.	■ Forecasts based on future business activity for each service individually and do not take into account IT activity or other IT services ■ Existing workloads not relevant.

Table 3.2 outlines some examples of the characteristics of positions at extreme ends of the spectrum. The purpose of this table is to assist organizations in identifying to which extreme they are closer, not to identify real-life positions to which organizations should aspire.

Building an IT organization that achieves a balance between stability and responsiveness in Service Operation will require the following actions:

■ Ensure investment in technologies and processes that are adaptive rather than rigid, e.g. virtual server and application technology and the use of Change Models (see Service Transition publication).
■ Build a strong Service Level Management (SLM) process which is active from the Service Design phase to the Continual Service Improvement phase of the ITSM Lifecycle.
■ Foster integration between SLM and the other Service Design processes to ensure proper mapping of business requirements to IT operational activities and components of the IT Infrastructure. This makes it easier to model the effect of changes and improvements.

■ Initiate changes at the earliest appropriate stage in the ITSM Lifecycle. This will ensure that both functional (business) and manageability (IT operational) requirements can be assessed and built or changed together.
■ Ensure IT involvement in business changes as early as possible in the change process to ensure scalability, consistency and achievability of IT services sustaining business changes.
■ Service Operation teams should provide input into the ongoing design and refinement of the architectures and IT services (see Service Design and Service Strategy publications).
■ Implement and use SLM to avoid situations where business and IT managers and staff negotiate informal agreements.

3.2.3 Quality of service versus cost of service

Service Operation is required consistently to deliver the agreed level of IT service to its customers and users, while at the same time keeping costs and resource utilization at an optimal level.

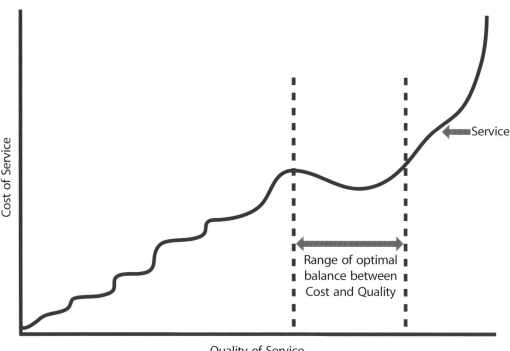

Figure 3.3 Balancing service quality and cost

Figure 3.3 represents the investment made to deliver a service at increasing levels of quality.

In Figure 3.3, an increase in the level of quality usually results in an increase in the cost of that service, and vice versa. However, the relationship is not always directly proportional:

■ Early in the service's lifecycle it is possible to achieve significant increases in service quality with a relatively small amount of money. For example, improving service availability from 55% to 75% is fairly straightforward and may not require a huge investment.

■ Later in the service's lifecycle, even small improvements in quality are very expensive. For example, improving the same service's availability from 96% to 99.9% may require large investments in high-availability technology and support staff and tools.

While this may seem straightforward, many organizations are under severe pressure to increase the quality of service while reducing their costs. In Figure 3.3, the relationship between cost and quality is sometimes inverse. It is possible (usually inside the range of optimization) to increase quality while reducing costs. This is normally

initiated within Service Operation and carried forward by Continual Service Improvement. Some costs can be reduced incrementally over time, but most cost savings can be made only once. For example, once a duplicate software tool has been eliminated, it cannot be eliminated again for further cost savings.

Achieving an optimal balance between cost and quality (shown between the dotted lines in Figure 3.3) is a key role of Service Management. There is no industry standard for what this range should be, since each service will have a different range of optimization, depending on the nature of the service and the type of business objective being met. For example, the business may be prepared to spend more to achieve high availability on a mission-critical service, while it is prepared to live with the lower quality of an administrative tool.

Determining the appropriate balance of cost and quality should be done during the Service Strategy and Service Design Lifecycle phases, although in many organizations it is left to the Service Operation teams – many of whom do not generally have all the facts or authority to be able to make this type of decision.

Unfortunately, it is also common to find organizations that are spending vast quantities of money without achieving any clear improvements in quality. Again, Continual Service Improvement will be able to identify the cause of the inefficiency, evaluate the optimal balance for that service and formulate a corrective plan.

Achieving the correct balance is important. Too much focus on quality will result in IT services that deliver more than necessary, at a higher cost, and could lead to a discussion on reducing the price of services. Too much focus on cost will result in IT delivering on or under budget, but putting the business at risk through sub-standard IT services.

Special note: just how far is too much?

Over the past several years, IT organizations have been under pressure to cut costs. In many cases this resulted in optimized costs and quality. But, in other cases, costs were cut to the point where quality started to suffer. At first, the signs were subtle – small increases in incident resolution times and a slight increase in the number of incidents. Over time, though, the situation became more serious as staff worked long hours to handle multiple workloads and services ran on ageing or outdated infrastructure.

There is no simple calculation to determine when costs have been cut too far, but good SLM is crucial to making customers aware of the impact of cutting too far, so recognizing these warning signs and symptoms can greatly enhance an organization's ability to correct this situation.

Service Level Requirements – together with a clear understanding of the business purpose of the service and the potential risks – will help to ensure that the service is delivered at the appropriate cost. They will also help to avoid 'over sizing' of the service just because budget is

available, or 'under sizing' because the business does not understand the manageability requirements of the solution. Either result will cause customer dissatisfaction and even more expense when the solution is re-engineered or retro-fitted to the requirements that should have been specified during Service Design.

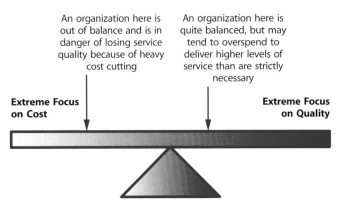

Figure 3.4 Achieving a balance between focus on cost and quality

Table 3.3 outlines some examples of the characteristics of positions at extreme ends of the cost/quality spectrum. The purpose of this table is to assist organizations in identifying to which extreme they are closer, not to identify real-life positions to which organizations should aspire.

Achieving a balance will ensure delivery of the level of service necessary to meet business requirements at an optimal (as opposed to lowest possible) cost. This will require the following:

■ A Financial Management process and tools that can account for the cost of providing IT services; and which model alternative methods of delivering services at differing levels of cost. For example, comparing the

Table 3.3 Examples of extreme focus on quality and cost

	Extreme focus on quality	Extreme focus on cost
Primary focus	Delivering the level of quality demanded by the business regardless of what it takes	Meeting budget and reducing costs
Typical problems experienced	■ Escalating budgets ■ IT services generally deliver more than is necessary for business success ■ Escalating demands for higher-quality services.	■ IT limits the quality of service based on their budget availability ■ Escalations from the business to get more service from IT.
Financial Management	IT usually does not have a method of communicating the cost of IT services. Accounting methods are based on an aggregated method (e.g. cost of IT per user).	Financial reporting is done purely on budgeted amounts. There is no way of linking activities in IT to the delivery of IT services.

cost of delivering a service at 98% availability or at 99.9% availability; or the cost of providing a service with or without additional functionality.

- Ensuring that decisions around cost versus quality are made by the appropriate managers during Service Strategy and Service Design. IT operational managers are generally not equipped to evaluate business opportunities and should only be asked to make financial decisions that are related to achieving operational efficiencies.

3.2.4 Reactive versus proactive

A reactive organization is one which does not act unless it is prompted to do so by an external driver, e.g. a new business requirement, an application that has been developed or escalation in complaints made by users and customers. An unfortunate reality in many organizations is the focus on reactive management mistakenly as the sole means to ensure services that are highly consistent and stable, actively discouraging proactive behaviour from operational staff. The unfortunate irony of this approach is that discouraging effort investment in proactive Service Management can ultimately increase the effort and cost of reactive activities and further risk stability and consistency in services.

A proactive organization is always looking for ways to improve the current situation. It will continually scan the internal and external environments, looking for signs of potentially impacting changes. Proactive behaviour is usually seen as positive, especially since it enables the organization to maintain competitive advantage in a changing environment. However, being too proactive can be expensive and can result in staff being distracted. The need for proper balance in reactive and proactive behaviour often achieves the optimal result.

Generally, it is better to manage IT services proactively, but achieving this is not easily planned or achieved. This is because building a proactive IT organization is dependent on many variables, including:

- The maturity of the organization. The longer the organization has been delivering a consistent set of IT services, the more likely it is to understand the relationship between IT and the business and the IT Infrastructure and IT services.
- The culture of the organization. Some organizations have a culture that is focused on innovation and are more likely to be proactive. Others are more likely to focus on the status quo and as such are likely to resist change and have more reactive focus.

- The role that IT plays in the business and the mandate that IT has to influence the strategy and tactics of the business. For example, a company where the CIO is a board member is likely to have an IT organization that is far more proactive and responsive than a company where IT is seen as an administrative overhead.
- The level of integration of management processes and tools. Higher levels of integration will facilitate better knowledge of opportunities.
- The maturity and scope of Knowledge Management in the organization; this is especially seen in organizations which have been able to store and organize historical data effectively – especially Availability and Problem Management data.

From a maturity perspective, it is clear that newer organizations will have different priorities and experiences from a more established organization – what is best practice for a mature organization may not suit a younger organization. Therefore an imbalance could result from an organization being either less or more mature. Consider the following:

- Less mature organizations (or organizations with newer IT services or technology) will generally be more reactive, simply because they do not know all the variables involved in running their business and providing IT services.
- IT staff in newer organizations tend to be generalists because it is unclear exactly what is required to deliver stable IT services to the business.
- Incidents and problems in newer organizations are fairly unpredictable because the technology is relatively new and changes quickly.
- More mature organizations tend to be more proactive, simply because they have more data and reporting available and know the typical patterns of incidents and workflows. Thus, they forecast exceptions far more easily.
- Staff working in mature organizations also generally tend to have more established relationships between IT staff and the business and so can be more proactive about meeting changing business requirements – this is especially true when IT is seen as a strategic component of the business.

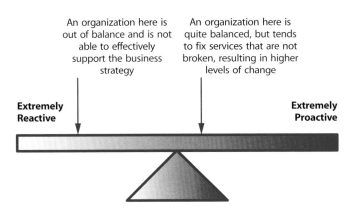

Figure 3.5 Achieving a balance between being too reactive or too proactive

Table 3.4 outlines some examples of the characteristics of positions at extreme ends of the spectrum. The purpose of this table is to assist organizations in identifying to which extreme they are closer, not to identify real-life positions to which organizations should aspire.

While proactive behaviour in Service Operation is generally good, there are also times where reactive behaviour is needed. The role of Service Operation is therefore to achieve a balance between being reactive and proactive. This will require:

■ Formal Problem Management and Incident Management processes, integrated between Service Operation and Continual Service Improvement.
■ The ability to be able to prioritize technical faults as well as business demands. This needs to be done during Service Operation, but the mechanisms need to be put in place during Service Strategy and Design. These mechanisms could include incident categorization systems, escalation procedures and tools to facilitate impact assessment for changes.
■ Data from Configuration and Asset Management to provide data where required, saving projects time and making decisions more accurate.
■ Ongoing involvement of SLM in Service Operation.

Table 3.4 Examples of extremely reactive and proactive behaviour

	Extremely reactive	Extremely proactive
Primary focus	Responds to business needs and incidents only after they are reported	Anticipates business requirements before they are reported and problems before they occur
Typical problems experienced	■ Preparing to deliver new services takes a long time because each project is dealt with as if it is the first ■ Similar incidents occur again and again, as there is no way of trending them ■ Staff turnover is high and morale is generally low, as IT staff keep moving from project to project without achieving a lasting, stable set of IT services	■ Money is spent before the requirements are stated. In some cases IT purchases items that will never be used because they anticipated the wrong requirements or because the project is stopped ■ IT staff tend to have been in the organization for a long time and tend to assume that they know the business requirements better than the business does
Capacity Planning	Wait until there are capacity problems and then purchase surplus capacity to last until the next capacity-related incident	Anticipate capacity problems and spend money on preventing these – even when the scenario is unlikely to happen
IT Service Continuity Planning	■ No plans exist until after a major event or disaster ■ IT Plans focus on recovering key systems, but without ensuring that the business can recover its processes	Over-planning (and over-spending) of IT Recovery options. Usually immediate recovery is provided for most IT services, regardless of their impact or priority
Change Management	■ Changes are often not logged, or logged at the last minute as Emergency Changes ■ Not enough time for proper impact and cost assessments ■ Changes are poorly tested and controlled, resulting in a high number of incidents	Changes are requested and implemented even when there is no real need, i.e. a significant amount of work done to fix items that are not broken

3.3 PROVIDING SERVICE

All Service Operation staff must be fully aware that they are there to 'provide service' to the business. They must provide a timely (rapid response and speedy delivery of requirements), professional and courteous service to allow the business to conduct its own activities – so that the commercial customer's needs are met and the business thrives.

It is important that staff are trained not only in how to deliver and support IT services, but also in the manner in which that service should be provided. For example, staff that are capable and deliver service effectively may still cause significant customer dissatisfaction if they are insensitive or dismissive. Conversely, no amount of being nice to a customer will help if the service is not being delivered.

A critical element of being a proficient service provider is placing as much emphasis on recruiting and training staff to develop competency in dealing with and managing customer relationships and interactions as they do on technical competencies for managing the IT environment.

3.4 OPERATION STAFF INVOLVEMENT IN SERVICE DESIGN AND SERVICE TRANSITION

It is extremely important that Service Operation staff are involved in Service Design and Service Transition and potentially also in Service Strategy where appropriate.

One key to achieving balance in Service Operation is an effective set of Service Design processes. These will provide IT Operations Management with:

- Clear definition of IT service objectives and performance criteria
- Linkage of IT service specifications to the performance of the IT Infrastructure
- Definition of operational performance requirements
- A mapping of services and technology
- The ability to model the effect of changes in technology and changes to business requirements
- Appropriate cost models (e.g. customer or service based) to evaluate Return on Investment and cost-reduction strategies.

The nature of IT Operations Management involvement should be carefully positioned. Service Design is a phase in the Service Management Lifecycle using a set of processes, not a function independent of Service Operation. As such, many of the people who are involved in Service Design will come from IT Operations Management.

This should not only be encouraged, but Service Operation staff should be measured on their involvement in Service Design activities – and such activities should be included in job descriptions and roles, etc. This will help to ensure continuity between business requirements and technology design and operation and it will also help to ensure that what is designed can also be operated. IT Operations Management staff should also be involved during Service Transition to ensure consistency and to ensure that both stated business and manageability requirements are met.

Resources must be made available for these activities and the time required should be taken into account, as appropriate.

3.5 OPERATIONAL HEALTH

Many organizations find it helpful to compare the monitoring and control of Service Operation to health monitoring and control.

In this sense, the IT Infrastructure is like an organism that has vital life signs that can be monitored to check whether it is functioning normally. This means that it is not necessary to monitor continuously every component of every IT system to ensure that it is functioning.

Operational Health can be determined by isolating a few important 'vital signs' on devices or services that are defined as critical for the successful execution of a Vital Business Function. This could be the bandwidth utilization on a network segment, or memory utilization on a major server. If these signs are within normal ranges, the system is healthy and does not require additional attention. This reduction in the need for extensive monitoring will result in cost reduction and operational teams and departments that are focused on the appropriate areas for service success.

However, as with organisms, it is important to check systems more thoroughly from time to time, to check for problems that do not immediately affect vital signs. For example a disk may be functioning perfectly, but it could be nearing its Mean Time Between Failures (MTBF) threshold. In this case the system should be taken out of service and given a thorough examination or 'health check'. At the same time, it should be stressed that the end result should be the healthy functioning of the service as a whole. This means that health checks on components should be balanced against checks of the 'end-to-end' service. The definition of what needs to be monitored and what is healthy versus unhealthy is defined during Service Design, especially Availability Management and SLM.

Operational Health is dependent on the ability to prevent incidents and problems by investing in reliable and maintainable infrastructure. This is achieved through good availability design and proactive Problem Management. At the same time, Operational Health is also dependent on the ability to identify faults and localize them effectively so that they have minimal impact on the service. This requires strong (preferably automated) Incident and Problem Management.

The idea of Operational Health has also led to a specialized area called 'Self Healing Systems'. This is an application of Availability, Capacity, Knowledge, Incident and Problem Management and refers to a system that has been designed to withstand the most severe operating conditions and to detect, diagnose and recover from most incidents and Known Errors. Self Healing Systems are known by different names, for example Autonomic Systems, Adaptive Systems and Dynamic Systems. Characteristics of Self Healing Systems include:

- Resilience is designed and built into the system, for example multiple redundant disks or multiple processors. This protects the system against hardware failure since it is able to continue operating using the duplicated hardware component.
- Software, data and operating system resilience is also designed into the system, for example mirrored databases (where a database is duplicated on a backup device) and disk-striping technology (where individual bits of data are distributed across a disk array – so that a disk failure results in the loss of only a part of data, which can be easily recovered using algorithms).
- The ability to shift processing from one physical device to another without any disruption to the service. This could be a response to a failure or because the device is reaching high utilization levels (some systems are designed to distribute processing workloads continuously, to make optimum use of available capacity, which is also known as virtualization).
- Built-in monitoring utilities which enable the system to detect events and to determine whether these represent normal operations or not.
- A correlation engine (see paragraph 4.1.5.6 on Event Management). This will enable the system to determine the significance of each event and also to determine whether there is any predefined response to that event.
- A set of diagnostic tools, such as diagnostic scripts, fault trees and a database of Known Errors and

common workarounds. These are used as soon as an error is detected, to determine the appropriate response.
- The ability to generate a call for human intervention by raising an alert or generating an incident.

While the concept of Operational Health is not a core concept of Service Operation, it is often a helpful metaphor to assist in determining what needs to be monitored and how frequently to perform preventive maintenance.

What and when to monitor for operational health should be determined in Service Design, tested and refined during Service Transition and optimized in Continual Service Improvement, as necessary.

3.6 COMMUNICATION

Good communication is needed with other IT teams and departments, with users and internal customers, and between the Service Operation teams and departments themselves. Issues can often be prevented or mitigated with appropriate communication.

This section is aimed at summarizing the communication that should take place in Service Operation. This is not a separate process, but a checklist of the type of communication that is required for effective Service Operation.

An important principle is that all communication must have an intended purpose or a resultant action. Information should not be communicated unless there is a clear audience. In addition, that audience should have been actively involved in determining the need for that communication and what they will do with the information.

A detailed description of the types of communication typical in Service Operation is contained in Appendix B of this publication, together with a description of the typical audience and the actions that are intended to be taken as a result of each communication. These include:

- Routine operational communication
- Communication between shifts
- Performance reporting
- Communication in projects
- Communication related to changes
- Communication related to exceptions
- Communication related to emergencies
- Training on new or customized processes and service designs

- Communication of strategy and design to Service Operation teams.

Please note that there is no definitive medium for communication, nor is there a fixed location or frequency. In some organizations communication has to take place in meetings. Other organizations prefer to use e-mail or the communication inherent in their Service Management tools.

There should therefore be a policy around communication within each team or department and for each process. Although this should be formal, the policy should not be cumbersome or complex. For example, a manager might require that all communications regarding changes must be sent by e-mail. As long as this is specified in the department's SOPs (in whatever form they exist), there is no need to create a separate policy for it.

Although the typical content of communication is fairly consistent once processes have been defined, the means of communication are changing with every new introduction of technology. The list of alternatives is growing and, today, includes:

- E-mail, to traditional clients or mobile devices
- SMS messages
- Pagers
- Instant messaging and web-based 'chats'
- Voice over Internet Protocol (VoIP) utilities that can turn any connected device to an inexpensive communication medium
- Teleconference and virtual meeting utilities, which have revolutionized meetings, which are now held across long distances
- Document-sharing utilities.

The means of communication itself is outside the scope of this publication. However, the following points should be noted:

- Communication is primary and the means of communication must ensure that they serve this goal. For example, the need for secure communication may eliminate the possibility of some of the above means. The need for quality may eliminate some VoIP options.
- It is possible to use any means of communication as long as all stakeholders understand how and when the communication will take place.

3.6.1 Meetings

Different organizations communicate in different ways. Where organizations are distributed, they will tend to rely on e-mail and teleconferencing facilities. Organizations that have more mature Service Management processes and tools will tend to rely on the tools and processes for communication (e.g. using an Incident Management tool to escalate and track incidents, instead of requesting e-mail or telephone calls for updates).

Other organizations prefer to communicate using meetings. However, it is important not to get into the mode whereby the only time work is done, or management is involved, is during a meeting. Also, face-to-face meetings tend to increase costs (e.g. travel, time spent in informal discussions, refreshments, etc.), so meeting organizers should balance the value of the meeting with the number and identity of the attendees and the time they will spend in, and getting to, the meeting.

The purpose of meetings is to communicate effectively to a group of people about a common set of objectives or activities. Meetings should be well controlled and brief, and the focus should be on facilitating action. A good rule is not to hold a meeting if the information can be communicated effectively by automated means.

A number of factors are essential for successful meetings. Although these may seem to be common sense, they are sometimes neglected:

- Establish and communicate a clear agenda to ensure that the meeting achieves its objective and to help the facilitator prevent attendees from 'hijacking' the meeting.
- Ensure that the rules for participating are understood. Organizations tend to have a formal set of meeting rules, ranging from relatively informal to very formal (e.g. Roberts Rules of Order).
- Make use of 'parking lots' or notes that record issues that are not directly relevant to the purpose of the meeting, but which can be called on if the need for discussion arises.
- Minutes of the meeting: rules should be set about when minutes are taken. Minutes are used to remind people who are assigned actions and to track the progress of delegated actions. They are also useful in ensuring that cross-functional decisions and actions are tracked and followed through.
- Use techniques to encourage the appropriate level of participation. One technique when discussing improvements, for example, is the 'keep, stop, start' technique. Participants are encouraged to list items that they would like to keep, things that need to be stopped and initiatives or actions that they would like to see started.

Examples of typical meetings are given below:

3.6.1.1 The Operations meeting

Operations meetings are normally held between the managers of the IT operational departments, teams or groups, at the beginning of each business day or week. The purpose of this type of meeting is to make staff aware of any issue relevant to Operations (such as change schedules, business events, maintenance schedules, etc.) and to provide an opportunity for staff to raise any issues of which they are aware. This is an opportunity to ensure that all departments in a data centre are synchronized.

In geographically dispersed organizations it may not be possible to have a single daily Operations meeting. In these cases it is important to coordinate the agenda of the meetings and to ensure that each meeting has two components:

1   The first part of the meeting will cover aspects that apply to the organization as a whole, e.g. new policies, changes that affect all regions and business events that span all regions.

2   The second part of the meeting will cover aspects that apply only to the local region, e.g. local operations schedules, changes to local equipment, etc.

The Operations meeting is usually chaired by the IT Operations Manager or a senior Operations Manager and attended by all managers and supervisors (except those whose shifts are not on duty). It is also helpful to have at least one representative from the Service Desk at the meeting so that they are aware of any situations that could give rise to incidents.

Opportunities to improve services or processes should be captured, if raised, and forwarded to the team responsible for Continual Service Improvement.

3.6.1.2 Department, group or team meetings

These meetings are essentially the same as the Operations meeting, but are aimed at a single IT department, group or team. Each manager or supervisor relays the information from the Operations meeting that is relevant to their team.

Additionally, these meetings will also cover the following:

- A more detailed discussion of incidents, problems and changes that are still being worked on, with information about:
  - Progress to date
  - Confirmation of what still needs to be done
  - Estimated completion times

- Request for additional resources, if required
- Discussion of potential problems or concerns
- Confirmation of staff availability for roster duties
- Confirmation of vacation schedules.

3.6.1.3 Customer meetings

From time to time it will be necessary to hold meetings with customers, apart from the regular Service Level Review meetings. Examples include:

- Follow-up after serious incidents. The purpose of these meetings is to repair the relationship with the customers, but also to ensure that IT has all the information required to prevent recurrence. Customers also have the opportunity to provide information about unforeseen business impacts. These meetings are helpful in agreeing actions for similar types of incident that may occur in future.

- A customer forum, which can be used for a range of purposes, including testing ideas for new services or solutions, or gathering requirements for new or revised services or procedures. A customer forum is generally a regular meeting with customers to discuss areas of common concern.

3.7   DOCUMENTATION

IT Operations Management and all of the Technical and Application Management teams and departments are involved in creating and maintaining a range of documents. These are detailed in Chapters 4, 5 and 6 of this publication and include the following:

- Participation in the definition and maintenance of process manuals for all processes they are involved in. These will include processes in other phases of the IT Service Management Lifecycle (e.g. Capacity Management, Change Management, Availability Management) as well as for all processes included in the Service Operation phase.

- Establishing their own technical procedures manuals. These must be kept up to date and new material must be added as it becomes relevant, under Change Control. It should be remembered that their procedures should always be structured to meet the objectives and constraints defined within higher-level Service Management processes, such as SLM. For example, a technical procedure for managing servers should always ensure that it aims at achieving the availability and performance levels agreed to in the Operational Level Agreements and Service Level Agreements (SLAs).

- Participation in the creation and maintenance of planning documents, e.g. the Capacity and Availability Plans and the IT Service Continuity Plans.
- Participation in the creation and maintenance of the Service Portfolio. This will include quantifying costs and establishing the operational feasibility of each proposed service.
- Participation in the definition and maintenance of Service Management tool work instructions in order to meet reporting requirements.

Service Operation processes

4

4 Service Operation processes

The processes listed in paragraph 2.4.5 are discussed in detail in this chapter. As a reference, the overall structure is briefly described here and then each of the processes is described in more detail later in the chapter. Please note that the roles for each process and the tools used for each process are described in Chapters 6 and 7 respectively.

■ **Event Management** is the process that monitors all events that occur through the IT infrastructure to allow for normal operation and also to detect and escalate exception conditions.

■ **Incident Management** concentrates on restoring the service to users as quickly as possible, in order to minimize business impact.

■ **Problem Management** involves root-cause analysis to determine and resolve the cause of events and incidents, proactive activities to detect and prevent future problems/incidents and a Known Error sub-process to allow quicker diagnosis and resolution if further incidents do occur.

NOTE: Without this distinction between incidents and problems, and keeping separate Incident and Problem Records, there is a danger that either:

● Incidents will be closed too early in the overall support cycle and there will be no actions taken to prevent recurrence – so the same incidents will have to be fixed over and over again, or

● Incidents will be kept open so that root cause analysis can be done and visibility will be lost of when the user's service was actually restored – so SLA targets may not be met even though the service has been restored within users' expectations. This often results in a large number of open incidents, many of which will never be closed unless a periodic 'purge' is undertaken. This can be very demotivating and can prevent effective visibility of current issues.

■ **Request Fulfilment** involves the management of customer or user requests that are not generated as an incident from an unexpected service delay or disruption. Some organizations may choose to handle such requests as a 'category' of incidents and manage the information through an Incident Management system – but others may choose (because of high volumes or business priority of such requests) to facilitate the provision of Request Fulfilment capabilities separately via the Request Fulfilment process. It has become popular practice to use a formal Request Fulfilment process to manage customer and user requests for all types of requests which include facilities, moves and supplies as well as those specific to IT services. These requests are not generally tied to the same SLA measures and separating the records and the process flow is emerging as best practice in many organizations.

■ **Access Management**: this is the process of granting authorized users the right to use a service, while restricting access to non-authorized users. It is based on being able accurately to identify authorized users and then manage their ability to access services as required during different stages of their human resources (HR) or contractual lifecycle. Access Management has also been called Identity or Rights Management in some organizations.

In addition, there are several other processes that will be executed or supported during Service Operation, but which are driven during other phases of the Service Management Lifecycle. The operational aspects of these processes will be discussed in the final part of this chapter and include:

■ Change Management, a major process which should be closely linked to Configuration Management and Release Management. These topics are primarily covered in the Service Transition publication.

■ Capacity and Availability Management, the operational aspects of which are covered in this publication, but which are covered in more detail in the Service Design publication.

■ Financial Management, which is covered in the Service Strategy publication.

■ Knowledge Management, which is covered in the Service Transition publication.

■ IT Service Continuity, which is covered in the Service Design publication.

■ Service Reporting and Measurement, which are covered in the Continual Service Improvement publication.

4.1 EVENT MANAGEMENT

An event can be defined as any detectable or discernible occurrence that has significance for the management of the IT Infrastructure or the delivery of IT service and evaluation of the impact a deviation might cause to the services. Events are typically notifications created by an IT service, Configuration Item (CI) or monitoring tool.

Effective Service Operation is dependent on knowing the status of the infrastructure and detecting any deviation from normal or expected operation. This is provided by good monitoring and control systems, which are based on two types of tools:

■ active monitoring tools that poll key CIs to determine their status and availability. Any exceptions will generate an alert that needs to be communicated to the appropriate tool or team for action
■ passive monitoring tools that detect and correlate operational alerts or communications generated by CIs.

4.1.1 Purpose/goal/objective

The ability to detect events, make sense of them and determine the appropriate control action is provided by Event Management. Event Management is therefore the basis for Operational Monitoring and Control (see Appendix B).

In addition, if these events are programmed to communicate operational information as well as warnings and exceptions, they can be used as a basis for automating many routine Operations Management activities, for example executing scripts on remote devices, or submitting jobs for processing, or even dynamically balancing the demand for a service across multiple devices to enhance performance.

Event Management therefore provides the entry point for the execution of many Service Operation processes and activities. In addition, it provides a way of comparing actual performance and behaviour against design standards and SLAs. As such, Event Management also provides a basis for Service Assurance and Reporting; and Service Improvement. This is covered in detail in the Continual Service Improvement publication.

4.1.2 Scope

Event Management can be applied to any aspect of Service Management that needs to be controlled and which can be automated. These include:

■ Configuration Items:
  ● Some CIs will be included because they need to stay in a constant state (e.g. a switch on a network needs to stay on and Event Management tools confirm this by monitoring responses to 'pings').
  ● Some CIs will be included because their status needs to change frequently and Event Management can be used to automate this and update the CMS (e.g. the updating of a file server).
■ Environmental conditions (e.g. fire and smoke detection)
■ Software licence monitoring for usage to ensure optimum/legal licence utilization and allocation
■ Security (e.g. intrusion detection)
■ Normal activity (e.g. tracking the use of an application or the performance of a server).

The difference between monitoring and Event Management

These two areas are very closely related, but slightly different in nature. Event Management is focused on generating and detecting meaningful notifications about the status of the IT Infrastructure and services.

While it is true that monitoring is required to detect and track these notifications, monitoring is broader than Event Management. For example, monitoring tools will check the status of a device to ensure that it is operating within acceptable limits, even if that device is not generating events.

Put more simply, Event Management works with occurrences that are specifically generated to be monitored. Monitoring tracks these occurrences, but it will also actively seek out conditions that do not generate events.

4.1.3 Value to business

Event Management's value to the business is generally indirect; however, it is possible to determine the basis for its value as follows:

■ Event Management provides mechanisms for early detection of incidents. In many cases it is possible for the incident to be detected and assigned to the appropriate group for action before any actual service outage occurs.

■ Event Management makes it possible for some types of automated activity to be monitored by exception – thus removing the need for expensive and resource intensive real-time monitoring, while reducing downtime.

■ When integrated into other Service Management processes (such as, for example, Availability or Capacity Management), Event Management can signal status changes or exceptions that allow the appropriate person or team to perform early response, thus improving the performance of the process. This, in turn, will allow the business to benefit from more effective and more efficient Service Management overall.

■ Event Management provides a basis for automated operations, thus increasing efficiencies and allowing expensive human resources to be used for more innovative work, such as designing new or improved functionality or defining new ways in which the business can exploit technology for increased competitive advantage.

4.1.4 Policies/principles/basic concepts

There are many different types of events, for example:

■ Events that signify regular operation:
  ● notification that a scheduled workload has completed
  ● a user has logged in to use an application
  ● an e-mail has reached its intended recipient.
■ Events that signify an exception
  ● a user attempts to log on to an application with the incorrect password
  ● an unusual situation has occurred in a business process that may indicate an exception requiring further business investigation (e.g. a web page

alert indicates that a payment authorization site is unavailable – impacting financial approval of business transactions)
  ● a device's CPU is above the acceptable utilization rate
  ● a PC scan reveals the installation of unauthorized software.
■ Events that signify unusual, but not exceptional, operation. These are an indication that the situation may require closer monitoring. In some cases the condition will resolve itself, for example in the case of an unusual combination of workloads – as they are completed, normal operation is restored. In other cases, operator intervention may be required if the situation is repeated or if it continues for too long. These rules or policies are defined in the Monitoring and Control Objectives for that device or service. Examples of this type of event are:
  ● A server's memory utilization reaches within 5% of its highest acceptable performance level
  ● The completion time of a transaction is 10% longer than normal.

Two things are significant about the above examples:

■ Exactly what constitutes normal versus unusual operation, versus an exception? There is no definitive rule about this. For example, a manufacturer may provide that a benchmark of 75% memory utilization is optimal for application X. However, it is discovered that, under the specific conditions of our organization, response times begin to degrade above 70% utilization. The next section will explore how these figures are determined.

■ Each relies on the sending and receipt of a message of some type. These are generally referred to as Event notifications and they don't just happen. The next paragraphs will explore exactly how events are defined, generated and captured.

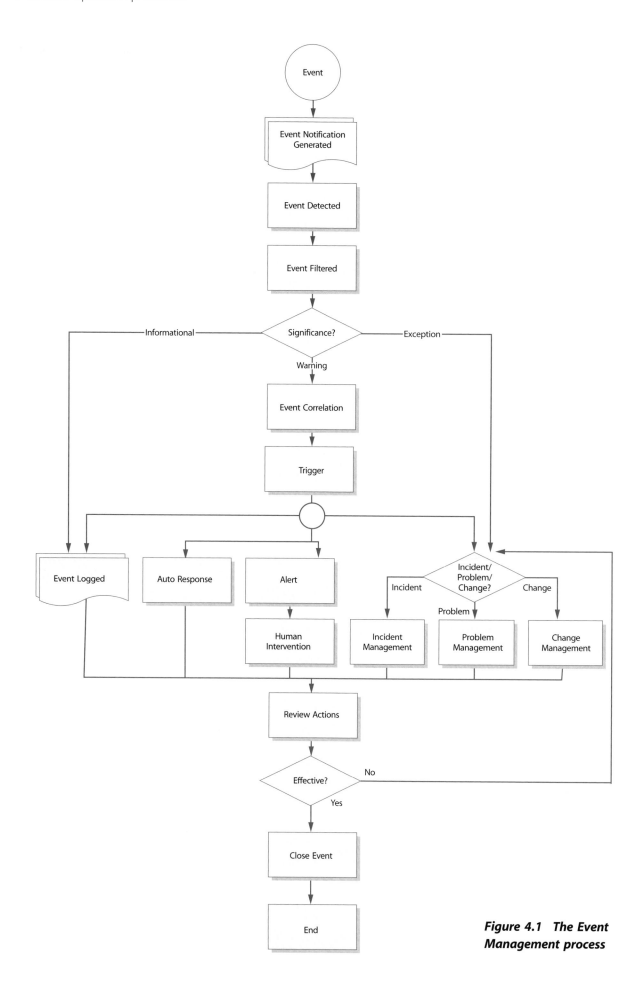

***Figure 4.1 The Event
Management process***

4.1.5 Process activities, methods and techniques

Figure 4.1 is a high-level and generic representation of Event Management. It should be used as a reference and definition point, rather than an actual Event Management flowchart. Each activity in this process is described below.

4.1.5.1 Event occurs

Events occur continuously, but not all of them are detected or registered. It is therefore important that everybody involved in designing, developing, managing and supporting IT services and the IT Infrastructure that they run on understands what types of event need to be detected.

This is discussed in paragraph 4.1.10.1, titled 'Instrumentation'.

4.1.5.2 Event notification

Most CIs are designed to communicate certain information about themselves in one of two ways:

- A device is interrogated by a management tool, which collects certain targeted data. This is often referred to as polling.
- The CI generates a notification when certain conditions are met. The ability to produce these notifications has to be designed and built into the CI, for example a programming hook inserted into an application.

Event notifications can be proprietary, in which case only the manufacturer's management tools can be used to detect events. Most CIs, however, generate Event notifications using an open standard such as SNMP (Simple Network Management Protocol).

Many CIs are configured to generate a standard set of events, based on the designer's experience of what is required to operate the CI, with the ability to generate additional types of event by 'turning on' the relevant event generation mechanism. For other CI types, some form of 'agent' software will have to be installed in order to initiate the monitoring. Often this monitoring feature is free, but sometimes there is a cost to the licensing of the tool.

In an ideal world, the Service Design process should define which events need to be generated and then specify how this can be done for each type of CI. During Service Transition, the event generation options would be set and tested.

In many organizations, however, defining which events to generate is done by trial and error. System managers use the standard set of events as a starting point and then tune the CI over time, to include or exclude events as required. The problem with this approach is that it only takes into account the immediate needs of the staff managing the device and does not facilitate good planning or improvement. In addition, it makes it very difficult to monitor and manage the service over all devices and staff. One approach to combating this problem is to review the set of events as part of continual improvement activities.

A general principle of Event notification is that the more meaningful the data it contains and the more targeted the audience, the easier it is to make decisions about the event. Operators are often confronted by coded error messages and have no idea how to respond to them or what to do with them. Meaningful notification data and clearly defined roles and responsibilities need to be articulated and documented during Service Design and Service Transition (see also paragraph 4.1.10.1 on 'Instrumentation'). If roles and responsibilities are not clearly defined, in a wide alert, no one knows who is doing what and this can lead to things being missed or duplicated efforts.

4.1.5.3 Event detection

Once an Event notification has been generated, it will be detected by an agent running on the same system, or transmitted directly to a management tool specifically designed to read and interpret the meaning of the event.

4.1.5.4 Event filtering

The purpose of filtering is to decide whether to communicate the event to a management tool or to ignore it. If ignored, the event will usually be recorded in a log file on the device, but no further action will be taken.

The reason for filtering is that it is not always possible to turn Event notification off, even though a decision has been made that it is not necessary to generate that type of event. It may also be decided that only the first in a series of repeated Event notifications will be transmitted.

During the filtering step, the first level of correlation is performed, i.e. the determination of whether the event is informational, a warning, or an exception (see next step). This correlation is usually done by an agent that resides on the CI or on a server to which the CI is connected.

The filtering step is not always necessary. For some CIs, every event is significant and moves directly into a management tool's correlation engine, even if it is duplicated. Also, it may have been possible to turn off all unwanted Event notifications.

4.1.5.5 Significance of events

Every organization will have its own categorization of the significance of an event, but it is suggested that at least these three broad categories be represented:

- **Informational**: This refers to an event that does not require any action and does not represent an exception. They are typically stored in the system or service log files and kept for a predetermined period. Informational events are typically used to check on the status of a device or service, or to confirm the successful completion of an activity. Informational events can also be used to generate statistics (such as the number of users logged on to an application during a certain period) and as input into investigations (such as which jobs completed successfully before the transaction processing queue hung). Examples of informational events include:
  - A user logs onto an application
  - A job in the batch queue completes successfully
  - A device has come online
  - A transaction is completed successfully.

- **Warning**: A warning is an event that is generated when a service or device is approaching a threshold. Warnings are intended to notify the appropriate person, process or tool so that the situation can be checked and the appropriate action taken to prevent an exception. Warnings are not typically raised for a device failure. Although there is some debate about whether the failure of a redundant device is a warning or an exception (since the service is still available). A good rule is that every failure should be treated as an exception, since the risk of an incident impacting the business is much greater. Examples of warnings are:
  - Memory utilization on a server is currently at 65% and increasing. If it reaches 75%, response times will be unacceptably long and the OLA for that department will be breached.
  - The collision rate on a network has increased by 15% over the past hour.

- **Exception**: An exception means that a service or device is currently operating abnormally (however that has been defined). Typically, this means that an OLA and SLA have been breached and the business is being impacted. Exceptions could represent a total failure, impaired functionality or degraded performance. Please note, though, that an exception does not always represent an incident. For example,

an exception could be generated when an unauthorized device is discovered on the network. This can be managed by using either an Incident Record or a Request for Change (or even both), depending on the organization's Incident and Change Management policies. Examples of exceptions include:

- A server is down
- Response time of a standard transaction across the network has slowed to more than 15 seconds
- More than 150 users have logged on to the General Ledger application concurrently
- A segment of the network is not responding to routine requests.

4.1.5.6 Event correlation

If an event is significant, a decision has to be made about exactly what the significance is and what actions need to be taken to deal with it. It is here that the meaning of the event is determined.

Correlation is normally done by a 'Correlation Engine', usually part of a management tool that compares the event with a set of criteria and rules in a prescribed order. These criteria are often called Business Rules, although they are generally fairly technical. The idea is that the event may represent some impact on the business and the rules can be used to determine the level and type of business impact.

A Correlation Engine is programmed according to the performance standards created during Service Design and any additional guidance specific to the operating environment.

Examples of what Correlation Engines will take into account include:

- Number of similar events (e.g. this is the third time that the same user has logged in with the incorrect password, a business application reports that there has been an unusual pattern of usage of a mobile telephone that could indicate that the device has been lost or stolen)
- Number of CIs generating similar events
- Whether a specific action is associated with the code or data in the event
- Whether the event represents an exception
- A comparison of utilization information in the event with a maximum or minimum standard (e.g. has the device exceeded a threshold?)
- Whether additional data is required to investigate the event further, and possibly even a collection of that data by polling another system or database

- Categorization of the event
- Assigning a priority level to the event.

4.1.5.7 Trigger

If the correlation activity recognizes an event, a response will be required. The mechanism used to initiate that response is called a trigger.

There are many different types of triggers, each designed specifically for the task it has to initiate. Some examples include:

- Incident Triggers that generate a record in the Incident Management system, thus initiating the Incident Management process
- Change Triggers that generate a Request for Change (RFC), thus initiating the Change Management process
- A trigger resulting from a approved RFC that has been implemented but caused the event, or from an unauthorised change that has been detected – in either case this will be referred to Change Management for investigation
- Scripts that execute specific actions, such as submitting batch jobs or rebooting a device
- Paging systems that will notify a person or team of the event by mobile phone
- Database triggers that restrict access of a user to specific records or fields, or that create or delete entries in the database.

4.1.5.8 Response selection

At this point in the process, there are a number of response options available. It is important to note that the response options can be chosen in any combination. For example, it may be necessary to preserve the log entry for future reference, but at the same time escalate the event to an Operations Management staff member for action.

The options in the flowchart are examples. Different organizations will have different options, and they are sure to be more detailed. For example, there will be a range of auto responses for each different technology. The process of determining which one is appropriate and how to execute it are not represented in this flowchart. Some of the options available are:

- **Event logged**: Regardless of what activity is performed, it is a good idea to have a record of the event and any subsequent actions. The event can be logged as an Event Record in the Event Management tool, or it can simply be left as an entry in the system log of the device or application that generated the event. If this is the case, though, there needs to be a

standing order for the appropriate Operations Management staff to check the logs on a regular basis and clear instructions about how to use each log. It should also be remembered that the event information in the logs may not be meaningful until an incident occurs; and where the Technical Management staff use the logs to investigate where the incident originated. This means that the Event Management procedures for each system or team need to define standards about how long events are kept in the logs before being archived and deleted.

- **Auto response**: Some events are understood well enough that the appropriate response has already been defined and automated. This is normally as a result of good design or of previous experience (usually Problem Management). The trigger will initiate the action and then evaluate whether it was completed successfully. If not, an Incident or Problem Record will be created. Examples of auto responses include:
  - Rebooting a device
  - Restarting a service
  - Submitting a job into batch
  - Changing a parameter on a device
  - Locking a device or application to protect it against unauthorized access.

  Note: locking a device may result in denial of service to authorized users, which could be exploited by a deliberate attacker – so great care should be taken when deciding whether this is an appropriate automated action. Where this response is used it may be prudent to also combine this with a call for human intervention, so that the automated action can be swiftly checked and approved.

- **Alert and human intervention**: If the event requires human intervention, it will need to be escalated. The purpose of the alert is to ensure that the person with the skills appropriate to deal with the event is notified. The alert will contain all the information necessary for that person to determine the appropriate action – including reference to any documentation required (e.g. user manuals). It is important to note that this is not necessarily the same as the functional escalation of an incident, where the emphasis is on restoring service within an agreed time (which may require a variety of activities). The alert requires a person, or team, to perform a specific action, possibly on a specific device and possibly at a specific time, e.g. changing a toner cartridge in a printer when the level is low.

- **Incident, problem or change?** Some events will represent a situation where the appropriate response will need to be handled through the Incident, Problem or Change Management process. These are discussed below, but it is important to note that a single incident may initiate any one or a combination of these three processes – for example, a non-critical server failure is logged as an incident, but as there is no workaround, a Problem Record is created to determine the root cause and resolution and an RFC is logged to relocate the workload onto an alternative server while the problem is resolved.

- **Open an RFC**: There are two places in the Event Management process where an RFC can be created:

  - **When an exception occurs**: For example, a scan of a network segment reveals that two new devices have been added without the necessary authorization. A way of dealing with this situation is to open an RFC, which can be used as a vehicle for the Change Management process to deal with the exception (as an alternative to the more conventional approach of opening an incident that would be routed via the Service Desk to Change Management). Investigation by Change Management is appropriate here since unauthorized changes imply that the Change Management process was not effective.

  - **Correlation identifies that a change is needed**: In this case the event correlation activity determines that the appropriate response to an event is for something to be changed. For example, a performance threshold has been reached and a parameter on a major server needs to be tuned. How does the correlation activity determine this? It was programmed to do so either in the Service Design process or because this has happened before and Problem Management or Operations Management updated the Correlation Engine to take this action.

- **Open an Incident Record**: As with an RFC, an incident can be generated immediately when an exception is detected, or when the Correlation Engine determines that a specific type or combination of events represents an incident. When an Incident Record is opened, as much information as possible should be included – with links to the events concerned and if possible a completed diagnostic script.

- **Open or link to a Problem Record**: It is rare for a Problem Record to be opened without related incidents (for example as a result of a Service Failure Analysis (see Service Design publication) or maturity assessment, or because of a high number of retry network errors, even though a failure has not yet occurred). In most cases this step refers to linking an incident to an existing Problem Record. This will assist the Problem Management teams to reassess the severity and impact of the problem, and may result in a changed priority to an outstanding problem. However, it is possible, with some of the more sophisticated tools, to evaluate the impact of the incidents and also to raise a Problem Record automatically, where this is warranted, to allow root-cause analysis to commence immediately.

- **Special types of incident**: In some cases an event will indicate an exception that does not directly impact any IT service, for example, a redundant air conditioning unit fails, or unauthorized entry to a data centre. Guidelines for these events are as follows:

  - An incident should be logged using an Incident Model that is appropriate for that type of exception, e.g. an Operations Incident or Security Incident (see paragraph 4.2.4.2 for more details of Incident Models).

  - The incident should be escalated to the group that manages that type of incident.

  - As there is no outage, the Incident Model used should reflect that this was an operational issue rather than a service issue. The statistics would not normally be reported to customers or users, unless they can be used to demonstrate that the money invested in redundancy was a good investment.

  - These incidents should not be used to calculate downtime, and can in fact be used to demonstrate how proactive IT has been in making services available.

4.1.5.9 Review actions

With thousands of events being generated every day, it is not possible formally to review every individual event. However, it is important to check that any significant events or exceptions have been handled appropriately, or to track trends or counts of event types, etc. In many cases this can be done automatically, for example polling a server that had been rebooted using an automated script to see that it is functioning correctly.

In the cases where events have initiated an incident, problem and/or change, the Action Review should not duplicate any reviews that have been done as part of those processes. Rather, the intention is to ensure that the handover between the Event Management process and other processes took place as designed and that the expected action did indeed take place. This will ensure that incidents, problems or changes originating within Operations Management do not get lost between the teams or departments.

The Review will also be used as input into continual improvement and the evaluation and audit of the Event Management process.

4.1.5.10 Close event

Some events will remain open until a certain action takes place, for example an event that is linked to an open incident. However, most events are not 'opened' or 'closed'.

Informational events are simply logged and then used as input to other processes, such as Backup and Storage Management. Auto-response events will typically be closed by the generation of a second event. For example, a device generates an event and is rebooted through auto response – as soon as that device is successfully back online, it generates an event that effectively closes the loop and clears the first event.

It is sometimes very difficult to relate the open event and the close notifications as they are in different formats. It is optimal that devices in the infrastructure produce 'open' and 'close' events in the same format and specify the change of status. This allows the correlation step in the process to easily match open and close notifications.

In the case of events that generated an incident, problem or change, these should be formally closed with a link to the appropriate record from the other process.

4.1.6 Triggers, input and output/inter-process interfaces

Event Management can be initiated by any type of occurrence. The key is to define which of these occurrences is significant and which need to be acted upon. Triggers include:

- Exceptions to any level of CI performance defined in the design specifications, OLAs or SOPs
- Exceptions to an automated procedure or process, e.g. a routine change that has been assigned to a build team has not been completed in time
- An exception within a business process that is being monitored by Event Management
- The completion of an automated task or job
- A status change in a device or database record

- Access of an application or database by a user or automated procedure or job
- A situation where a device, database or application, etc. has reached a predefined threshold of performance.

Event Management can interface to any process that requires monitoring and control, especially those that do not require real-time monitoring, but which do require some form of intervention following an event or group of events. Examples of interfaces with other processes include:

- Interface with business applications and/or business processes to allow potentially significant business events to be detected and acted upon (e.g. a business application reports abnormal activity on a customer's account that may indicate some sort of fraud or security breach).
- The primary ITSM relationships are with Incident, Problem and Change Management. These interfaces are described in some detail in paragraph 4.1.5.8.
- Capacity and Availability Management are critical in defining what events are significant, what appropriate thresholds should be and how to respond to them. In return, Event Management will improve the performance and availability of services by responding to events when they occur and by reporting on actual events and patterns of events to determine (by comparison with SLA targets and KPIs) if there is some aspect of the infrastructure design or operation that can be improved.
- Configuration Management is able to use events to determine the current status of any CI in the infrastructure. Comparing events with the authorized baselines in the Configuration Management System (CMS) will help to determine whether there is unauthorized Change activity taking place in the organization (see Service Transition publication).
- Asset Management (covered in more detail in the Service Design and Transition publications) can use Event Management to determine the lifecycle status of assets. For example, an event could be generated to signal that a new asset has been successfully configured and is now operational.
- Events can be a rich source of information that can be processed for inclusion in Knowledge Management systems. For example, patterns of performance can be correlated with business activity and used as input into future design and strategy decisions.

- Event Management can play an important role in ensuring that potential impact on SLAs is detected early and any failures are rectified as soon as possible so that impact on service targets is minimized.

4.1.7 Information Management

Key information involved in Event Management includes the following:

- SNMP messages, which are a standard way of communicating technical information about the status of components of an IT Infrastructure.
- Management Information Bases (MIBs) of IT devices. An MIB is the database on each device that contains information about that device, including its operating system, BIOS version, configuration of system parameters, etc. The ability to interrogate MIBs and compare them to a norm is critical to being able to generate events.
- Vendor's monitoring tools agent software.
- Correlation Engines contain detailed rules to determine the significance and appropriate response to events. Details on this are provided in paragraph 4.1.5.6.
- There is no standard Event Record for all types of event. The exact contents and format of the record depend on the tools being used, what is being monitored (e.g. a server and the Change Management tools will have very different data and probably use a different format). However, there is some key data that is usually required from each event to be useful in analysis. It should typically include the:
  - Device
  - Component
  - Type of failure
  - Date/time
  - Parameters in exception
  - Value.

4.1.8 Metrics

For each measurement period in question, the metrics to check on the effectiveness and efficiency of the Event Management process should include the following:

- Number of events by category
- Number of events by significance
- Number and percentage of events that required human intervention and whether this was performed
- Number and percentage of events that resulted in incidents or changes

- Number and percentage of events caused by existing problems or Known Errors. This may result in a change to the priority of work on that problem or Known Error
- Number and percentage of repeated or duplicated events. This will help in the tuning of the Correlation Engine to eliminate unnecessary event generation and can also be used to assist in the design of better event generation functionality in new services
- Number and percentage of events indicating performance issues (for example, growth in the number of times an application exceeded its transaction thresholds over the past six months)
- Number and percentage of events indicating potential availability issues (e.g. failovers to alternative devices, or excessive workload swapping)
- Number and percentage of each type of event per platform or application
- Number and ratio of events compared with the number of incidents.

4.1.9 Challenges, Critical Success Factors and risks

4.1.9.1 Challenges

There are a number of challenges that might be encountered:

- An initial challenge may be to obtain funding for the necessary tools and effort needed to install and exploit the benefits of the tools.
- One of the greatest challenges is setting the correct level of filtering. Setting the level of filtering incorrectly can result in either being flooded with relatively insignificant events, or not being able to detect relatively important events until it is too late.
- Rolling out of the necessary monitoring agents across the entire IT infrastructure may be a difficult and time-consuming activity requiring an ongoing commitment over quite a long period of time – there is a danger that other activities may arise that could divert resources and delay the rollout.
- Acquiring the necessary skills can be time consuming and costly.

4.1.9.2 Critical Success Factors

In order to obtain the necessary funding a compelling Business Case should be prepared showing how the benefits of effective Event Management can far outweigh the costs – giving a positive return on investment.

One of the most important CSFs is achieving the correct level of filtering. This is complicated by the fact that the significance of events changes. For example, a user logging into a system today is normal, but if that user leaves the organization and tries to log in it is a security breach.

There are three keys to the correct level of filtering, as follows:

■ Integrate Event Management into all Service Management processes where feasible. This will ensure that only the events significant to these processes are reported.
■ Design new services with Event Management in mind (this is discussed in detail in paragraph 4.1.10).
■ Trial and error. No matter how thoroughly Event Management is prepared, there will be classes of events that are not properly filtered. Event Management must therefore include a formal process to evaluate the effectiveness of filtering.

Proper planning is needed for the rollout of the monitoring agent software across the entire IT Infrastructure. This should be regarded as a project with realistic timescales and adequate resources being allocated and protected throughout the duration of the project.

4.1.9.3 Risks

The key risks are really those already mentioned above: failure to obtain adequate funding; ensuring the correct level of filtering; and failure to maintain momentum in rolling out the necessary monitoring agents across the IT Infrastructure. If any of these risks is not addressed it could adversely impact on the success of Event Management.

4.1.10 Designing for Event Management

Effective Event Management is not designed once a service has been deployed into Operations. Since Event Management is the basis for monitoring the performance and availability of a service, the exact targets and mechanisms for monitoring should be specified and agreed during the Availability and Capacity Management processes (see Service Design publication).

However, this does not mean that Event Management is designed by a group of remote system developers and then released to Operations Management together with the system that has to be managed. Nor does it mean that, once designed and agreed, Event Management becomes static – day-to-day operations will define additional events, priorities, alerts and other improvements

that will feed through the Continual Improvement process back into Service Strategy, Service Design etc.

Service Operation functions will be expected to participate in the design of the service and how it is measured (see section 3.4).

For Event Management, the specific design areas include the following.

4.1.10.1 Instrumentation

Instrumentation is the definition of what can be monitored about CIs and the way in which their behaviour can be affected. In other words, instrumentation is about defining and designing exactly how to monitor and control the IT Infrastructure and IT services.

Instrumentation is partly about a set of decisions that need to be made and partly about designing mechanisms to execute these decisions.

Decisions that need to be made include:

■ What needs to be monitored?
■ What type of monitoring is required (e.g. active or passive; performance or output)?
■ When do we need to generate an event?
■ What type of information needs to be communicated in the event?
■ Who are the messages intended for?

Mechanisms that need to be designed include:

■ How will events be generated?
■ Does the CI already have event generation mechanisms as a standard feature and, if so, which of these will be used? Are they sufficient or does the CI need to be customized to include additional mechanisms or information?
■ What data will be used to populate the Event Record?
■ Are events generated automatically or does the CI have to be polled?
■ Where will events be logged and stored?
■ How will supplementary data be gathered?

Note: A strong interface exists here with the application's design. All applications should be coded in such a way that meaningful and detailed error messages/codes are generated at the exact point of failure – so that these can be included in the event and allow swift diagnosis and resolution of the underlying cause. The need for the inclusion and testing of such error messaging is covered in more detail in the Service Transition publication.

4.1.10.2 Error messaging

Error messaging is important for all components (hardware, software, networks, etc.). It is particularly important that all software applications are designed to support Event Management. This might include the provision of meaningful error messages and/or codes that clearly indicate the specific point of failure and the most likely cause. In such cases the testing of new applications should include testing of accurate event generation.

Newer technologies such as Java Management Extensions (JMX) or HawkNL™ provide the tools for building distributed, web-based, modular and dynamic solutions for managing and monitoring devices, applications and service-driven networks. These can be used to reduce or eliminate the need for programmers to include error messaging within the code – allowing a valuable level of normalization and code-independence.

4.1.10.3 Event Detection and Alert Mechanisms

Good Event Management design will also include the design and population of the tools used to filter, correlate and escalate Events.

The Correlation Engine specifically will need to be populated with the rules and criteria that will determine the significance and subsequent action for each type of event.

Thorough design of the event detection and alert mechanisms requires the following:

- Business knowledge in relationship to any business processes being managed via Event Management
- Detailed knowledge of the Service Level Requirements of the service being supported by each CI
- Knowledge of who is going to be supporting the CI
- Knowledge of what constitutes normal and abnormal operation of the CI
- Knowledge of the significance of multiple similar events (on the same CI or various similar CIs
- An understanding of what they need to know to support the CI effectively
- Information that can help in the diagnosis of problems with the CI
- Familiarity with incident prioritization and categorization codes so that if it is necessary to create an Incident Record, these codes can be provided
- Knowledge of other CIs that may be dependent on the affected CI, or those CIs on which it depends
- Availability of Known Error information from vendors or from previous experience.

4.1.10.4 Identification of thresholds

Thresholds themselves are not set and managed through Event Management. However, unless these are properly designed and communicated during the instrumentation process, it will be difficult to determine which level of performance is appropriate for each CI.

Also, most thresholds are not constant. They typically consist of a number of related variables. For example, the maximum number of concurrent users before response time slows will vary depending on what other jobs are active on the server. This knowledge is often only gained by experience, which means that Correlation Engines have to be continually tuned and updated through the process of Continual Service Improvement.

4.2 INCIDENT MANAGEMENT

In ITIL terminology, an 'incident' is defined as:

An unplanned interruption to an IT service or reduction in the quality of an IT service. Failure of a configuration item that has not yet impacted service is also an incident, for example failure of one disk from a mirror set.

Incident Management is the process for dealing with all incidents; this can include failures, questions or queries reported by the users (usually via a telephone call to the Service Desk), by technical staff, or automatically detected and reported by event monitoring tools.

4.2.1 Purpose/goal/objective

The primary goal of the Incident Management process is to restore normal service operation as quickly as possible and minimize the adverse impact on business operations, thus ensuring that the best possible levels of service quality and availability are maintained. 'Normal service operation' is defined here as service operation within SLA limits.

4.2.2 Scope

Incident Management includes any event which disrupts, or which could disrupt, a service. This includes events which are communicated directly by users, either through the Service Desk or through an interface from Event Management to Incident Management tools.

Incidents can also be reported and/or logged by technical staff (if, for example, they notice something untoward with a hardware or network component they may report or log an incident and refer it to the Service Desk). This does not mean, however, that all events are incidents. Many classes of events are not related to disruptions at all, but are indicators of normal operation or are simply informational (see section 4.1).

Although both incidents and service requests are reported to the Service Desk, this does not mean that they are the same. Service requests do not represent a disruption to agreed service, but are a way of meeting the customer's needs and may be addressing an agreed target in an SLA. Service requests are dealt with by the Request Fulfilment process (see section 4.3).

4.2.3 Value to business

The value of Incident Management includes:

■ The ability to detect and resolve incidents, which results in lower downtime to the business, which in turn means higher availability of the service. This means that the business is able to exploit the functionality of the service as designed.

■ The ability to align IT activity to real-time business priorities. This is because Incident Management includes the capability to identify business priorities and dynamically allocate resources as necessary.

■ The ability to identify potential improvements to services. This happens as a result of understanding what constitutes an incident and also from being in contact with the activities of business operational staff.

■ The Service Desk can, during its handling of incidents, identify additional service or training requirements found in IT or the business.

Incident Management is highly visible to the business, and it is therefore easier to demonstrate its value than most areas in Service Operation. For this reason, Incident Management is often one of the first processes to be implemented in Service Management projects. The added benefit of doing this is that Incident Management can be used to highlight other areas that need attention – thereby providing a justification for expenditure on implementing other processes.

4.2.4 Policies/principles/basic concepts

There are some basic things that need to be taken into account and decided when considering Incident Management. These are covered in this section.

4.2.4.1 Timescales

Timescales must be agreed for all incident-handling stages (these will differ depending upon the priority level of the incident) – based upon the overall incident response and resolution targets within SLAs – and captured as targets within OLAs and Underpinning Contracts (UCs). All support groups should be made fully aware of these timescales. Service Management tools should be used to automate timescales and escalate the incident as required based on pre-defined rules.

4.2.4.2 Incident Models

Many incidents are not new – they involve dealing with something that has happened before and may well happen again. For this reason, many organizations will find it helpful to pre-define 'standard' Incident Models – and apply them to appropriate incidents when they occur.

An Incident Model is a way of pre-defining the steps that should be taken to handle a process (in this case a process for dealing with a particular type of incident) in an agreed way. Support tools can then be used to manage the required process. This will ensure that 'standard' incidents are handled in a pre-defined path and within pre-defined timescales.

Incidents which would require specialized handling can be treated in this way (for example, security-related incidents can be routed to Information Security Management and capacity- or performance-related incidents that would be routed to Capacity Management.

The Incident Model should include:

■ The steps that should be taken to handle the incident

■ The chronological order these steps should be taken in, with any dependences or co-processing defined

■ Responsibilities; who should do what

■ Timescales and thresholds for completion of the actions

■ Escalation procedures; who should be contacted and when

■ Any necessary evidence-preservation activities (particularly relevant for security- and capacity-related incidents).

The models should be input to the incident-handling support tools in use and the tools should then automate the handling, management and escalation of the process.

4.2.4.3 Major incidents

A separate procedure, with shorter timescales and greater urgency, must be used for 'major' incidents. A definition of what constitutes a major incident must be agreed and ideally mapped on to the overall incident prioritization system – such that they will be dealt with through the major incident process.

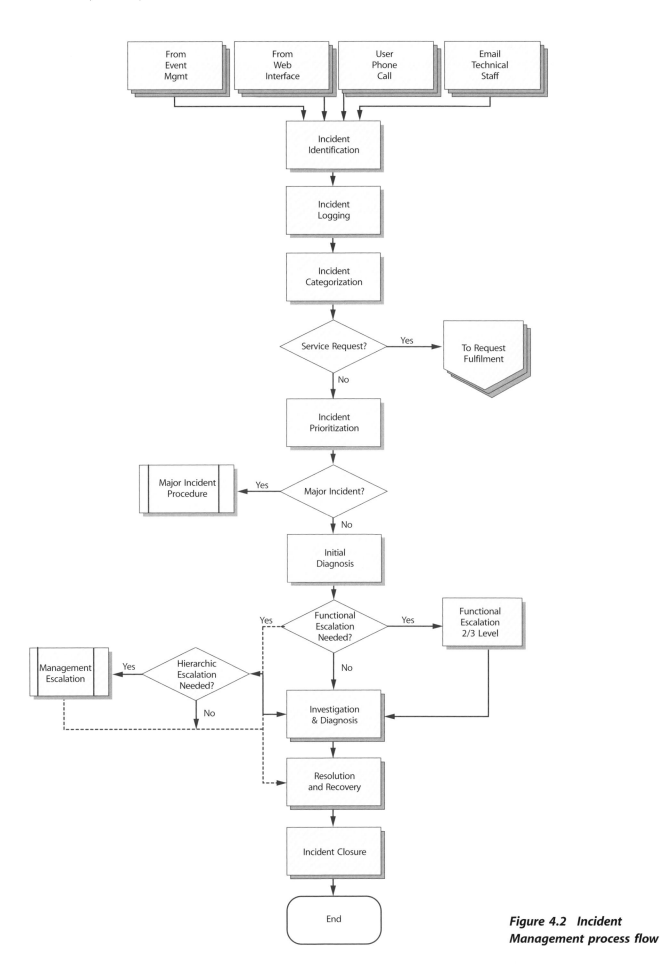

Figure 4.2 Incident Management process flow

Note: People sometimes use loose terminology and/or confuse a major incident with a problem. In reality, an incident remains an incident forever – it may grow in impact or priority to become a major incident, but an incident never 'becomes' a problem. A problem is the underlying cause of one or more incidents and remains a separate entity always!

Some lower-priority incidents may also have to be handled through this procedure – due to potential business impact – and some major incidents may not need to be handled in this way if the cause and resolutions are obvious and the normal incident process can easily cope within agreed target resolution times – provided the impact remains low!

Where necessary, the major incident procedure should include the dynamic establishment of a separate major incident team under the direct leadership of the Incident Manager, formulated to concentrate on this incident alone to ensure that adequate resources and focus are provided to finding a swift resolution. If the Service Desk Manager is also fulfilling the role of Incident Manager (say in a small organization), then a separate person may need to be designated to lead the major incident investigation team – so as to avoid conflict of time or priorities – but should ultimately report back to the Incident Manager.

If the cause of the incident needs to be investigated at the same time, then the Problem Manager would be involved as well but the Incident Manager must ensure that service restoration and underlying cause are kept separate. Throughout, the Service Desk would ensure that all activities are recorded and users are kept fully informed of progress.

4.2.5 Process activities, methods and techniques

The process to be followed during the management of an incident is shown in Figure 4.2. The process includes the following steps.

4.2.5.1 Incident identification

Work cannot begin on dealing with an incident until it is known that an incident has occurred. It is usually unacceptable, from a business perspective, to wait until a user is impacted and contacts the Service Desk. As far as possible, all key components should be monitored so that failures or potential failures are detected early so that the incident management process can be started quickly. Ideally, incidents should be resolved before they have an impact on users!

Please see section 4.1 for further details.

4.2.5.2 Incident logging

All incidents must be fully logged and date/time stamped, regardless of whether they are raised through a Service Desk telephone call or whether automatically detected via an event alert.

Note: If Service Desk and/or support staff visit the customers to deal with one incident, they may be asked to deal with further incidents 'while they are there'. It is important that if this is done, a separate Incident Record is logged for each additional incident handled – to ensure that a historical record is kept and credit is given for the work undertaken.

All relevant information relating to the nature of the incident must be logged so that a full historical record is maintained – and so that if the incident has to be referred to other support group(s), they will have all relevant information to hand to assist them.

The information needed for each incident is likely to include:

- Unique reference number
- Incident categorization (often broken down into between two and four levels of sub-categories)
- Incident urgency
- Incident impact
- Incident prioritization
- Date/time recorded
- Name/ID of the person and/or group recording the incident
- Method of notification (telephone, automatic, e-mail, in person, etc.)
- Name/department/phone/location of user
- Call-back method (telephone, mail, etc.)
- Description of symptoms
- Incident status (active, waiting, closed, etc.)
- Related CI
- Support group/person to which the incident is allocated
- Related problem/Known Error
- Activities undertaken to resolve the incident
- Resolution date and time
- Closure category
- Closure date and time.

Note: If the Service Desk does not work 24/7 and responsibility for first-line incident logging and handling passes to another group, such as IT Operations or Network

Support, out of Service Desk hours, then these staff need to be equally rigorous about logging of incident details. Full training and awareness needs to be provided to such staff on this issue.

4.2.5.3 Incident categorization

Part of the initial logging must be to allocate suitable incident categorization coding so that the exact type of the call is recorded. This will be important later when looking at incident types/frequencies to establish trends for use in Problem Management, Supplier Management and other ITSM activities.

Please note that the check for Service Requests in this process does not imply that Service Requests are incidents. This is simply recognition of the fact that Service Requests are sometimes incorrectly logged as incidents (e.g. a user incorrectly enters the request as an incident from the web interface). This check will detect any such requests and ensure that they are passed to the Request Fulfilment process.

Multi-level categorization is available in most tools – usually to three or four levels of granularity. For example, an incident may be categorized as shown in Figure 4.3.

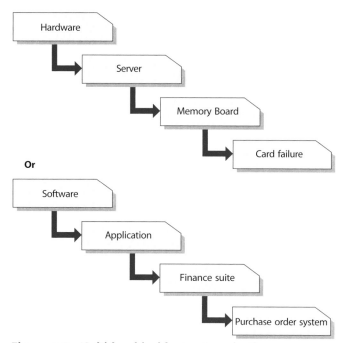

Figure 4.3   Multi-level incident categorization

All organizations are unique and it is therefore difficult to give generic guidance on the categories an organization should use, particularly at the lower levels. However, there is a technique that can be used to assist an organization

to achieve a correct and complete set of categories – if they are starting from scratch! The steps involve:

1   Hold a brainstorming session among the relevant support groups, involving the SD Supervisor and Incident and Problem Managers.

2   Use this session to decide the 'best guess' top-level categories – and include an 'other' category. Set up the relevant logging tools to use these categories for a trial period.

3   Use the categories for a short trial period (long enough for several hundred incidents to fall into each category, but not too long that an analysis will take too long to perform).

4   Perform an analysis of the incidents logged during the trial period. The number of incidents logged in each higher-level category will confirm whether the categories are worth having – and a more detailed analysis of the 'other' category should allow identification of any additional higher-level categories that will be needed.

5   A breakdown analysis of the incidents within each higher-level category should be used to decide the lower-level categories that will be required.

6   Review and repeat these activities after a further period – of, say, one to three months – and again regularly to ensure that they remain relevant. Be aware that any significant changes to categorization may cause some difficulties for incident trending or management reporting – so they should be stabilized unless changes are genuinely required.

If an existing categorization scheme is in use, but it is not thought to be working satisfactorily, the basic idea of the technique suggested above can be used to review and amend the existing scheme.

NOTE: Sometimes the details available at the time an incident is logged may be incomplete, misleading or incorrect. It is therefore important that the categorization of the incident is checked, and updated if necessary, at call closure time (in a separate closure categorization field, so as not to corrupt the original categorization) – please see paragraph 4.2.5.9.

4.2.5.4 Incident prioritization

Another important aspect of logging every incident is to agree and allocate an appropriate prioritization code – as this will determine how the incident is handled both by support tools and support staff.

Prioritization can normally be determined by taking into account both the urgency of the incident (how quickly the business needs a resolution) and the level of impact it is causing. An indication of impact is often (but not always) the number of users being affected. In some cases, and very importantly, the loss of service to a single user can have a major business impact – it all depends upon who is trying to do what – so numbers alone is not enough to evaluate overall priority! Other factors that can also contribute to impact levels are:

- Risk to life or limb
- The number of services affected – may be multiple services
- The level of financial losses
- Effect on business reputation
- Regulatory or legislative breaches.

An effective way of calculating these elements and deriving an overall priority level for each incident is given in Table 4.1:

Table 4.1 Simple priority coding system

		Impact		
		High	Medium	Low
	High	1	2	3
Urgency	Medium	2	3	4
	Low	3	4	5

Priority code	Description	Target resolution time
1	Critical	1 hour
2	High	8 hours
3	Medium	24 hours
4	Low	48 hours
5	Planning	Planned

In all cases, clear guidance – with practical examples – should be provided for all support staff to enable them to determine the correct urgency and impact levels, so the correct priority is allocated. Such guidance should be produced during service level negotiations.

However, it must be noted that there will be occasions when, because of particular business expediency or whatever, normal priority levels have to be overridden. When a user is adamant that an incident's priority level should exceed normal guidelines, the Service Desk should comply with such a request – and if it subsequently turns out to be incorrect this can be resolved as an off-line management level issue, rather than a dispute occurring when the user is on the telephone.

Some organizations may also recognize VIPs (high-ranking executives, officers, diplomats, politicians, etc.) whose incidents would be handled on a higher priority than normal – but in such cases this is best catered for and documented within the guidance provided to the Service Desk staff on how to apply the priority levels, so they are all aware of the agreed rules for VIPs, and who falls into this category.

It should be noted that an incident's priority may be dynamic – if circumstances change, or if an incident is not resolved within SLA target times, then the priority must be altered to reflect the new situation.

Note: some tools may have constraints that make it difficult automatically to calculate performance against SLA targets if a priority is changed during the lifetime of an incident. However, if circumstances do change, the change in priority should be made – and if necessary manual adjustments made to reporting tools. Ideally, tools with such constraints should not be selected.

4.2.5.5 Initial diagnosis

If the incident has been routed via the Service Desk, the Service Desk Analyst must carry out initial diagnosis, typically while the user is still on the telephone – if the call is raised in this way – to try to discover the full symptoms of the incident and to determine exactly what has gone wrong and how to correct it. It is at this stage that diagnostic scripts and known error information can be most valuable in allowing earlier and accurate diagnosis.

If possible, the Service Desk Analyst will resolve the incident while the user is still on the telephone – and close the incident if the resolution is successful.

If the Service Desk Analyst cannot resolve the incident while the user is still on the telephone, but there is a prospect that the Service Desk may be able to do so within the agreed time limit without assistance from other support groups, the Analyst should inform the user of their intentions, give the user the incident reference number and attempt to find a resolution.

4.2.5.6 Incident escalation

- **Functional escalation**. As soon as it becomes clear that the Service Desk is unable to resolve the incident itself (or when target times for first-point resolution have been exceeded – whichever comes first!) the incident must be immediately escalated for further support.

  If the organization has a second-level support group and the Service Desk believes that the incident can be resolved by that group, it should refer the incident to them. If it is obvious that the incident will need deeper technical knowledge, or when the second-level group has not been able to resolve the incident within agreed target times (whichever comes first), the incident must be immediately escalated to the appropriate third-level support group. Note that third-level support groups may be internal – but they may also be third parties such as software suppliers or hardware manufacturers or maintainers. The rules for escalation and handling of incidents must be agreed in OLAs and UCs with internal and external support groups respectively.

Note: Incident Ownership remains with the Service Desk! Regardless of where an incident is referred to during its life, ownership of the incident remains with the Service Desk at all times. The Service Desk remains responsible for tracking progress, keeping users informed and ultimately for Incident Closure.

■ **Hierarchic escalation**. If incidents are of a serious nature (for example Priority 1 incidents) the appropriate IT managers must be notified, for informational purposes at least. Hierarchic escalation is also used if the 'Investigation and Diagnosis' and 'Resolution and Recovery' steps are taking too long or proving too difficult. Hierarchic escalation should continue up the management chain so that senior managers are aware and can be prepared and take any necessary action, such as allocating additional resources or involving suppliers/maintainers. Hierarchic escalation is also used when there is contention about to whom the incident is allocated.

Hierarchic escalation can, of course, be initiated by the affected users or customer management, as they see fit – that is why it is important that IT managers are made aware so that they can anticipate and prepare for any such escalation.

The exact levels and timescales for both functional and hierarchic escalation need to be agreed, taking into account SLA targets, and embedded within support tools which can then be used to police and control the process flow within agreed timescales.

The Service Desk should keep the user informed of any relevant escalation that takes place and ensure the Incident Record is updated accordingly to keep a full history of actions.

Note regarding Incident allocation

There may be many incidents in a queue with the same priority level – so it will be the job of the Service Desk

and/or Incident Management staff initially, in conjunction with managers of the various support groups to which incidents are escalated, to decide the order in which incidents should be picked up and actively worked on. These managers must ensure that incidents are dealt with in true business priority order and that staff are not allowed to 'cherry-pick' the incidents they choose!

4.2.5.7 Investigation and Diagnosis

In the case of incidents where the user is just seeking information, the Service Desk should be able to provide this fairly quickly and resolve the service request – but if a fault is being reported, this is an incident and likely to require some degree of investigation and diagnosis.

Each of the support groups involved with the incident handling will investigate and diagnose what has gone wrong – and all such activities (including details of any actions taken to try to resolve or re-create the incident) should be fully documented in the incident record so that a complete historical record of all activities is maintained at all times.

Note: Valuable time can often be lost if investigation and diagnostic action (or indeed resolution or recovery actions) are performed serially. Where possible, such activities should be performed in parallel to reduce overall timescales – and support tools should be designed and/or selected to allow this. However, care should be taken to coordinate activities, particularly resolution or recovery activities, otherwise the actions of different groups may conflict or further complicate a resolution!

This investigation is likely to include such actions as:

■ Establishing exactly what has gone wrong or being sought by the user
■ Understanding the chronological order of events
■ Confirming the full impact of the incident, including the number and range of users affected
■ Identifying any events that could have triggered the incident (e.g. a recent change, some user action?)
■ Knowledge searches looking for previous occurrences by searching previous Incident/Problem Records and/or Known Error Databases or manufacturers'/suppliers' Error Logs or Knowledge Databases.

4.2.5.8 Resolution and Recovery

When a potential resolution has been identified, this should be applied and tested. The specific actions to be undertaken and the people who will be involved in taking the recovery actions may vary, depending upon the nature of the fault – but could involve:

- Asking the user to undertake directed activities on their own desk top or remote equipment
- The Service Desk implementing the resolution either centrally (say, rebooting a server) or remotely using software to take control of the user's desktop to diagnose and implement a resolution
- Specialist support groups being asked to implement specific recovery actions (e.g. Network Support reconfiguring a router)
- A third-party supplier or maintainer being asked to resolve the fault.

Even when a resolution has been found, sufficient testing must be performed to ensure that recovery action is complete and that the service has been fully restored to the user(s).

NOTE: in some cases it may be necessary for two or more groups to take separate, though perhaps coordinated, recovery actions for an overall resolution to be implemented. In such cases Incident Management must coordinate the activities and liaise with all parties involved.

Regardless of the actions taken, or who does them, the Incident Record must be updated accordingly with all relevant information and details so that a full history is maintained.

The resolving group should pass the incident back to the Service Desk for closure action.

4.2.5.9 Incident Closure

The Service Desk should check that the incident is fully resolved and that the users are satisfied and willing to agree the incident can be closed. The Service Desk should also check the following:

- **Closure categorization**. Check and confirm that the initial incident categorization was correct or, where the categorization subsequently turned out to be incorrect, update the record so that a correct closure categorization is recorded for the incident – seeking advise or guidance from the resolving group(s) as necessary.
- **User satisfaction survey**. Carry out a user satisfaction call-back or e-mail survey for the agreed percentage of incidents.
- **Incident documentation**. Chase any outstanding details and ensure that the Incident Record is fully documented so that a full historic record at a sufficient level of detail is complete.

- **Ongoing or recurring problem?** Determine (in conjunction with resolver groups) whether it is likely that the incident could recur and decide whether any preventive action is necessary to avoid this. In conjunction with Problem Management, raise a Problem Record in all such cases so that preventive action is initiated.
- **Formal closure**. Formally close the Incident Record.

Note: Some organizations may chose to utilize an automatic closure period on specific, or even all, incidents (e.g. incident will be automatically closed after two working days if no further contact is made by the user). Where this approach is to be considered, it must first be fully discussed and agreed with the users – and widely publicized so that all users and IT staff are aware of this. It may be inappropriate to use this method for certain types of incidents – such as major incidents or those involving VIPs, etc.

Rules for re-opening incidents

Despite all adequate care, there will be occasions when incidents recur even though they have been formally closed. Because of such cases, it is wise to have pre-defined rules about if and when an incident can be re-opened. It might make sense, for example, to agree that if the incident recurs within one working day then it can be re-opened – but that beyond this point a new incident must be raised, but linked to the previous incident(s).

The exact time threshold/rules may vary between individual organizations – but clear rules should be agreed and documented and guidance given to all Service Desk staff so that uniformity is applied.

4.2.6 Triggers, input and output/inter-process interfaces

Incidents can be triggered in many ways. The most common route is when a user rings the Service Desk or completes a web-based incident-logging screen, but increasingly incidents are raised automatically via Event Management tools. Technical staff may notice potential failures and raise an incident, or ask the Service Desk to do so, so that the fault can be addressed. Some incidents may also arise at the initiation of suppliers – who may send some form of notification of a potential or actual difficulty that needs attention.

The interfaces with Incident Management include:

- **Problem Management**: Incident Management forms part of the overall process of dealing with problems in the organization. Incidents are often caused by underlying problems, which must be solved to prevent the incident from recurring. Incident Management provides a point where these are reported.

- **Configuration Management** provides the data used to identify and progress incidents. One of the uses of the CMS is to identify faulty equipment and to assess the impact of an incident. It is also used to identify the users affected by potential problems. The CMS also contains information about which categories of incident should be assigned to which support group. In turn, Incident Management can maintain the status of faulty CIs. It can also assist Configuration Management to audit the infrastructure when working to resolve an incident.

- **Change Management**: Where a change is required to implement a workaround or resolution, this will need to be logged as an RFC and progressed through Change Management. In turn, Incident Management is able to detect and resolve incidents that arise from failed changes.

- **Capacity Management**: Incident Management provides a trigger for performance monitoring where there appears to be a performance problem. Capacity Management may develop workarounds for incidents.

- **Availability Management**; will use Incident Management data to determine the availability of IT services and look at where the incident lifecycle can be improved.

- **SLM**: The ability to resolve incidents in a specified time is a key part of delivering an agreed level of service. Incident Management enables SLM to define measurable responses to service disruptions. It also provides reports that enable SLM to review SLAs objectively and regularly. In particular, Incident Management is able to assist in defining where services are at their weakest, so that SLM can define actions as part of the Service Improvement Plan (SIP) – please see the Continual Service Improvement publication for more details. SLM defines the acceptable levels of service within which Incident Management works, including:
  - Incident response times
  - Impact definitions
  - Target fix times
  - Service definitions, which are mapped to users
  - Rules for requesting services
  - Expectations for providing feedback to users.

4.2.7 Information Management

Most information used in Incident Management comes from the following sources:

- **The Incident Management tools**, which contain information about:
  - Incident and problem history
  - Incident categories
  - Action taken to resolve incidents
  - Diagnostic scripts which can help first-line analysts to resolve the incident, or at least gather information that will help second- or third-line analysts resolve it faster.

- **Incident Records**, which include the following data:
  - Unique reference number
  - Incident classification
  - Date and time of recording and any subsequent activities
  - Name and identity of the person recording and updating the Incident Record
  - Name/organization/contact details of affected user(s)
  - Description of the incident symptoms
  - Details of any actions taken to try to diagnose, resolve or re-create the incident
  - Incident category, impact, urgency and priority
  - Relationship with other incidents, problems, changes or Known Errors
  - Closure details, including time, category, action taken and identity of person closing the record.

Incident Management also requires access to the CMS. This will help it to identify the CIs affected by the incident and also to estimate the impact of the incident.

The Known Error Database provides valuable information about possible resolutions and workarounds. This is discussed in detail in paragraph 4.4.7.2.

4.2.8 Metrics

The metrics that should be monitored and reported upon to judge the efficiency and effectiveness of the Incident Management process, and its operation, will include:

- Total numbers of Incidents (as a control measure)
- Breakdown of incidents at each stage (e.g. logged, work in progress, closed etc)
- Size of current incident backlog
- Number and percentage of major incidents
- Mean elapsed time to achieve incident resolution or circumvention, broken down by impact code
- Percentage of incidents handled within agreed response time (incident response-time targets may be specified in SLAs, for example, by impact and urgency codes)

- Average cost per incident
- Number of incidents reopened and as a percentage of the total
- Number and percentage of incidents incorrectly assigned
- Number and percentage of incidents incorrectly categorized
- Percentage of Incidents closed by the Service Desk without reference to other levels of support (often referred to as 'first point of contact')
- Number and percentage the of incidents processed per Service Desk agent
- Number and percentage of incidents resolved remotely, without the need for a visit
- Number of incidents handled by each Incident Model
- Breakdown of incidents by time of day, to help pinpoint peaks and ensure matching of resources.

Reports should be produced under the authority of the Incident Manager, who should draw up a schedule and distribution list, in collaboration with the Service Desk and support groups handling incidents. Distribution lists should at least include IT Services Management and specialist support groups. Consider also making the data available to users and customers, for example via SLA reports.

4.2.9 Challenges, Critical Success Factors and risks

4.2.9.1 Challenges

The following challenges will exist for successful Incident Management:

- The ability to detect incidents as early as possible. This will require education of the users reporting incidents, the use of Super Users (see paragraph 6.2.4.5) and the configuration of Event Management tools.
- Convincing all staff (technical teams as well as users) that all incidents must be logged, and encouraging the use of self-help web-based capabilities (which can speed up assistance and reduce resource requirements).
- Availability of information about problems and Known Errors. This will enable Incident Management staff to learn from previous incidents and also to track the status of resolutions.
- Integration into the CMS to determine relationships between CIs and to refer to the history of CIs when performing first-line support.

- Integration into the SLM process. This will assist Incident Management correctly to assess the impact and priority of incidents and assists in defining and executing escalation procedures. SLM will also benefit from the information learned during Incident Management, for example in determining whether service level performance targets are realistic and achievable.

4.2.9.2 Critical Success Factors

The following factors will be critical for successful Incident Management:

- A good Service Desk is key to successful Incident Management
- Clearly defined targets to work to – as defined in SLAs
- Adequate customer-oriented and technically training support staff with the correct skill levels, at all stages of the process
- Integrated support tools to drive and control the process
- OLAs and UCs that are capable of influencing and shaping the correct behaviour of all support staff.

4.2.9.3 Risks

The risks to successful Incident Management are actually similar to some of the challenges and the reverse of some of the Critical Success Factors mentioned above. They include:

- Being inundated with incidents that cannot be handled within acceptable timescales due to a lack of available or properly trained resources
- Incidents being bogged down and not progressed as intended because of inadequate support tools to raise alerts and prompt progress
- Lack of adequate and/or timely information sources because of inadequate tools or lack of integration
- Mismatches in objectives or actions because of poorly aligned or non-existent OLAs and/or UCs.

4.3 REQUEST FULFILMENT

The term 'Service Request' is used as a generic description for many varying types of demands that are placed upon the IT Department by the users. Many of these are actually small changes – low risk, frequently occurring, low cost, etc. (e.g. a request to change a password, a request to install an additional software application onto a particular workstation, a request to relocate some items of desktop equipment) or maybe just a question requesting information – but their scale and frequent, low-risk nature means that they are better handled by a separate process, rather than being allowed to congest and obstruct the normal Incident and Change Management processes.

4.3.1 Purpose/goal/objective

Request Fulfilment is the processes of dealing with Service Requests from the users. The objectives of the Request Fulfilment process include:

■ To provide a channel for users to request and receive standard services for which a pre-defined approval and qualification process exists

■ To provide information to users and customers about the availability of services and the procedure for obtaining them

■ To source and deliver the components of requested standard services (e.g. licences and software media)

■ To assist with general information, complaints or comments.

4.3.2 Scope

The process needed to fulfil a request will vary depending upon exactly what is being requested – but can usually be broken down into a set of activities that have to be performed. Some organizations will be comfortable to let the Service Requests be handled through their Incident Management processes (and tools) – with Service Requests being handled as a particular type of 'incident' (using a high-level categorization system to identify those 'incidents' that are in fact Service Requests).

Note, however, that there is a significant difference here – an incident is usually an unplanned event whereas a Service Request is usually something that can and should be planned!

Therefore, in an organization where large numbers of Service Requests have to be handled, and where the actions to be taken to fulfil those requests are very varied or specialized, it may be appropriate to handle Service Requests as a completely separate work stream – and to record and manage them as a separate record type.

This may be particularly appropriate if the organization has chosen to widen the scope of the Service Desk to expand upon just IT-related issues and use the desk as a focal point for other types or request for service – for example, a request to service a photocopier or even going so far as to include, for example, building management issues, such as a need to replace a light fitment or repair a leak in the plumbing.

Note: It will ultimately be up to each organization to decide and document which request it will handle

through the Request Fulfilment process and which others will have to go through more formal Change Management. There will always be grey areas which prevent generic guidance from being usefully prescribed.

4.3.3 Value to business

The value of Request Fulfilment is to provide quick and effective access to standard services which business staff can use to improve their productivity or the quality of business services and products.

Request Fulfilment effectively reduces the bureaucracy involved in requesting and receiving access to existing or new services, thus also reducing the cost of providing these services. Centralizing fulfilment also increases the level of control over these services. This in turn can help reduce costs through centralized negotiation with suppliers, and can also help to reduce the cost of support.

4.3.4 Policies/principles/basic concepts

Many Service Requests will be frequently recurring, so a predefined process flow (a model) can be devised to include the stages needed to fulfil the request, the individuals or support groups involved, target timescales and escalation paths. Service Requests will usually be satisfied by implementing a Standard Change (see the Service Transition publication for further details on Standard Changes). The ownership of Service Requests resides with the Service Desk, which monitors, escalates, dispatches and often fulfils the user request.

4.3.4.1 Request Models

Some Service Requests will occur frequently and will require handling in a consistent manner in order to meet agreed service levels. To assist this, many organizations will wish to create pre-defined Request Models (which typically include some form of pre-approval by Change Management). This is similar in concept to the idea of Incident Models already described in paragraph 4.2.4.2, but applied to Service Requests.

4.3.5 Process activities, methods and techniques

4.3.5.1 Menu selection

Request Fulfilment offers great opportunities for self-help practices where users can generate a Service Request using technology that links into Service Management tools. Ideally, users should be offered a 'menu'-type selection via a web interface, so that they can select and input details of Service Requests from a pre-defined list –

appropriate expectations can be set by giving target delivery and/or implementation targets/dates (in line with SLA targets). Where organizations are offering a self-help IT support capability to the users, it would make sense to combine this with a Request Fulfilment system as described.

Specialist web tools to offer this type of 'shopping basket' experience can be used together with interfaces directly to the back-end integrated ITSM tools, or other more general business process automation or Enterprise Resource Planning (ERP) tools that may be used for management of the Request Fulfilment activities.

4.3.5.2 Financial approval

One important extra step that is likely to be needed when dealing with a service request is that of financial approval.

Most requests will have some form of financial implications, regardless of the type of commercial arrangements in place. The cost of fulfilling the request must first be established. It may be possible to agree fixed prices for 'standard' requests – and prior approval for such requests may be given as part of the organization's overall annual financial management. In all other cases, an estimate of the cost must be produced and submitted to the user for financial approval (the user may need to seek approval up their management/financial chain). If approval is given, in addition to fulfilling the request, the process must also include charging (billing or cross-charging) for the work done – if charging is in place.

4.3.5.3 Other approval

In some cases further approval may be needed – such as compliance-related or wider business approval. Request Fulfilment must have the ability to define and check such approvals where needed.

4.3.5.4 Fulfilment

The actual fulfilment activity will depend upon the nature of the Service Request. Some simpler requests may be completed by the Service Desk, acting as first-line support, while others will have to be forwarded to specialist groups and/or suppliers for fulfilment.

Some organizations may have specialist fulfilment groups (to 'pick, pack and dispatch') – or may have outsourced some fulfilment activities to a third-party supplier(s). The Service Desk should monitor and chase progress and keep users informed throughout, regardless of the actual fulfilment source.

4.3.5.5 Closure

When the Service Request has been fulfilled it must be referred back to the Service Desk for closure. The Service Desk should go through the same closure process as described earlier in paragraph 4.2.5.9 – checking that the user is satisfied with the outcome.

4.3.6 Triggers, input and output/inter-process interfaces

Most requests will be triggered through either a user calling the Service Desk or a user completing some form of self-help web-based input screen to make their request. The latter will often involve a selection from a portfolio of available request types.

The primary interfaces with Request Fulfilment include:

- **Service Desk/Incident Management**: Many Service Requests may come in via the Service Desk and may be initially handled through the Incident Management process. Some organizations may choose that all requests are handled via this route – but others may choose to have a separate process, for reasons already discussed earlier in this chapter.

- A strong link is also needed between **Request Fulfilment, Release, Asset and Configuration Management** – as some requests will be for the deployment of new or upgraded components that can be automatically deployed. In such cases the 'release' can be pre-defined, built and tested but only deployed upon request by those who want the 'release'. Upon deployment, the CMS will have to be updated to reflect the change. Where appropriate, software licence checks/updates will also be necessary.

Where appropriate, it will be necessary to relate IT-related Service Requests to any incidents or problems that have initiated the need for the request (as would be the case for any other type of change).

4.3.7 Information Management

Request Fulfilment is dependent on information from the following sources:

- **The Service Requests** will contain information about:
  - What service is being requested
  - Who requested and authorized the service
  - Which process will be used to fulfil the request
  - To whom it was assigned to and what action was taken

- The date and time when the request was logged as well as the date and time of all actions taken
- Closure details.
- **Requests for Change**: In some cases the Request Fulfilment process will be initiated by an RFC. This is typical where the Service Request relates to a CI
- **The Service Portfolio**, to enable the scope of agreed Service Request to be identified
- **Security Policies** will prescribe any controls to be executed or adhered to when providing the service, e.g. ensuring that the requester is authorized to access the service, or that the software is licensed.

4.3.8 Metrics

The metrics needed to judge the effectiveness and efficiency of Request Fulfilment will include the following (each metric will need to be broken down by request type, within the period):

- The total number of Service Requests (as a control measure)
- Breakdown of service requests at each stage (e.g. logged, WIP, closed, etc.)
- The size of current backlog of outstanding Service Requests
- The mean elapsed time for handling each type of Service Request
- The number and percentage of Service Requests completed within agreed target times
- The average cost per type of Service Request
- Level of client satisfaction with the handling of Service Requests (as measured in some form of satisfaction survey).

4.3.9 Challenges, Critical Success Factors and risks

4.3.9.1 Challenges

The following challenges will be faced when introducing Request Fulfilment:

- Clearly defining and documenting the type of requests that will be handled within the Request Fulfilment process (and those that will either go through the Service Desk and be handled as incidents or those that will need to go through formal Change Management) – so that all parties are absolutely clear on the scope.
- Establishing self-help front-end capabilities that allow the users to interface successfully with the Request Fulfilment process.

4.3.9.2 Critical Success Factors

Request Fulfilment depends on the following Critical Success Factors:

- Agreement of what services will be standardized and who is authorized to request them. The cost of these services must also be agreed. This may be done as part of the SLM process. Any variances of the services must also be defined.
- Publication of the services to users as part of the Service Catalogue. It is important that this part of the Service Catalogue must be easily accessed, perhaps on the Intranet, and should be recognized as the first source of information for users seeking access to a service.
- Definition of a standard fulfilment procedure for each of the services being requested. This includes all procurement policies and the ability to generate purchase orders and work orders
- A single point of contact which can be used to request the service. This is often provided by the Service Desk or through an Intranet request, but could be through an automated request directly into the Request Fulfilment or procurement system.
- Self-service tools needed to provide a front-end interface to the users. It is essential that these integrate with the back-end fulfilment tools, often managed through Incident or Change Management.

4.3.9.3 Risks

Risks that may be encountered with Request Fulfilment include:

- Poorly defined scope, where people are unclear about exactly what the process is expected to handle
- Poorly designed or implemented user interfaces so that users have difficulty raising the requests that they need
- Badly designed or operated back-end fulfilment processes that are incapable of dealing with the volume or nature of the requests being made
- Inadequate monitoring capabilities so that accurate metrics cannot be gathered.

4.4 PROBLEM MANAGEMENT

ITIL defines a 'problem' as the unknown cause of one or more incidents.

4.4.1 Purpose/goal/objective

Problem Management is the process responsible for managing the lifecycle of all problems. The primary objectives of Problem Management are to prevent problems and resulting incidents from happening, to eliminate recurring incidents and to minimize the impact of incidents that cannot be prevented.

4.4.2 Scope

Problem Management includes the activities required to diagnose the root cause of incidents and to determine the resolution to those problems. It is also responsible for ensuring that the resolution is implemented through the appropriate control procedures, especially Change Management and Release Management.

Problem Management will also maintain information about problems and the appropriate workarounds and resolutions, so that the organization is able to reduce the number and impact of incidents over time. In this respect, Problem Management has a strong interface with Knowledge Management, and tools such as the Known Error Database will be used for both.

Although Incident and Problem Management are separate processes, they are closely related and will typically use the same tools, and may use similar categorization, impact and priority coding systems. This will ensure effective communication when dealing with related incidents and problems.

4.4.3 Value to business

Problem Management works together with Incident Management and Change Management to ensure that IT service availability and quality are increased. When incidents are resolved, information about the resolution is recorded. Over time, this information is used to speed up the resolution time and identify permanent solutions, reducing the number and resolution time of incidents. This results in less downtime and less disruption to business critical systems.

Additional value is derived from the following:

- Higher availability of IT services
- Higher productivity of business and IT staff
- Reduced expenditure on workarounds or fixes that do not work
- Reduction in cost of effort in fire-fighting or resolving repeat incidents.

4.4.4 Policies/principles/basic concepts

There are some important concepts of Problem Management that must be taken into account from the outset. These include:

4.4.4.1 Problem Models

Many problems will be unique and will require handling in an individual way – but it is conceivable that some incidents may recur because of dormant or underlying problems (for example, where the cost of a permanent resolution will be high and a decision has been taken not to go ahead with an expensive solution – but to 'live with' the problem).

As well as creating a Known Error Record in the Known Error Database (see paragraph 4.4.5.7) to ensure quicker diagnosis, the creation of a Problem Model for handling such problems in the future may be helpful. This is very similar in concept to the idea of Incident Models already described in paragraph 4.2.4.2, but applied to problems as well as incidents.

4.4.5 Process activities, methods and techniques

Problem Management consists of two major processes:

- **Reactive** Problem Management, which is generally executed as part of Service Operation – and is therefore covered in this publication
- **Proactive** Problem Management which is initiated in Service Operation, but generally driven as part of Continual Service Improvement (see this publication for fuller details).

The reactive Problem Management process is shown in Figure 4.4. This is a simplified chart to show the normal process flow, but in reality some of the states may be iterative or variations may have to be made in order to handle particular situations.

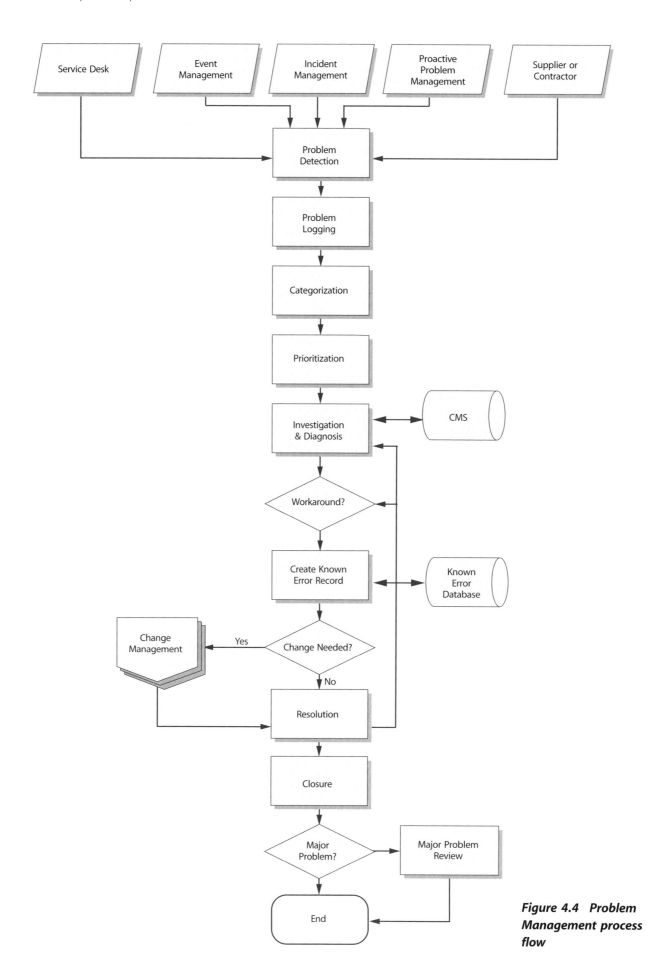

***Figure 4.4 Problem
Management process
flow***

4.4.5.1 Problem detection

It is likely that multiple ways of detecting problems will exist in all organizations. These will include:

- Suspicion or detection of an unknown cause of one or more incidents by the Service Desk, resulting in a Problem Record being raised – the desk may have resolved the incident but has not determined a definitive cause and suspects that it is likely to recur, so will raise a Problem Record to allow the underlying cause to be resolved. Alternatively, it may be immediately obvious from the outset that an incident, or incidents, has been caused by a major problem, so a Problem Record will be raised without delay.
- Analysis of an incident by a technical support group which reveals that an underlying problem exists, or is likely to exist.
- Automated detection of an infrastructure or application fault, using event/alert tools automatically to raise an incident which may reveal the need for a Problem Record.
- A notification from a supplier or contractor that a problem exists that has to be resolved.
- Analysis of incidents as part of proactive Problem Management – resulting in the need to raise a Problem Record so that the underlying fault can be investigated further.

Frequent and regular analysis of incident and problem data must be performed to identify any trends as they become discernible. This will require meaningful and detailed categorization of incidents/problems and regular reporting of patterns and areas of high occurrence. 'Top ten' reporting, with drill-down capabilities to lower levels, is useful in identifying trends.

Further details of how detected trends should be handled are included in the Continual Service Improvement publication.

4.4.5.2 Problem logging

Regardless of the detection method, all the relevant details of the problem must be recorded so that a full historic record exists. This must be date and time stamped to allow suitable control and escalation.

A cross-reference must be made to the incident(s) which initiated the Problem Record – and all relevant details must be copied from the Incident Record(s) to the Problem Record. It is difficult to be exact, as cases may vary, but typically this will include details such as:

- User details
- Service details
- Equipment details
- Date/time initially logged
- Priority and categorization details
- Incident description
- Details of all diagnostic or attempted recovery actions taken.

4.4.5.3 Problem Categorization

Problems must be categorized in the same way as incidents (and it is advisable to use the same coding system) so that the true nature of the problem can be easily traced in the future and meaningful management information can be obtained.

4.4.5.4 Problem Prioritization

Problems must be prioritized in the same way and for the same reasons as incidents – but the frequency and impact of related incidents must also be taken into account. The coding system described earlier in Table 4.1 (which combines impact with urgency to give an overall priority level) can be used to prioritize problems in the same way that it might be used for incidents, though the definitions and guidance to support staff on what constitutes a problem, and the related service targets at each level, must obviously be devised separately.

Problem prioritization should also take into account the severity of the problems. Severity in this context refers to how serious the problem is from an infrastructure perspective, for example:

- Can the system be recovered, or does it need to be replaced?
- How much will it cost?
- How many people, with what skills, will be needed to fix the problem?
- How long will it take to fix the problem?
- How extensive is the problem (e.g. how many CIs are affected)?

4.4.5.5 Problem Investigation and Diagnosis

An investigation should be conducted to try to diagnose the root cause of the problem – the speed and nature of this investigation will vary depending upon the impact, severity and urgency of the problem – but the appropriate level of resources and expertise should be applied to finding a resolution commensurate with the priority code allocated and the service target in place for that priority level.

There are a number of useful problem solving techniques that can be used to help diagnose and resolve problems –

and these should be used as appropriate. Such techniques are described in more detail later in this section.

The CMS must be used to help determine the level of impact and to assist in pinpointing and diagnosing the exact point of failure. The Know Error Database (KEDB) should also be accessed and problem-matching techniques (such as key word searches) should be used to see if the problem has occurred before and, if so, to find the resolution.

It is often valuable to try to recreate the failure, so as to understand what has gone wrong, and then to try various ways of finding the most appropriate and cost-effective resolution to the problem. To do this effectively without causing further disruption to the users, a test system will be necessary that mirrors the production environment.

There are many problem analysis, diagnosis and solving techniques available and much research has been done in this area. Some of the most useful and frequently used techniques include:

- **Chronological Analysis**: When dealing with a difficult problem, there are often conflicting reports about exactly what has happened and when. It is therefore very helpful briefly to document all events in chronological order – to provide a timeline of events. This often makes it possible to see which events may have been triggered by others – or to discount any claims that are not supported by the sequence of events.

- **Pain Value Analysis**: This is where a broader view is taken of the impact of an incident or problem, or incident/problem type. Instead of just analysing the number of incidents/problems of a particular type in a particular period, a more in-depth analysis is done to determine exactly what level of pain has been caused to the organization/business by these incidents/problems. A formula can be devised to calculate this pain level. Typically this might include taking into account:
  - The number of people affected
  - The duration of the downtime caused
  - The cost to the business (if this can be readily calculated or estimated).

  By taking all of these factors into account, a much more detailed picture of those incidents/problems or incident/problem types that are causing most pain can be determined – to allow a better focus on those things that really matter and deserve highest priority in resolving.

- **Kepner and Tregoe**: Charles Kepner and Benjamin Tregoe developed a useful way of problem analysis which can be used formally to investigate deeper-rooted problems. They defined the following stages:
  - defining the problem
  - describing the problem in terms of identity, location, time and size
  - establishing possible causes
  - testing the most probable cause
  - verifying the true cause.

  The method is described in fuller detail in Appendix C.

- **Brainstorming**: It can often be valuable to gather together the relevant people, either physically or by electronic means, and to 'brainstorm' the problem – with people throwing in ideas on what the potential cause may be and potential actions to resolve the problem. Brainstorming sessions can be very constructive and innovative but it is equally important that someone, perhaps the Problem Manager, documents the outcome and any agreed actions and keeps a degree of control in the session(s).

- **Ishikawa Diagrams**: Kaoru Ishikawa (1915–89), a leader in Japanese quality control, developed a method of documenting causes and effects which can be useful in helping identify where something may be going wrong, or be improved. Such a diagram is typically the outcome of a brainstorming session where problem solvers can offer suggestions. The main goal is represented by the trunk of the diagram, and primary factors are represented as branches. Secondary factors are then added as stems, and so on. Creating the diagram stimulates discussion and often leads to increased understanding of a complex problem. An example diagram is given in Appendix D.

- **Pareto Analysis**: This is a technique for separating important potential causes from more trivial issues. The following steps should be taken:
  1. Form a table listing the causes and their frequency as a percentage.
  2. Arrange the rows in the decreasing order of importance of the causes, i.e. the most important cause first.
  3. Add a cumulative percentage column to the table. By this step, the chart should look something like Table 4.2, which illustrates 10 causes of network failure in an organization.
  4. Create a bar chart with the causes, in order of their percentage of total.

Table 4.2   Pareto cause ranking chart

Causes	Percentage of total	Network failures	
		Computation	Cumulative %
Network Controller	35	0+35%	35
File corruption	26	35%+26%	61
Addressing conflicts	19	61%+19%	80
Server OS	6	80%+6%	86
Scripting error	5	86%+5%	91
Untested change	3	91%+3%	94
Operator error	2	94%+2%	96
Backup failure	2	96%+2%	98
Intrusion attempts	1	98%+1%	99
Disk failure	1	99%+1%	100

5   Superimpose a line chart of the cumulative percentages. The completed graph is illustrated in Figure 4.5.

6   Draw line at 80% on the y-axis parallel to the x-axis. Then drop the line at the point of intersection with the curve on the x-axis. This point on the x-axis separates the important causes and trivial causes. This line is represented as a dotted line in Figure 4.5.

From this chart it is clear to see that there are three primary causes for network failure in the organization. These should therefore be targeted first.

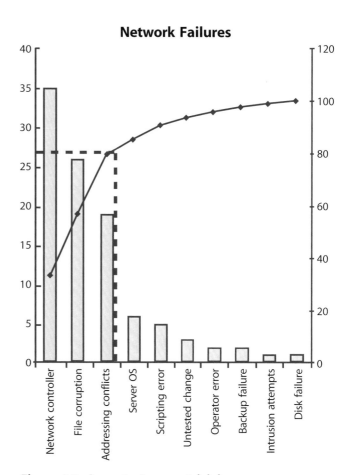

Figure 4.5   Important versus trivial causes

4.4.5.6 Workarounds

In some cases it may be possible to find a workaround to the incidents caused by the problem – a temporary way of overcoming the difficulties. For example, a manual amendment may be made to an input file to allow a program to complete its run successfully and allow a billing process to complete satisfactorily, but it is important that work on a permanent resolution continues where this is justified – in this example the reason for the file becoming corrupted in the first place must be found and corrected to prevent this happening again.

In cases where a workaround is found, it is therefore important that the problem record remains open, and details of the workaround are always documented within the Problem Record.

4.4.5.7 Raising a Known Error Record

As soon as the diagnosis is complete, and particularly where a workaround has been found (even though it may not yet be a permanent resolution), a Known Error Record must be raised and placed in the Known Error Database – so that if further incidents or problems arise, they can be identified and the service restored more quickly.

However, in some cases it may be advantageous to raise a Known Error Record even earlier in the overall process – just for information purposes, for example – even though the diagnosis may not be complete or a workaround found, so it is inadvisable to set a concrete procedural point exactly when a Known Error Record must be raised. It should be done as soon as it becomes useful to do so!

The Known Error Database and the way it should be used are described in more detail in paragraph 4.4.7.2.

4.4.5.8 Problem resolution

Ideally, as soon as a solution has been found, it should be applied to resolve the problem – but in reality safeguards may be needed to ensure that this does not cause further difficulties. If any change in functionality is required this will require an RFC to be raised and approved before the resolution can be applied. If the problem is very serious and an urgent fix is needed for business reasons, then an Emergency RFC should be handled by the Change Advisory Board Emergency Committee (CAB/EC) to facilitate this urgent action. Otherwise, the RFC should follow the established Change Management process for that type of change – and the resolution should be applied only when the change has been approved and scheduled for release. In the meantime, the KEDB should be used to help resolve quickly any further occurrences of the incidents/problems that occur.

Note: There may be some problems for which a Business Case for resolution cannot be justified (e.g. where the impact is limited but the cost of resolution would be extremely high). In such cases a decision may be taken to leave the Problem Record open but to use a workaround description in the Known Error Record to detect and resolve any recurrences quickly. Care should be taken to use the appropriate code to flag the open Problem Record so that it does not count against the performance of the team performing the process and so that unauthorized rework does not take place.

4.4.5.9 Problem Closure

When any change has been completed (and successfully reviewed), and the resolution has been applied, the Problem Record should be formally closed – as should any related Incident Records that are still open. A check should be performed at this time to ensure that the record contains a full historical description of all events – and if not, the record should be updated.

The status of any related Known Error Record should be updated to shown that the resolution has been applied.

4.4.5.10 Major Problem Review

After every major problem (as determined by the organization's priority system), while memories are still fresh a review should be conducted to learn any lessons for the future. Specifically, the review should examine:

- Those things that were done correctly
- Those things that were done wrong
- What could be done better in the future
- How to prevent recurrence
- Whether there has been any third-party responsibility and whether follow-up actions are needed.

Such reviews can be used as part of training and awareness activities for support staff – and any lessons learned should be documented in appropriate procedures, work instructions, diagnostic scripts or Known Error Records. The Problem Manager facilitates the session and documents any agreed actions.

The knowledge learned from the review should be incorporated into a service review meeting with the business customer to ensure the customer is aware of the actions taken and the plans to prevent future major incidents from occurring. This helps to improve customer satisfaction and assure the business that Service Operations is handling major incidents responsibly and actively working to prevent their future recurrence.

4.4.5.11 Errors detected in the development environment

It is rare for any new applications, systems or software releases to be completely error-free. It is more likely that during testing of such new applications, systems or releases a prioritization system will be used to eradicate the more serious faults, but it is possible that minor faults are not rectified – often because of the balance that has to be made between delivering new functionality to the business as quickly as possible and ensuring totally fault-free code or components.

Where a decision is made to release something into the production environment that includes known deficiencies, these should be logged as Known Errors in the KEDB, together with details of workarounds or resolution activities. There should be a formal step in the testing sign-off that ensures that this handover always takes place (see Service Transition publication).

Experience has shown if this does not happen, it will lead to far higher support costs when the users start to experience the faults and raise incidents that have to be re-diagnosed and resolved all over again!

4.4.6 Triggers, input and output/inter-process interfaces

The vast majority of Problem Records will be triggered in reaction to one or more incidents, and many will be raised or initiated via Service Desk staff. Other Problem Records, and corresponding Known Error Records, may be triggered in testing, particularly the latter stages of testing such as User Acceptance Testing/Trials (UAT), if a decision is made to go ahead with a release even though some faults are known. Suppliers may trigger the need for some Problem Records through the notification of potential faults or known deficiencies in their products or services (e.g. a warning may be given regarding the use of a particular CI and a Problem Record may be raised to facilitate the investigation by technical staff of the condition of such CIs within the organization's IT Infrastructure).

The primary relationship between Incident and Problem Management has been discussed in detail in paragraphs 4.2.6 and 4.4.5.1. Other key interfaces include the following:

- Service Transition
  - **Change Management**: Problem Management ensures that all resolutions or workarounds that require a change to a CI are submitted through Change Management through an RFC. Change Management will monitor the progress of these changes and keep Problem Management advised. Problem Management is also involved in rectifying the situation caused by failed changes.
  - **Configuration Management**: Problem Management uses the CMS to identify faulty CIs and also to determine the impact of problems and resolutions. The CMS can also be used to form the basis for the KEDB and hold or integrate with the Problem Records.
  - **Release and Deployment Management**: Is responsible for rolling problem fixes out into the live environment. It also assists in ensuring that the associated known errors are transferred from the development Known Error Database into the live Known Error Database. Problem Management will assist in resolving problems caused by faults during the release process.
- Service Design
  - **Availability Management**: Is involved with determining how to reduce downtime and increase uptime. As such, it has a close relationship with Problem Management, especially the proactive areas. Much of the management information available in Problem Management will be communicated to Availability Management.
  - **Capacity Management**: Some problems will require investigation by Capacity Management teams and techniques, e.g. performance issues. Capacity Management will also assist in assessing proactive measures. Problem Management provides management information relative to the quality of decisions made during the Capacity Planning process.
  - **IT Service Continuity**: Problem Management acts as an entry point into IT Service Continuity Management where a significant problem is not resolved before it starts to have a major impact on the business.
- Continual Service Improvement
  - **Service Level Management**: The occurrence of incidents and problems affects the level of service delivery measured by SLM. Problem Management contributes to improvements in service levels, and its management information is used as the basis of some of the SLA review components. SLM also provides parameters within which Problem Management works, such as impact information and the effect on services of proposed resolutions and proactive measures.

- Service Strategy
  - **Financial Management**: Assists in assessing the impact of proposed resolutions or workarounds, as well as Pain Value Analysis. Problem Management provides management information about the cost of resolving and preventing problems, which is used as input into the budgeting and accounting systems and Total Cost of Ownership calculations.

4.4.7 Information Management

4.4.7.1 CMS

The CMS will hold details of all of the components of the IT Infrastructure as well as the relationships between these components. It will act as a valuable source for problem diagnosis and for evaluating the impact of problems (e.g. if this disk is down, what data is on that disk; which services use that data; which users use those services?). As it will also hold details of previous activities, it can also be used as a valuable source of historical data to help identify trends or potential weaknesses – a key part of proactive Problem Management (see Continual Service Improvement publication).

4.4.7.2 Known Error Database

The purpose of a Known Error Database is to allow storage of previous knowledge of incidents and problems – and how they were overcome – to allow quicker diagnosis and resolution if they recur.

The Known Error Record should hold exact details of the fault and the symptoms that occurred, together with precise details of any workaround or resolution action that can be taken to restore the service and/or resolve the problem. An incident count will also be useful to determine the frequency with which incidents are likely to recur and influence priorities, etc.

It should be noted that a Business Case for a permanent resolution for some problems may not exist. For example, if a problem does not cause serious disruption and a workaround exists and/or the cost of resolving the problem far outweighs the benefits of a permanent resolution – then a decision may be taken to tolerate the existence of the problem. However, it will still be desirable to diagnose and implement a workaround as quickly as possible, which is where the KEDB can be of assistance.

It is essential that any data put into the database can be quickly and accurately retrieved. The Problem Manager should be fully trained and familiar with the search methods/algorithms used by the selected database and should carefully ensure that when new records are added, the relevant search key criteria are correctly included.

Care should be taken to avoid duplication of records (i.e. the same problem described in two or more ways as separate records). To avoid this, the Problem Manager should be the only person able to enter a new record. Other support groups should be allowed, indeed encouraged, to propose new records, but these should be vetted by the Problem Manager before entry to the KEDB. In large organizations where Problem Management staff exist in multiple locations but a single KEDB is used (recommended!), a procedure must be agreed between all Problem Management staff to ensure that such duplication cannot occur. This may involve designating just one staff member as the central KEDB Manager.

The KEDB should be used during the Incident and Problem Diagnosis phases to try to speed up the resolution process – and new records should be added as quickly as possible when a new problem has been identified and diagnosed.

All support staff should be fully trained and conversant with the value that the KEDB can offer and the way it should be used. They should be able readily to retrieve and use data.

Note: Some tools/implementations may choose to delineate Known Errors simply by changing a field in the original Problem Record. This is acceptable provided the same level of functionality is available.

The KEDB, like the CMS, forms part of a larger Service Knowledge Management System (SKMS) illustrated in Figure 4.6. More information on the SKMS can be found in the Service Transition publication.

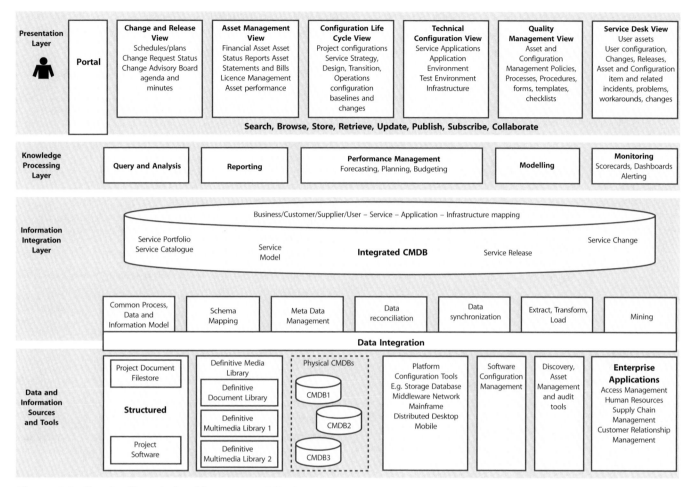

Figure 4.6 Service Knowledge Management System

4.4.8 Metrics

The following metrics should be used to judge the effectiveness and efficiency of the Problem Management process, or its operation:

- The total number of problems recorded in the period (as a control measure)
- The percentage of problems resolved within SLA targets (and the percentage that are not!)
- The number and percentage of problems that exceeded their target resolution times
- The backlog of outstanding problems and the trend (static, reducing or increasing?)
- The average cost of handling a problem
- The number of major problems (opened and closed and backlog)
- The percentage of Major Problem Reviews successfully performed
- The number of Known Errors added to the KEDB
- The percentage accuracy of the KEDB (from audits of the database)

- The percentage of Major Problem Reviews completed successfully and on time.

All metrics should be broken down by category, impact, severity, urgency and priority level and compared with previous periods.

4.4.9 Challenges, Critical Success Factors and risks

A major dependency for Problem Management is the establishment of an effective Incident Management process and tools. This will ensure that problems are identified as soon as possible and that as much work is done on pre-qualification as possible. However, it is also critical that the two processes have formal interfaces and common working practices. This implies the following:

- Linking Incident and Problem Management tools
- The ability to relate Incident and Problem Records
- The second- and third-line staff should have a good working relationship with staff on the first line
- Making sure that business impact is well understood by all staff working on problem resolution.

In addition it is important that Problem Management is able to use all Knowledge and Configuration Management resources available.

Another CSF is the ongoing training of technical staff in both technical aspects of their job as well as the business implications of the services they support and the processes they use.

4.5 ACCESS MANAGEMENT

Access Management is the process of granting authorized users the right to use a service, while preventing access to non-authorized users. It has also been referred to as Rights Management or Identity Management in different organizations.

4.5.1 Purpose/goal/objective

Access Management provides the right for users to be able to use a service or group of services. It is therefore the execution of policies and actions defined in Security and Availability Management.

4.5.2 Scope

Access Management is effectively the execution of both Availability and Information Security Management, in that it enables the organization to manage the confidentiality, availability and integrity of the organization's data and intellectual property.

Access Management ensures that users are given the right to use a service, but it does not ensure that this access is available at all agreed times – this is provided by Availability Management.

Access Management is a process that is executed by all Technical and Application Management functions and is usually not a separate function. However, there is likely to be a single control point of coordination, usually in IT Operations Management or on the Service Desk.

Access Management can be initiated by a Service Request through the Service Desk.

4.5.3 Value to business

Access Management provides the following value:

- Controlled access to services ensures that the organization is able to maintain more effectively the confidentiality of its information
- Employees have the right level of access to execute their jobs effectively

- There is less likelihood of errors being made in data entry or in the use of a critical service by an unskilled user (e.g. production control systems)
- The ability to audit use of services and to trace the abuse of services
- The ability more easily to revoke access rights when needed – an important security consideration
- May be needed for regulatory compliance (e.g. SOX, HIPAA, COBIT).

4.5.4 Policies/principles/basic concepts

Access Management is the process that enables users to use the services that are documented in the Service Catalogue. It comprises the following basic concepts:

- **Access** refers to the level and extent of a service's functionality or data that a user is entitled to use.
- **Identity** refers to the information about them that distinguishes them as an individual and which verifies their status within the organization. By definition, the Identity of a user is unique to that user. (This is covered in more detail in paragraph 4.5.7.1.)
- **Rights** (also called privileges) refer to the actual settings whereby a user is provided access to a service or group of services. Typical rights, or levels of access, include read, write, execute, change, delete.
- **Services or service groups**. Most users do not use only one service, and users performing a similar set of activities will use a similar set of services. Instead of providing access to each service for each user separately, it is more efficient to be able to grant each user – or group of users – access to the whole set of services that they are entitled to use at the same time. (This is discussed in more detail in paragraph 4.5.7.2.)
- **Directory Services** refers to a specific type of tool that is used to manage access and rights. These are discussed in section 5.8.

4.5.5 Process activities, methods and techniques

4.5.5.1 Requesting access

Access (or restriction) can be requested using one of any number of mechanisms, including:

- A standard request generated by the Human Resource system. This is generally done whenever a person is hired, promoted, transferred or when they leave the company
- A Request for Change
- A Service Request submitted via the Request Fulfilment system

- By executing a pre-authorized script or option (e.g. downloading an application from a staging server as and when it is needed).

Rules for requesting access are normally documented as part of the Service Catalogue.

4.5.5.2 Verification

Access Management needs to verify every request for access to an IT service from two perspectives:

- That the user requesting access is who they say they are
- That they have a legitimate requirement for that service.

The first category is usually achieved by the user providing their username and password. Depending on the organization's security policies, the use of the username and password are usually accepted as proof that the person is a legitimate user. However, for more sensitive services further identification may be required (biometric, use of an electronic access key or encryption device, etc.).

The second category will require some independent verification, other than the user's request. For example:

- Notification from Human Resources that the person is a new employee and requires both a username and access to a standard set of services
- Notification from Human Resources that the user has been promoted and requires access to additional resources
- Authorization from an appropriate (defined in the process) manager
- Submission of a Service Request (with supporting evidence) through the Service Desk
- Submission of an RFC (with supporting evidence) through Change Management, or execution of a pre-defined Standard Change
- A policy stating that the user may have access to an optional service if they need it.

For new services the Change Record should specify which users or groups of users will have access to the Service. Access Management will then check to see that all the users are still valid and automatically provide access as specified in the RFC.

4.5.5.3 Providing rights

Access Management does not decide who has access to which IT services. Rather, Access Management executes the policies and regulations defined during Service Strategy and Service Design. Access Management enforces

decisions to restrict or provide access, rather than making the decision.

As soon as a user has been verified, Access Management will provide that user with rights to use the requested service. In most cases this will result in a request to every team or department involved in supporting that service to take the necessary action. If possible, these tasks should be automated.

The more roles and groups that exist, the more likely that Role Conflict will arise. Role Conflict in this context refers to a situation where two specific roles or groups, if assigned to a single user, will create issues with separation of duties or conflict of interest. Examples of this include:

- One role requires detailed access, while another role prevents that access
- Two roles allow a user to perform two tasks that should not be combined (e.g. a contractor can log their time sheet for a project and then approve all payment on work for the same project).

Role Conflict can be avoided by careful creation of roles and groups, but more often they are caused by policies and decisions made outside of Service Operation – either by the business or by different project teams working during Service Design. In each case the conflict must be documented and escalated to the stakeholders to resolve.

Whenever roles and groups are defined, it is possible that they could be defined too broadly or too narrowly. There will always be users who need something slightly different from the pre-defined roles. In these cases, it is possible to use standard roles and then add or subtract specific rights as required – similar to the concept of Baselines and Variants in Configuration Management (see Service Transition publication). However, the decision to do this is not in the hands of individual operational staff members. Each exception should be coordinated by Access Management and approved through the originating process.

Access Management should perform a regular review of the roles and groups that it has created and manage to ensure that they are appropriate for the services that IT delivers and supports – and obsolete or unwanted roles/groups should be removed.

4.5.5.4 Monitoring identity status

As users work in the organization, their roles change and so also do their needs to access services. Examples of changes include:

- **Job changes**. In this case the user will possibly need access to different or additional services.
- **Promotions or demotions**. The user will probably use the same set of services, but will need access to different levels of functionality or data.
- **Transfers**. In this situation, the user may need access to exactly the same set of services, but in a different region with different working practices and different sets of data.
- **Resignation or death**. Access needs to be completely removed to prevent the username being used as a security loophole.
- **Retirement**. In many organizations, an employee who retires may still have access to a limited set of services, including benefits systems or systems that allow them to purchase company products at a reduced rate.
- **Disciplinary action**. In some cases the organization will require a temporary restriction to prevent the user from accessing some or all of the services that they would normally have access to. There should be a feature in the process and tools to do this, rather than having to delete and reinstate the user's access rights.
- **Dismissals**. Where an employee or contractor is dismissed, or where legal action is taken against a customer (for example for defaulting on payment for products purchased on the Internet), access should be revoked immediately. In addition, Access Management, working together with Information Security Management, should take active measures to prevent and detect malicious action against the organization from that user.

Access Management should understand and document the typical User Lifecycle for each type of user and use it to automate the process. Access Management tools should provide features that enable a user to be moved from one state to another, or from one group to another, easily and with an audit trail.

4.5.5.5 Logging and tracking access

Access Management should not only respond to requests. It is also responsible for ensuring that the rights that they have provided are being properly used.

In this respect, Access Monitoring and Control must be included in the monitoring activities of all Technical and Application Management functions and all Service Operation processes.

Exceptions should be handled by Incident Management, possibly using Incident Models specifically designed to deal with abuse of access rights. It should be noted that the visibility of such actions should be restricted. Making

this information available to all who have access to the Incident Management system will expose vulnerabilities.

Information Security Management plays a vital role in detecting unauthorized access and comparing it with the rights that were provided by Access Management. This will require Access Management involvement in defining the parameters for use in Intrusion Detection tools.

Access Management may also be required to provide a record of access for specific Services during forensic investigations. If a user is suspected of breaches of policy, inappropriate use of resources, or fraudulent use of data, Access Management may be required to provide evidence of dates, times and even content of that user's access to specific Services. This is normally provided by the Operational staff of that service, but working as part of the Access Management process.

4.5.5.6 Removing or restricting rights

Just as Access Management provides rights to use a Service, it is also responsible for revoking those rights. Again, this is not a decision that it makes on its own. Rather, it will execute the decisions and policies made during Service Strategy and Design and also decisions made by managers in the organization.

Removing access is usually done in the following circumstances:

- Death
- Resignation
- Dismissal
- When the user has changed roles and no longer requires access to the service
- Transfer or travel to an area where different regional access applies.

In other cases it is not necessary to remove access, but just to provide tighter restrictions. These could include reducing the level, time or duration of access. Situations in which access should be restricted include:

- When the user has changed roles or been demoted and no longer requires the same level of access
- When the user is under investigation, but still requires access to basic services, such as e-mail. In this case their e-mail may be subject to additional scanning (but this would need to be handled very carefully and in full accordance with the organization's security policy)
- When a user is away from the organization on temporary assignment and will not require access to that service for some time.

4.5.6 Triggers, input and output/inter-process interfaces

Access Management is triggered by a request for a user or users to access a service or group of services. This could originate from any of the following:

- **An RFC**. This is most frequently used for large-scale service introductions or upgrades where the rights of a significant number of users need to be updated as part of the project.
- **A Service Request**. This is usually initiated through the Service Desk, or directly into the Request Fulfilment system, and executed by the relevant Technical or Application Management teams.
- A request from the appropriate **Human Resources Management** personnel (which should be channelled via the Service Desk). This is usually generated as part of the process for hiring, promoting, relocating and termination or retirement.
- A request from the **manager of a department**, who could be performing an HR role, or who could have made a decision to start using a service for the first time.

Access Management should be linked to the Human Resource processes to verify the user's identify as well as to ensure that they are entitled to the services being requested.

Information Security Management is a key driver for Access Management as it will provide the security and data protection policies and tools needed to execute Access Management.

Change Management plays an important role as the means to control the actual requests for access. This is because any request for access to a service is a change, although it is usually processed as a Standard Change or Service Request (possibly using a model) once the criteria for access have been agreed through SLM.

SLM maintains the agreements for access to each service. This will include the criteria for who is entitled to access each service, what the cost of that access will be, if appropriate and what level of access will be granted to different types of user (e.g. managers or staff).

There is also a strong relationship between Access Management and Configuration Management. The CMS can be used for data storage and interrogated to determine current access details.

4.5.7 Information Management

4.5.7.1 Identity

The identity of a user is the information about them that distinguishes them as an individual and which verifies their status within the organization. By definition, the identity of a user is unique to that user. Since there are cases where two users share a common piece of information (e.g. they have the same name), identity is usually established using more than one piece of information, for example:

- Name
- Address
- Contact details, e.g. telephone, e-mail address, etc.
- Physical documentation, e.g. driver's licence, passport, marriage certificate, etc.
- Numbers that refer to a document or an entry in a database, e.g. employee number, tax number, government identity number, driver's licence number, etc.
- Biometric information, e.g. fingerprints, retinal images, voice recognition patterns, DNA, etc.
- Expiration date (if relevant).

A user identity is provided to anyone with a legitimate requirement to access IT services or organizational information. These could include:

- Employees
- Contractors
- Vendor staff (e.g. account managers, support personnel, etc.)
- Customers (especially when purchasing products or services over the Internet).

Most organizations will verify a user's identity before they join the organization by requesting a subset of the above information. The more secure the organization, the more types of information are required and the more thoroughly they are checked.

Many organizations will be faced with the need to provide access rights to temporary or occasional staff or contractors/suppliers. The management of access to such personnel often proves problematic – closing access after use is often as difficult to manage, or more so, than providing access initially. Well-defined procedures between IT and HR should be established that include fail-safe checks that ensure access rights are removed immediately they are no longer justified or required.

When a user is granted access to an application, it should already have been established by the organization (usually the Human Resources or Security Department) that the user is who they say they are.

At this point, all that information is filed and the file is associated with a corporate identity, usually an employee or contractor number and an identity that can be used to access corporate resources and information, usually a user identity or 'username' and an associated password.

4.5.7.2 Users, groups, roles and service groups

While each user has an individual identity, and each IT service can be seen as an entity in its own right, it is often helpful to group them together so that they can be managed more easily. Sometimes the terms 'user profile' or 'user template' or 'user role' are used to describe this type of grouping.

Most organizations have a standard set of services for all individual users, regardless of their position or job (excluding customers – who do not have any visibility to internal services and processes). These will include services such as messaging, office automation, Desktop Support, telephony, etc. New users are automatically provided with rights to use these services.

However, most users also have some specialized role that they perform. For example, in addition to the standard services, the user also performs a Marketing Management role, which requires that they have access to some specialized marketing and financial modelling tools and data.

Some groups may have unique requirements – such as field or home workers who may have to dial in or use Virtual Private Network (VPN) connections, with security implications that may have to be more tightly managed.

To make it easier for Access Management to provide the appropriate rights, it uses a catalogue of all the roles in the organization and which services support each role. This catalogue of roles should be compiled and maintained by Access Management in conjunction with HR and will often be automated in the Directory Services tools (see section 5.8).

In addition to playing different roles, users may also belong to different groups. For example, all contractors are required to log their timesheets in a dedicated Time Card System, which is not used by employees. Access Management will assess all the roles that a user plays as well as the groups that they belong to and ensure that they provide rights to use all associated services.

Note: All data held on users will be subject to data protection legislation (this exists in most geographic locations in some form or other) so should be handled

and protected as part of the organization's security procedures.

4.5.8 Metrics

Metrics that can be used to measure the efficiency and effectiveness of Access Management include:

- Number of requests for access (Service Request, RFC, etc.)
- Instances of access granted, by service, user, department, etc.
- Instances of access granted by department or individual granting rights
- Number of incidents requiring a reset of access rights
- Number of incidents caused by incorrect access settings.

4.5.9 Challenges, Critical Success Factors and risks

Conditions for successful Access Management include:

- The ability to verify the identity of a user (that the person is who they say they are)
- The ability to verify the identity of the approving person or body
- The ability to verify that a user qualifies for access to a specific service
- The ability to link multiple access rights to an individual user
- The ability to determine the status of the user at any time (e.g. to determine whether they are still employees of the organization when they log on to a system)
- The ability to manage changes to a user's access requirements
- The ability to restrict access rights to unauthorized users
- A database of all users and the rights that they have been granted.

4.6 OPERATIONAL ACTIVITIES OF PROCESSES COVERED IN OTHER LIFECYCLE PHASES

4.6.1 Change Management

Change Management is primarily covered in the Service Transition publication, but there are some aspects of Change Management which Service Operation staff will be involved with on a day-to-day basis. These include:

- Raising and submitting RFCs as needed to address Service Operation issues
- Participating in CAB or CAB/EC meetings to ensure that Service Operation risks, issues and views are taken into account
- Implementing changes as directed by Change Management where they involve Service Operation component or services
- Backing out changes as directed by Change Management where they involve Service Operation component or services
- Helping define and maintain change models relating to Service Operation components or services
- Receiving change schedules and ensuring that all Service Operation staff are made aware of and prepared for all relevant changes
- Using the Change Management process for standard, operational-type changes.

4.6.2 Configuration Management

Configuration Management is primarily covered in the Service Transition publication, but there are some aspects of Configuration Management which Service Operation staff will be involved with on a day-to-day basis. These include:

- Informing Configuration Management of any discrepancies found between any CIs and the CMS
- Making any amendments necessary to correct any discrepancies, under the authority of Configuration Management, where they involve any Service Operation components or services.

Responsibility for updating the CMS remains with Configuration Management, but in some cases Operations staff might be asked, under the direction of Configuration Management, to update relationships, or even to add new CIs or mark CIs as 'disposed' in the CMS, if these updates are related to operational activities actually performed by Operations staff.

4.6.3 Release and Deployment Management

Release and Deployment Management is primarily covered in the Service Transition publication, but there are some aspects of this process which Service Operation staff will be involved with on a day-to-day basis. These may include:

- Actual implementation actions regarding the deployment of new releases, under the direction of Release and Deployment Management, where they relate to Service Operation components or services

- Participation in the planning stages of major new releases to advise on Service Operation issues
- The physical handling of CIs from/to the DML as required to fulfil their operational roles – while adhering to relevant Release and Deployment Management procedures, such as ensure that all items are properly booked out and back in.

4.6.4 Capacity Management

Capacity Management should operate at three levels: Business Capacity Management, Service Capacity Management and Component Capacity Management.

- **Business Capacity Management** involves working with the business to plan and anticipate both longer-term strategic issues and shorter-term tactical initiatives that are likely to have an impact on IT capacity.
- **Service Capacity Management** is about understanding the characteristics of each of the IT services, and then the demands that different types of users or transactions have on the underlying infrastructure – and how these vary over time and might be impacted by business change.
- **Component Capacity Management** involves understanding the performance characteristics and capabilities and current utilization levels of all the technical components (CIs) that make up the IT Infrastructure, and predicting the impact of any changes or trends.

Many of these activities are of a strategic or longer-term planning nature and are covered in the Service Strategy, Service Design and Service Transition publications. However, there are a number of operational Capacity Management activities that must be performed on a regular ongoing basis as part of Service Operation. These include the following.

4.6.4.1 Capacity and Performance Monitoring

All components of the IT Infrastructure should be continually monitored (in conjunction with Event Management) so that any potential problems or trends can be identified before failures or performance degradation occurs. Ideally, such monitoring should be automated and thresholds should be set so that exception alerts are raised in good time to allow appropriate avoiding or recovery action to be taken before adverse impact occurs.

The components and elements to be monitored will vary depending upon the infrastructure in use, but will typically include:

- CPU utilization (overall and broken down by system/service usage)
- Memory utilization
- IO rates (physical and buffer) and device utilization
- Queue length (maximum and average)
- File store utilization (disks, partitions, segments)
- Applications (throughput rates, failure rates)
- Databases (utilization, record locks, indexing, contention)
- Network transaction rates, error and retry rates
- Transaction response time
- Batch duration profiles
- Internet/intranet site/page hit rates
- Internet response times (external and internal to firewalls)
- Number of system/application log-ons and concurrent users
- Number of network nodes in use, and utilization levels.

There are different kinds of monitoring tools needed to collect and interpret data at each level. For example, some tools will allow performance of business transactions to be monitored, while others will monitor CI behaviour.

Capacity Management must set up and calibrate alarm thresholds (where necessary in conjunction with Event Management, as it is often Event Monitoring tools that may be used) so that the correct alert levels are set and that any filtering is established as necessary so that only meaningful events are raised. Without such filtering it is possible that 'information only' alerts can obscure more significant alerts that require immediate attention. In addition, it is possible for serious failures to cause 'alert storms' due to very high volumes of repeat alerts, which again must be filtered so that the most meaningful messages are not obscured.

It may be appropriate to use external, third-party, monitoring capabilities for some CIs or components of the IT Infrastructure (e.g. key internet sites/pages). Capacity Management should be involved in helping specify and select any such monitoring capabilities and in integrating the results or any alerts with other monitoring and handling systems.

Capacity Management must work with all appropriate support groups to make decisions on where alarms are routed and on escalation paths and timescales. Alerts should be logged to the Service Desk as well as to appropriate support staff, so that appropriate Incident Records can be raised so a permanent record of the event exists – and Service Desk staff have a view of how well the

support group(s) are dealing with the fault and can intervene if necessary.

Manufacturers' claimed performance capabilities and agreed service level targets, together with actual historical monitored performance and capacity data, should be used to set alert levels. This may need to be an iterative process initially, performing some trial-and-error adjustments until the correct levels are achieved.

Note: Capacity Management may have to become involved in the capacity requirements and capabilities of IT Service Management. Whether the organization has enough Service Desk staff to handle the rate of incidents; whether the CAB structure can handle the number of changes it is being asked to review and approve; whether support tools can handle the volume of data being gathered are Capacity Management issues, which the Capacity Management team may be asked to help investigate and answer.

4.6.4.2 Handling capacity- or performance-related incidents

If an alert is triggered, or an incident is raised at the Service Desk, caused by a current or ongoing Capacity or Performance Management problem, Capacity Management must become involved to identify the cause and find a resolution. Working together with appropriate technical support groups, and alongside Problem Management, all necessary investigations must be performed to detect exactly what has gone wrong and what is needed to correct the situation.

It may be necessary to switch to more detailed monitoring during the investigation phase to determine the exact cause. Monitoring is often set at a 'background' level during normal circumstances due to the large amount of data that can be generated and to avoid placing too high a burden on the IT Infrastructure – but when specific difficulties are being investigated more detailed monitoring may be needed to pinpoint the exact cause.

When a solution, or potential solution, has been found, any changes necessary to resolve the problem must be approved via formal Change Management prior to implementation. If the fault is causing serious disruption and an urgent resolution is needed, the urgent change process should be used. It is very important that no 'tuning' takes place without submission through Change Management, as even apparently small adjustments can often have very large cumulative effects – sometimes across the entire IT Infrastructure.

4.6.4.3 Capacity and performance trends

Capacity Management has a role to play in identifying any capacity or performance trends as they become discernible. Further details of actions needed to address such trends are included in the Continual Service Improvement publication.

4.6.4.4 Storage of Capacity Management data

Large amounts of data are usually generated through capacity and performance monitoring. Monitoring of meters and tables of just a few Kbytes each can quickly grown into huge files if many components are being monitored at relatively short intervals. Another problem with very short-term monitoring is that it is not possible to gather meaningful information without looking over a longer period. For example, a single snapshot of a CPU will show the device to be either 'busy' or 'idle' – but a summary over, say, a 5-minute period will show the average utilization level over that period, which is a much more meaningful measure of whether the device is able to work comfortably, or whether potential performance problems are likely to occur.

In any organization it is likely that the monitoring tools used will vary greatly – with a combination of system-specific tools, many of them part of the basic operating system, and specialist monitoring tools being used. In order to coordinate the data being generated and allow the retention of meaningful data for analysis and trending purposes, some form of central repository for holding this summary data is needed: a Capacity Management Information System (CMIS).

The format, location and design of such a database should be planned and implemented in advance – see the Service Design publication for further details – but there will be some operational aspects to handle, such as database housekeeping and backups.

4.6.4.5 Demand Management

Demand Management is the name given to a number of techniques that can be used to modify demand for a particular resource or service. Some techniques for Demand Management can be planned in advance – and these are covered in more detail in the Service Design publication. However, there are other aspects of Demand Management that are of a more operational nature, requiring shorter-term action.

If, for example, the performance of a particular service is causing concern, and short-term restrictions on concurrency of users are needed to allow performance improvements for a smaller restricted group, then Service Operation functions will have to take action to implement such restrictions – usually accompanied by concurrent action to implement the logging-out of users who have been inactive for an agreed period of time to free up resources for others.

4.6.4.6 Workload Management

There may be occasions when optimization of infrastructure resources is needed to maintain or improve performance or throughput. This can often be done through Workload Management, which is a generic term to cover such actions as:

■ Rescheduling a particular service or workload to run at a different time of day, or day of the week etc. (usually away from peak-times to off-peak windows) – which will often mean having to make adjustments to job-scheduling software.

■ Moving a service or workload from one location or set of CIs to another – often to balance utilization or traffic.

■ Technical Virtualization: setting up and using virtualization systems to allow movement of processing around the infrastructure to give better performance/resilience in a dynamic fashion.

■ Limiting or moving demand for resources through Demand Management techniques (see above and also the Service Design publication).

It will only be possible to manage workloads effectively if a good understanding exists of which workloads will run at what time and how much resource utilization each workload places upon the IT Infrastructure. Diligent monitoring and analysis of workloads is therefore needed on an ongoing operational basis.

4.6.4.7 Modelling and applications sizing

Modelling and/or sizing of new services and/or applications must, where appropriate, be done during the planning and transition phases – see the Service Design and Service Transition publications. However, the Service Operation functions have a role to play in evaluating the accuracy of the predictions and feeding back any issues or discrepancies.

4.6.4.8 Capacity Planning

During Service Design and Service Transition, the capacity requirements of IT services are calculated. A forward-looking capacity plan should be maintained and regularly updated and Service Operation will have a role to play in this. Such a plan should look forward up to two years or more, but should be reviewed regularly every three to 12 months, depending upon volatility and resources available.

The plan should be linked to the organization's financial planning cycle, so that any required expenditure for infrastructure upgrades, enhancements or additions can be included in budget estimates and approved in advance.

The plan should predict the future but must also examine and report upon previous predictions, particularly to give some confidence in further predictions. Where any discrepancies have been encountered, these should be explained and future remedial action described.

The Capacity Plan might typically cover:

- Current performance and utilization details, with recent trends for all key CIs, including
    - Backbone networks
    - LANs
    - Mainframes (if still used)
    - Key servers
    - Main data storage devices
    - Selected (representative) desktop and laptop equipment
    - Key websites
    - Key databases
    - Key applications
    - Operational capacity – electricity, floor space, environmental capacity (air condition), floor weighting, heat generation and output, electrical and water demand and supply etc.
    - Magnetic media.
- Estimated performance and utilization for all such CIs during the planning period (e.g. the next three months)
- Comparative data with previous estimates – to allow confidence in future estimates to be judged
- Reports on any specific capacity difficulties encountered in the past period, with details of recovery and preventive actions taken for the future
- Details of any required upgrades or procurements needed and planned for the future, with indicative costs and timescales.
- Any potential capacity risks that are likely – with suggested countermeasures should they arise.

4.6.5 Availability Management

During Service Design and Service Transition, IT services are designed for availability and recovery. Service Operation is responsible for actually making the IT service available to the specified users at the required time and at the agreed levels.

During Service Operation the IT teams and users are in the best position to detect whether services actually meet the agreed requirements and whether the design of these services is effective.

What seems like a good idea during the Design phase may not actually be practical or optimal. The experience of the users and operational functions makes them a primary input into the ongoing improvement of existing services and the design.

However, there are a number of challenges with gaining access to this knowledge:

- Most of the experiences of the operational teams and users are either informal, or spread across multiple sources.
- The process for collecting and collating this data needs to be formalized.
- Users and operational staff are usually fully occupied with their regular activities and tasks and it is very difficult for them to be involved in regular planning and design activities. One argument often made here is that if design is improved, the operational teams will be less busy resolving problems and will therefore have more time to be involved in design activities. However, practice shows that as soon as staff are freed up, they often become the target of workforce reduction exercises.

Having said this, there are three key opportunities for operational staff to be involved in Availability Improvement, since these are generally viewed as part of their ongoing responsibility:

- **Review of maintenance activities**. Service Design will define detailed maintenance schedules and activities, which are required to keep IT services functioning at the required level of performance and availability. Regular comparison of actual maintenance activities and times with the plans will highlight potential areas for improvement. One of the sources of this information is a review of whether Service Maintenance Objectives were met and, if not, why not.
- **Major problem reviews**. Problems could be the result of any number of factors, one of which is poor design. Problem reviews therefore may include opportunities to identify improvements to the design of IT services, which will include availability and capacity improvement.

■ Involvement in **specific initiatives** using techniques such as Service Failure Analysis (SFA), Component Failure Impact Analysis (CFIA), or Fault Tree Analysis (FTA) or as members of Technical Observation (TO) activities – either as part of the follow-up to major problems or as part of an ongoing Service Improvement Plan, in collaboration with dedicated Availability Management staff. These Availability Management techniques are explained in more detail in the Service Design publication.

There may be occasions when Operational Staff themselves need downtime of one or more services to enable them to conduct their operational or maintenance activities – which may impact on availability if not properly scheduled and managed. In such cases they must liaise with SLM and Availability Management staff – who will negotiate with the business/users, often using the Service Desk to perform this role, to agree and schedule such activities.

4.6.6 Knowledge Management

It is vitally important that all data and information that can be useful for future Service Operation activities are properly gathered, stored and assessed. Relevant data, metrics and information should be passed up on the management chain and to other Service Lifecycle phases so that it can feed into the knowledge and wisdom layers of the organization's Service Knowledge Management System, the structures of which have to be defined in Service Strategy and Service Design and refined in Continual Service Improvement (see other ITIL publications in this series).

Key repositories of Service Operation, which have been frequently mentioned elsewhere, are the CMS and the KEDB, but this must be widened out to include all of the Service Operation teams' and departments' documentation, such as operations manuals, procedures manuals, work instructions, etc.

4.6.7 Financial Management for IT services

Service Operation staff must participate in and support the overall IT budgeting and accounting system – and may be actively involved in any charging system that may be in place.

Proper planning is necessary so that capital expenditure (Capex) and operational expenditure (Opex) budget estimates can be prepared and agreed in good time to meet the budgetary cycles.

The Service Operation Manager must also be involved in regular, at least monthly, reviews of expenditure against budgets – as part of the ongoing IT budgeting and accounting process. Any discrepancies must be identified and necessary adjustments made. All committed expenditure must go through the organization's purchase order system so that commitments can be accrued and proper checks must be made on all goods received so that invoices and payments can be correctly authorized – or discrepancies investigated and rectified.

It should be noted that some proposed cost reductions by the business may actually increase IT costs, or at least unit costs. Care should therefore be taken to ensure that IT is involved in discussing all cost-saving measures and contribute to overall decisions. Financial Management is covered in detail in the Service Strategy publication.

4.6.8 IT Service Continuity Management

Service Operation functions are responsible for the testing and execution of system and service recovery plans as determined in the IT Service Continuity plans for the organization. In addition, managers of all Service Operation functions must be on the Business Continuity Central Coordination team.

This is discussed in detail in Service Strategy and Service Design and will not be repeated here, except to indicate that it is important that Service Operation functions must be involved in the following areas:

■ Risk assessment, using its knowledge of the infrastructure and techniques such as CFIA and access to information in the CMS to identify single points of failure or other high-risk situations

■ Execution of any Risk Management measures that are agreed, e.g. implementation of countermeasures, or increased resilience to components of the infrastructures, etc.

■ Assistance in writing the actual recovery plans for systems and services under its control

■ Participation in testing of the plans (such as involvement in off-site testing, simulations etc) on an ongoing basis under the direction of the IT Service Continuity Manager (ITSCM)

■ Ongoing maintenance of the plans under the control of ITSCM and Change Management

■ Participation in training and awareness campaigns to ensure that they are able to execute the plans and understand their roles in a disaster

■ The Service Desk will play a key role in communicating with staff, customers and users during an actual disaster.

Common Service
Operation activities

5

5 Common Service Operation activities

Chapter 4 dealt with the processes required for effective Service Operation and Chapter 6 will deal with the organizational aspects. This chapter focuses on a number of operational activities that ensure that technology is aligned with the overall Service and Process objectives. These activities are sometimes described as processes, but in reality they are sets of specialized technical activities all aimed at ensuring that the technology required to deliver and support services is operating effectively and efficiently.

These activities will usually be technical in nature – although the exact technology will vary depending on the type of services being delivered. This publication will focus on the activities required to manage IT.

Important note on managing technology

It is tempting to divorce the concept of Service Management from the management of the infrastructure that is used to deliver those services.

In reality, it is impossible to achieve quality services without aligning and 'gearing' every level of technology (and the people who manage it) to the services being provided. Service Management involves people, process and technology.

In other words, the common Service Operation activities are not about managing the technology for the sake of having good technology performance. They are about achieving performance that will integrate the technology component with the people and process components to achieve service and business objectives. See Figure 5.1 for examples of how technology is managed in maturing organizations.

Figure 5.1 illustrates the steps involved in maturing from a technology-centric organization to an organization that harnesses technology as part of its business strategy. Figure 5.1 further outlines the role of Technology Managers in organizations of differing maturity. The diagram is not comprehensive, but it does provide examples of the way in which technology is managed

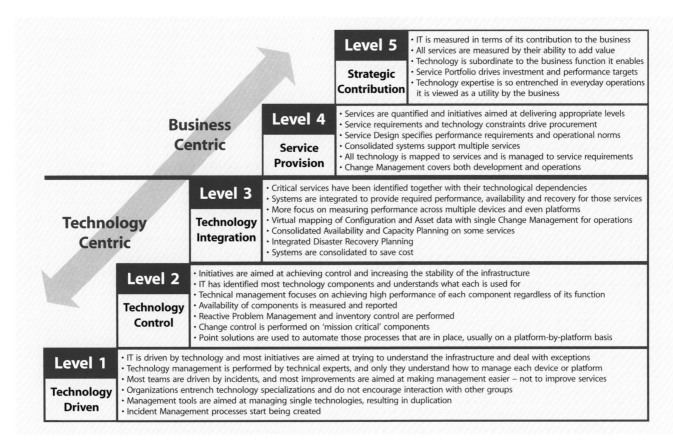

Figure 5.1 Achieving maturity in Technology Management

in each type of organization. The bold headings indicate the major role played by IT in managing technology. The text in the rows describes the characteristics of an IT department at each level.

The purpose of this diagram in this chapter is as follows:

■ This chapter focuses on Technical Management activities, but there is no single way of representing them. A less mature organization will tend to see these activities as ends in themselves, not a means to an end. A more mature organization will tend to subordinate these activities to higher-level Service Management objectives. For example, the Server Management team will move from an insulated department, focused purely on managing servers, to a team that works closely with other Technology Managers to find ways of increasing their value to the business.

■ To make and reinforce the point that there is no 'right' way of grouping and organizing the departments that perform these services. Some readers might interpret the headings in this chapter as the names of departments, but this is not the case. The aim of this chapter is to identify the typical technical activities involved in Service Operation. Organizational aspects are discussed in Chapter 6.

■ The Service Operation activities described in the rest of this chapter are not typical of any one of the levels of maturity. Rather, the activities are usually all present in some form at all levels. They are just organized and managed differently at each level.

In some cases a dedicated group may handle all of a process or activity while in other cases processes or activities may be shared or split between groups. However, by way of broad guidance, the following sections list the required activities under the functional groups most likely to be involved in their operation. This does not mean that all organizations have to use these divisions. Smaller organizations will tend to assign groups of these activities (if they are needed at all) to single departments, or even individuals.

Finally, the purpose of this chapter is not to provide a detailed analysis of all the activities. They are specialized, and detailed guidance is available from the platform vendors and other, more technical, frameworks; new categories will be added continually as technology evolves. This chapter simply aims to highlight the importance and nature of technology management for Service Management in the IT context.

5.1 MONITORING AND CONTROL

The measurement and control of services is based on a continual cycle of monitoring, reporting and subsequent action. This cycle is discussed in detail in this section because it is fundamental to the delivery, support and improvement of services.

It is also important to note that, although this cycle takes place during Service Operation, it provides a basis for setting strategy, designing and testing services and achieving meaningful improvement. It is also the basis for SLM measurement. Therefore, although monitoring is performed by Service Operation functions, it should not be seen as a purely operational matter. All phases of the Service Lifecycle should ensure that measures and controls are clearly defined, executed and acted upon.

5.1.1 Definitions

> Monitoring refers to the activity of observing a situation to detect changes that happen over time.

In the context of Service Operation, this implies the following:

■ Using tools to monitor the status of key CIs and key operational activities

■ Ensuring that specified conditions are met (or not met) and, if not, to raise an alert to the appropriate group (e.g. the availability of key network devices)

■ Ensuring that the performance or utilization of a component or system is within a specified range (e.g. disk space or memory utilization)

■ To detect abnormal types or levels of activity in the infrastructure (e.g. potential security threats)

■ To detect unauthorized changes (e.g. introduction of software)

■ To ensure compliance with the organization's policies (e.g. inappropriate use of e-mail)

■ To track outputs to the business and ensure that they meet quality and performance requirements

■ To track any information that is used to measure Key Performance Indicators (KPIs).

> Reporting refers to the analysis, production and distribution of the output of the monitoring activity.

In the context of Service Operation, this implies the following:

■ Using tools to collate the output of monitoring information that can be disseminated to various groups, functions or processes

- Interpreting the meaning of that information
- Determining where that information would best be used
- Ensuring that decision makers have access to the information that will enable them to make decisions
- Routing the reported information to the appropriate person, group or tool.

Control refers to the process of managing the utilization or behaviour of a device, system or service. It is important to note, though, that simply manipulating a device is not the same as controlling it. Control requires three conditions:

- The action must ensure that behaviour conforms to a defined standard or norm
- The conditions prompting the action must be defined, understood and confirmed
- The action must be defined, approved and appropriate for these conditions.

In the context of Service Operation, control implies the following:

- Using tools to define what conditions represent normal operations or abnormal operations
- Regulate performance of devices, systems or services
- Measure availability
- Initiate corrective action, which could be automated (e.g. reboot a device remotely or run a script), or manual (e.g. notify operations staff of the status).

5.1.2 Monitor Control Loops

The most common model for defining control is the Monitor Control Loop. Although it is a simple model, it has many complex applications within IT Service Management. This section will define the basic concepts of the Monitor Control Loop Model and subsequent sections will show how important these concepts are for the Service Management Lifecycle.

Figure 5.2 outlines the basic principles of control. A single activity and its output are measured using a predefined norm, or standard, to determine whether it is within an acceptable range of performance or quality. If not, action is taken to rectify the situation or to restore normal performance.

Typically there are two types of Monitor Control Loops:

- **Open Loop Systems** are designed to perform a specific activity regardless of environmental conditions. For example, a backup can be initiated at a given time

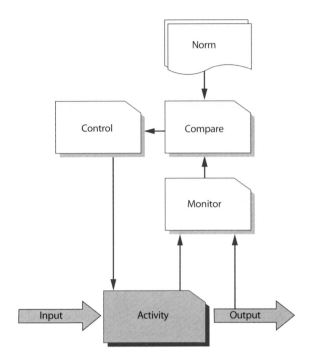

Figure 5.2 The Monitor Control Loop

and frequency – and will run regardless of other conditions.

- **Closed Loop Systems** monitor an environment and respond to changes in that environment. For example, in network load balancing a monitor will evaluate the traffic on a circuit. If network traffic exceeds a certain range, the control system will begin to route traffic across a backup circuit. The monitor will continue to provide feedback to the control system, which will continue to regulate the flow of network traffic between the two circuits.

To help clarify the difference, solving Capacity Management through over-provisioning is open loop; a load-balancer that detects congestion/failure and redirects capacity is closed loop.

5.1.2.1 Complex Monitor Control Loop

The Monitor Control Loop in Figure 5.2 is a good basis for defining how Operations Management works, but within the context of ITSM the situation is far more complex. Figure 5.3 illustrates a process consisting of three major activities. Each one has an input and an output, and the output becomes an input for the next activity.

In this diagram, each activity is controlled by its own Monitor Control Loop, using a set of norms for that specific activity. The process as a whole also has its own Monitor Control Loop, which spans all the activities and ensures that all norms are appropriate and are being followed.

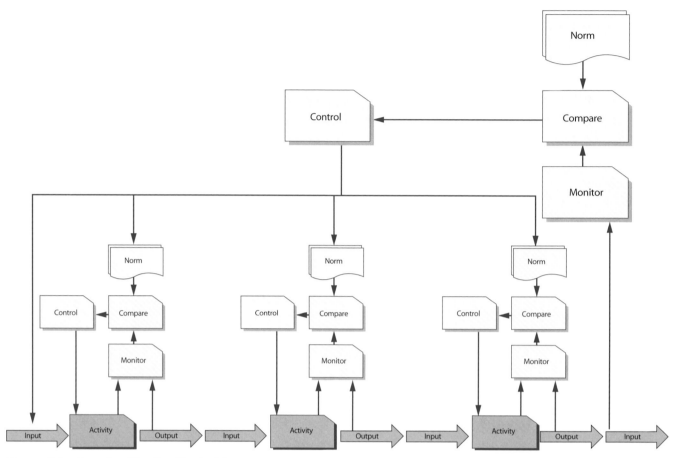

Figure 5.3 Complex Monitor Control Loop

In Figure 5.3 there is a double feedback loop. One loop focuses purely on executing a defined standard, and the second evaluates the performance of the process and also the standards whereby the process is executed. An example of this would be if the first set of feedback loops at the bottom of the diagram represented individual stations on an assembly line and the higher-level loop represented Quality Assurance.

The Complex Monitor Control Loop is a good organizational learning tool (as defined by Chris Argyris (1976, *Increasing Leadership Effectiveness*. New York: Wiley). The first level of feedback at individual activity level is concerned with monitoring and responding to data (single facts, codes or pieces of information). The second level is concerned with monitoring and responding to information (a collection of a number of facts about which a conclusion may be drawn). Refer to the Service Transition publication for a full discussion on Data, Information, Knowledge and Wisdom.

All of this is interesting theory, but does not explain how the Monitor Control Loop concept can be used to operate IT services. And especially – who defines the norm? Based

on what has been described so far, Monitor Control Loops can be used to manage:

■ **The performance of activities in a process or procedure**. Each activity and its related output can potentially be measured to ensure that problems with the process are identified before the process as a whole is completed. For example, in Incident Management, the Service Desk monitors whether a technical team has accepted an incident in a specified time. If not, the incident is escalated. This is done well before the target resolution time for that incident because the aim of escalating that one activity is to ensure that the process as whole is completed in time.

■ **The effectiveness of a process or procedure as a whole**. In this case the 'activity' box represents the entire process as a single entity. For example, Change Management will measure the success of the process by checking whether a change was implemented on time, to specification and within budget.

■ **The performance of a device**. For example, the 'activity' box could represent the response time of a server under a given workload.

■ **The performance of a series of devices**. For example, the end user response time of an application across the network.

To define how to use the concept of Monitor Control Loops in Service Management, the following questions need to be answered:

■ How do we define what needs to be monitored?
■ What are the appropriate thresholds for each of these?
■ How will monitoring be performed (manual or automated)?
■ What represents normal operation?
■ What are the dependencies for normal operation?
■ What happens before we get the input?
■ How frequently should the measurement take place?
■ Do we need to perform active measurement to check whether the item is within the norm or do we wait until an exception is reported (passive measurement)?
■ Is Operations Management the only function that performs monitoring?

■ If not, how are the other instances of monitoring related to Operations Management?
■ If there are multiple loops, which processes are responsible for each loop?

The following sections will expand on the concept of Monitor Control Loops and demonstrate how these questions are answered.

5.1.2.2 The ITSM Monitor Control Loop

In ITSM, the complex Monitor Control Loop can be represented as shown in Figure 5.4.

Figure 5.4 can be used to illustrate the control of a process or of the components used to deliver a service. In this diagram the word 'activity' implies that it refers to a process. To apply it to a service, an 'activity' could also be a 'CI'. There are a number of significant features in Figure 5.4 as given overleaf.

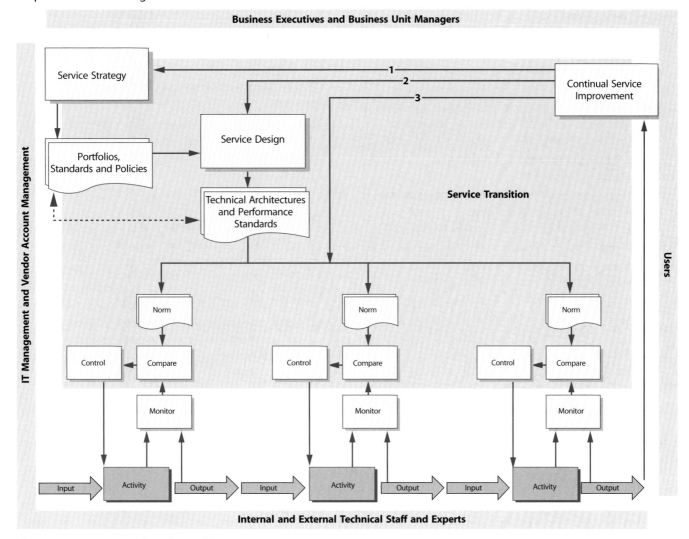

Figure 5.4 ITSM Monitor Control Loop

■ Each activity in a Service Management process (or each component used to provide a service) is monitored as part of the Service Operation processes. The operational team or department responsible for each activity or component will apply the Monitor Control Loop as defined in the process, and using the norms that were defined during the Service Design processes. The role of Operational Monitoring and Control is to ensure that the process or service functions exactly as specified, which is why they are primarily concerned with maintaining the status quo.

■ The norms and Monitoring and Control mechanisms are defined in Service Design, but they are based on the standards and architectures defined during Service Strategy. Any changes to the organization's Service Strategy, architecture, service portfolios or Service Level Requirements will precipitate changes to what is monitored and how it is controlled.

■ The Monitor Control Loops are placed within the context of the organization. This implies that Service Strategy will primarily be executed by Business and IT Executives with support from vendor account managers. Service Design acts as the bridge between Service Strategy and Service Operation and will typically involve representatives from all groups. The activities and controls will generally be executed by IT staff (sometimes involving users) and supported by IT Managers and the vendors. Service Improvement spans all areas, but primarily represents the interests of the business and its users.

■ Notice that the second level of monitoring in this complex Monitor Control Loop is performed by the CSI processes through Service Strategy and Service Design. These relationships are represented by the numbered arrows in Figure 5.4 as follows:

● **Arrow 1**. In this case CSI has recognized that the service will be improved by making a change to the Service Strategy. This could be the result of the business needing a change to the Service Portfolio, or that the architecture does not deliver what was expected.

● **Arrow 2**. In this case the Service Level Requirements need to be adjusted. It could be that the service is too expensive; or that the configuration of the infrastructure needs to be changed to enhance performance; or because Operations Management is unable to maintain service quality in the current architecture.

● **Arrow 3**. In this case the norms specified in Service Design are not being adhered to. This could be because they are not appropriate or executable, or because of a lack of education or a lack of communication. The norms and the lack of compliance need to be investigated and action taken to rectify the situation.

Service Transition provides a major set of checks and balances in these processes. It does so as follows:

■ For **new** services, Service Transition will ensure that the technical architectures are appropriate; and that the Operational Performance Standards can be executed. This in turn will ensure that the Service Operation teams or departments are able to meet the Service Level Requirements.

■ For **existing** services, Change Management will manage any of the changes that are required as part of a control (e.g. tuning) as well as any changes represented by the arrows labelled 1, 2 and 3. Although Service Transition does not define strategy and design services per se, it provides coordination and assurance that the services are working, and will continue to work, as planned.

Why is this loop covered under Service Operation?

Figure 5.4 represents Monitoring and Control for the whole of IT Service Management. Some readers of the Service Operation publication may feel that it should be more suitably covered in the Service Strategy publication.

However, Monitoring and Control can only effectively be deployed when the service is operational. This means that the quality of the entire set of IT Service Management processes depends on how they are monitored and controlled in Service Operation.

The implications of this are as follows:

■ Service Operation staff are not the only people with an interest in what is monitored and how they are controlled.

■ While Service Operation is responsible for monitoring and control of services and components, they are acting as stewards of a very important part of the set of ITSM Monitoring and Control loops.

■ If Service Operation staff define and execute Monitoring and Control procedures in isolation, none of the Service Management processes or functions will be fully effective. This is because the Service Operation functions will not support the priorities and information requirements of the other processes, e.g. attempting to negotiate an SLA when the only data available is page-swap rates on a server and detailed bandwidth utilization of a network.

5.1.2.3 Defining what needs to be monitored

The definition of what needs to be monitored is based on understanding the desired outcome of a process, device or system. IT should focus on the service and its impact on the business, rather than just the individual components of technology. The first question that needs to be asked is 'What are we trying to achieve?'.

5.1.2.4 Internal and External Monitoring and Control

At the outset, it will become clear that there are two levels of monitoring:

■ **Internal Monitoring and Control**: Most teams or departments are concerned about being able to execute effectively and efficiently the tasks that have been assigned to them. Therefore, they will monitor the items and activities that are directly under their control. This type of monitoring and control focuses on activities that are self-contained within that team or department. For example, the Service Desk Manager will monitor the volume of calls to determine how many staff need to be available to answer the telephone.

■ **External Monitoring and Control**: Although each team or department is responsible for managing its own area, they do not act independently. Every task that they perform, or device that they manage, has an impact on the success of the organization as a whole. Each team or department will also be controlling items and activities on behalf of other groups, processes or functions. For example, the Server Management team will monitor the CPU performance on key servers and perform workload balancing so that a critical application is able to stay within performance thresholds set by Application Management.

The distinction between Internal and External Monitoring is an important one. If Service Operation focuses only on Internal Monitoring, it will have very well-managed infrastructure, but no way of understanding or influencing the quality of services. If it focuses only on External Monitoring, it will understand how poor the service quality is, but will have no idea what is causing it or how to change it.

In reality, most organizations have a combination of Internal and External Monitoring, but in many cases these are not linked. For example, the Server Management team knows exactly how well the servers are performing and the Service Level Manager knows exactly how the users perceive the quality of service provided by the servers. However, neither of them knows how to link these metrics to define what level of server performance represents good quality service. This becomes even more confusing when server performance that is acceptable in the middle of the month, is not acceptable at month-end.

5.1.2.5 Defining objectives for Monitoring and Control

Many organizations start by asking the question 'What are we managing?'. This will invariably lead to a strong Internal Monitoring System, with very little linkage to the real outcome or service that is required by the business.

The more appropriate question is 'What is the end result of the activities and equipment that my team manages?'. Therefore the best place to start, when defining what to monitor, is to determine the required outcome.

The definition of Monitoring and Control objectives should ideally start with the definition of the Service Level Requirements documents (see Service Design publication). These will specify how the customers and users will measure the performance of the service, and are used as input into the Service Design processes. During Service Design, various processes will determine how the service will be delivered and managed. For example, Capacity Management will determine the most appropriate and cost-effective way to deliver the levels of performance required. Availability Management will determine how the infrastructure can be configured to provide the fewest points of failure.

If there is any doubt about the validity or completeness of objectives, the COBIT framework provides a comprehensive, high-level set of objectives as a checklist. More information on COBIT is provided in Appendix A of this publication.

The Service Design Process will help to identify the following sets of inputs for defining Operational Monitoring and Control norms and mechanisms:

■ They will work with customers and users to determine how the output of the service will be measured. This will include measurement mechanisms, frequency and sampling. This part of Service Design will focus specifically on the Functional Requirements.

■ They will identify key CIs, how they should be configured and what level of performance and availability is required in order to meet the agreed Service Levels.

■ They will work with the developers and vendors of the CIs that make up each service to identify any constraints or limitations in those components.

■ All support and delivery teams and departments will need to identify what information will help them to execute their role effectively. Part of the Service Design and development will be to instrument each service so that it can be monitored to provide this information, or so that it can generate meaningful events.

All of this means that a very important part of defining what Service Operation monitors and how it exercises control is to identify the stakeholders of each service.

Stakeholders can be defined as anyone with an interest in the successful delivery and receipt of IT services. Each stakeholder will have a different perspective of what it will take to deliver or receive an IT service. Service Operation will need to understand each of these perspectives in order to determine exactly what needs to be monitored and what to do with the output.

Service Operation will therefore rely on SLM to define exactly who these stakeholders are and how they contribute to or use the service. This is discussed more fully in the Service Design and Continual Service Improvement publications.

> **Note on Internal and External Monitoring Objectives**
>
> The required outcome could be internal or external to the Service Operation functions, although it should always be remembered that an internal action will often have an external result. For example, consolidating servers to make them easier to manage may result in a cost saving, which will affect the SLM negotiation and review cycle as well as the Financial Management processes.

5.1.2.6 Types of monitoring

There are many different types of monitoring tool and different situations in which each will be used. This section focuses on some of the different types of monitoring that can be performed and when they would be appropriate.

Active versus Passive Monitoring

■ **Active Monitoring** refers to the ongoing 'interrogation' of a device or system to determine its status. This type of monitoring can be resource intensive and is usually reserved to proactively monitor the availability of critical devices or systems; or as a diagnostic step when attempting to resolve an Incident or diagnose a problem.

■ **Passive Monitoring** is more common and refers to generating and transmitting events to a 'listening device' or monitoring agent. Passive Monitoring depends on successful definition of events and instrumentation of the system being monitored (see section 4.1).

Reactive versus Proactive

■ **Reactive Monitoring** is designed to request or trigger action following a certain type of event or failure. For example, server performance degradation may trigger a reboot, or a system failure will generate an incident. Reactive monitoring is not only used for exceptions. It can also be used as part of normal operations procedures, for example a batch job completes successfully, which prompts the scheduling system to submit the next batch job.

■ **Proactive Monitoring** is used to detect patterns of events which indicate that a system or service may be about to fail. Proactive monitoring is generally used in more mature environments where these patterns have been detected previously, often several times. Proactive Monitoring tools are therefore a means of automating the experience of seasoned IT staff and are often created through the Proactive Problem Management process (see Continual Service Improvement publication).

Please note that Reactive and Proactive Monitoring could be active or passive, as per Table 5.1 overleaf.

Table 5.1   Active and Passive Reactive and Proactive Monitoring

	Active	Passive
Reactive	Used to diagnose which device is causing the failure and under what conditions (e.g. 'ping' a device, or run and track a sample transaction through a series of devices) Requires knowledge of the infrastructure topography and the mapping of services to CIs	Detects and correlates event records to determine the meaning of the events and the appropriate action (e.g. a user logs in three times with the incorrect password, which generates represents a security exception and is escalated through Information Security Management procedures) Requires detailed knowledge of the normal operation of the infrastructure and services
Proactive	Used to determine the real-time status of a device, system or service – usually for critical components or following the recovery of a failed device to ensure that it is fully recovered (i.e. is not going to cause further incidents)	Event records are correlated over time to build trends for Proactive Problem Management. Patterns of events are defined and programmed into correlation tools for future recognition

Continuous Measurement versus Exception-Based Measurement

■ **Continuous Measurement** is focused on monitoring a system in real time to ensure that it complies with a performance norm (for example, an application server is available for 99.9% of the agreed service hours). The difference between Continuous Measurement and Active Monitoring is that Active Monitoring does not have to be continuous. However, as with Active Monitoring, this is resource intensive and is usually reserved for critical components or services. In most cases the cost of the additional bandwidth and processor power outweighs the benefit of continuous measurement. In these cases monitoring will usually be based on sampling and statistical analysis (e.g. the system performance is reported every 30 seconds and extrapolated to represent overall performance). In these cases, the method of measurement will have to be documented and agreed in the OLAs to ensure that it is adequate to support the Service Reporting Requirements (see Continual Service Improvement publication).

■ **Exception-Based Measurement** does not measure the real-time performance of a service or system, but detects and reports against exceptions. For example, an event is generated if a transaction does not complete, or if a performance threshold is reached. This is more cost-effective and easier to measure, but could result in longer service outages. Exception-Based Measurement is used for less critical systems or on systems where cost is a major issue. It is also used where IT tools are not able to determine the status or quality of a service (e.g. if printing quality is part of the service specification, the only way to measure this

is physical inspection – often performed by the user rather than IT staff). Where Exception-Based Measurement is used, it is important that both the OLA and the SLA for that service reflect this, as service outages are more likely to occur, and users are often required to report the exception.

Performance versus output

There is an important distinction between the reporting used to track the performance of components or teams or department used to deliver a service and the reporting used to demonstrate the achievement of service quality objectives.

IT managers often confuse these by reporting to the business on the performance of their teams or departments (e.g. number of calls taken per Service Desk Analyst), as if that were the same thing as quality of service (e.g. incidents solved within the agreed time).

Performance Monitoring and metrics should be used internally by the Service Management to determine whether people, process and technology are functioning correctly and to standard.

Users and customers would rather see reporting related to the quality and performance of the service.

Although Service Operation is concerned with both types of reporting, the primary concern of this publication is Performance Monitoring, whereas monitoring of Service Quality (or Output-Based Monitoring) will be discussed in detail in the Continual Service Improvement publication.

5.1.2.7 Monitoring in Test Environments

As with any IT Infrastructure, a Test Environment will need to define how it will use monitoring and control. These controls are more fully discussed in the Service Transition publication.

- **Monitoring the Test Environment itself**: A Test Environment consists of infrastructure, applications and processes that have to be managed and controlled just as any other environment. It is tempting to think that the Test Environment does not need rigorous monitoring and control because it is not a live environment. However, this argument is not valid. If a Test Environment is not properly monitored and controlled, there is a danger of running the tests on equipment that deviates from the standards defined in Service Design.

- **Monitoring items being tested**: The results of testing have to be accurately tracked and checked. Also it is important that any monitoring tools that have been built into new or changed services have to be tested as well.

5.1.2.8 Reporting and action

> 'A report alone creates awareness; a report with an action plan achieves results.'

Reporting and dysfunction

Practical experience has shown that there is more reporting in dysfunctional organizations than in effective organizations. This is because reports are not being used to initiate pre-defined action plans, but rather:

- to shift the blame for an incident

- to try to find out who is responsible for making a decision

- as input to creating action plans for future occurrences.

In dysfunctional organizations a lot of reports are produced which no one has the time to look at or query.

Monitoring without control is irrelevant and ineffective. Monitoring should always be aimed at ensuring that service and operational objectives are being met. This means that unless there is a clear purpose for monitoring a system or service, it should not be monitored.

This also means that when monitoring is defined, so too should any required actions. For example, being able to detect that a major application has failed is not sufficient.

The relevant Application Management team should also have defined the exact steps that it will take when the application fails.

In addition, it should also be recognized that action may need to be taken by different people, for example a single event (such as an application failure) may trigger action by the Application Management team (to restore service), the users (to initiate manual processing) and management (to determine how this event can be prevented in future).

The implications of this principle are outlined in more detail in relation to Event Management (see section 4.1).

5.1.2.9 Service Operation audits

Regular audits must be performed on the Service Operation processes and activities to ensure:

- They are being performed as intended
- There is no circumvention
- They are still fit for purpose, or to identify any required changes or improvements.

Service Operation Managers may choose to perform such audits themselves, but ideally some form of independent element to the audits is preferable.

The organization's internal IT audit team or department may be asked to be involved or some organizations may choose to engage third-party consultancy/audit/ assessment companies so that an entirely independent expert view is obtained.

Service Operation audits are part of the ongoing measurement that takes place as part of Continual Service Improvement and are discussed in more detail in that publication.

5.1.2.10 Measurement, metrics and KPIs

This section has focused primarily on the monitoring and control as a basis for Service Operation. Other sections of the publication have covered some basic metrics that could be used to measure the effectiveness and efficiency of a process.

Although this publication is not primarily about measurement and metrics, it is important that organizations using these guidelines have robust measurement techniques and metrics that support the objectives of their organization. This section is a summary of these concepts.

Measurement

> Measurement refers to any technique that is used to evaluate the extent, dimension or capacity of an item in relation to a standard or unit.
>
> ■ Extent refers to the degree of compliance or completion (e.g. are all changes formally authorized by the appropriate authority)
>
> ■ Dimension refers to the size of an item, e.g. the number of incidents resolved by the Service Desk
>
> ■ Capacity refers to the total capability of an item, for example maximum number of standard transactions that can be processed by a server per minute.

Measurement only becomes meaningful when it is possible to measure the actual output or dimensions of a system, function or process against a standard or desired level, e.g. the server must be capable of processing a minimum of 100 standard transactions per minute. This needs to be defined in Service Design, and refined over time through Continual Service Improvement, but the measurement itself takes place during Service Operation.

Metrics

> Metrics refer to the quantitative, periodic assessment of a process, system or function, together with the procedures and tools that will be used to make these assessments and the procedures for interpreting them.

This definition is important because it not only specifies what needs to be measured, but also how to measure it, what the acceptable range of performance will be and what action will need to be taken as a result of normal performance or an exception. From this, it is clear that any metric given in the previous section of this publication is a very basic one and will need to be applied and expanded within the context of each organization before it can be effective.

Key Performance Indicators

> A KPI refers to a specific, agreed level of performance that will be used to measure the effectiveness of an organization or process.

KPIs are unique to each organization and have to be related to specific inputs, outputs and activities. They are not generic or universal and thus have not been included in this publication.

A further reason for not including them is the fact that similar metrics can be used to achieve very different KPIs. For example, one organization used the metric 'Percentage of Incidents resolved by the Service Desk' to evaluate the performance of the Service Desk. This worked effectively for about two years, after which the IT manager began to realize that this KPI was being used to prevent effective Problem Management, i.e. if, after two years, 80% of all incidents are easy enough to be resolved in 10 minutes on the first call, why have we not come up with a solution for them? In effect, the KPI now became a measure for how ineffective the Problem Management teams were.

5.1.2.11 Interfaces to other Service Lifecycle practices

Operational Monitoring and Continual Service Improvement

This section has focused on Operational Monitoring and Reporting, but monitoring also forms the starting point for Continual Service Improvement. This is covered in the Continual Service Improvement publication, but key differences are outlined here.

Quality is the key objective of monitoring for Continual Service Improvement (CSI). Monitoring will therefore focus on the effectiveness of a service, process, tool, organization or CI. The emphasis is not on assuring real-time service performance; rather it is on identifying where improvements can be made to the existing level of service, or IT performance.

Monitoring for CSI will therefore tend to focus on detecting exceptions and resolutions. For example, CSI is not as interested in whether an incident was resolved, but whether it was resolved within the agreed time and whether future incidents can be prevented.

CSI is not only interested in exceptions, though. If an SLA is consistently met over time, CSI will also be interested in determining whether that level of performance can be sustained at a lower cost or whether it needs to be upgraded to an even better level of performance. CSI may therefore also need access to regular performance reports.

However, since CSI is unlikely to need, or be able to cope with, the vast quantities of data that are produced by all monitoring activity, they will most likely focus on a specific subset of monitoring at any given time. This could be determined by input from the business or improvements to technology.

This has two main implications:

■ Monitoring for CSI will change over time. They may be interested in monitoring the e-mail service one quarter and then move on to look at HR systems in the next quarter.

■ This means that Service Operation and CSI need to build a process which will help them to agree on what areas need to be monitored and for what purpose.

5.2 IT OPERATIONS

5.2.1 Console Management/Operations Bridge

These provide a central coordination point for managing various classes of events, detecting incidents, managing routine operational activities and reporting on the status or performance of technology components.

Observation and monitoring of the IT Infrastructure can occur from a centralized console – to which all system events are routed. Historically, this involved the monitoring of the master operations console of one or more mainframes – but these days is more likely to involve monitoring of a server farm(s), storage devices, network components, applications, databases, or any other CIs, including any remaining mainframe(s), from a single location, known as the Operations Bridge.

There are two theories about how the Operations Bridge was so named. One is that it resembles the bridge of a large, automated ship (such as spaceships commonly seen in science fiction movies). The other theory is that the Operations Bridge represents a link between the IT Operations teams and the traditional Help Desk. In some organizations this means that the functions of Operational Control and the Help Desk were merged into the Service Desk, which performed both sets of duties in a single physical location.

Regardless of how it was named, an Operations Bridge will pull together all of the critical observation points within the IT Infrastructure so that they can be monitored and managed from a centralised location with minimal effort. The devices being monitored are likely to be physically dispersed and may be located in centralized computer installations or dispersed within the user community, or both.

The Operations Bridge will combine many activities, which might include Console Management, event handling, first-line network management, Job Scheduling and out-of-hours support (covering for the Service Desk and/or

second-line support groups if they do not work 24/7). In some organizations, the Service Desk is part of the Operations Bridge.

The physical location and layout of the Operation's Bridge needs to be carefully designed to give the correct accessibility and visibility of all relevant screens and devices to authorised personnel. However, this will become a very sensitive area where controlled access and tight security will be essential.

Smaller organizations may not have a physical Operations Bridge, but there will certainly still be the need for Console Management, usually combined with other technical roles. For example, a single team of technical staff will manage the network, servers and applications. Part of their role will be to monitor the consoles for those systems – often using virtual consoles so that they can perform the activity from any location. However, it should be noted that these virtual consoles are powerful tools and, if used in insecure locations or over unsecured connections, could represent a significant security threat.

5.2.2 Job Scheduling

IT Operations will perform standard routines, queries or reports delegated to it as part of delivering services; or as part of routine housekeeping delegated by Technical and Application Management teams.

Job Scheduling involves defining and initiating job-scheduling software packages to run batch and real-time work. This will normally involve daily, weekly, monthly, annual and ad hoc schedules to meet business needs.

In addition to the initial design, or periodic redesign, of the schedules, there are likely to be frequent amendments or adjustments to make during which job dependencies have to be identified and accommodated. There will also be a role to play in defining alerts and Exception Reports to be used for monitoring/checking job schedules. Change Management plays an important role in assessing and validating major changes to schedules, as well as creating Standard Change procedures for more routine changes.

Run-time parameters and/or files have to be received (or expedited if delayed) and input – and all run-time logs have to be checked and any failures identified.

If failures do occur, then re-runs will have to be initiated, under the guidance of the appropriate business units, often with different parameters or amended data/file versions. This will require careful communications to ensure correct parameters and files are used.

Many organizations are faced with increasing overnight batch schedules which can, if they overrun the overnight batch slot, adversely impact upon the online day services – so are seeking ways of utilizing maximum overnight capacity and performance, in conjunction with Capacity Management. This is where Workload Management techniques can be useful, such as:

- Re-scheduling of work to avoid contention on specific devices or at specific times and improve overall throughput
- Migration of workloads to alternative platforms/environments to gain improved performance and/or throughput (virtualization capabilities make this far more achievable by allowing dynamic, automated migration)
- Careful timing and 'interleaving' of jobs to gain maximum utilization of available resources.

Anecdote

One large organization, which was faced with batch overrun/utilization problems, identified that, due to human nature where people were seeking to be 'tidy', all jobs were being started on the hour or at 15-minute intervals during the hour (i.e. n o'clock, 15 minutes past, half past, 15 minutes to, etc.).

By re-scheduling of work so that it started as soon as other work finished, and staggering the start times of other work, it was able to gain significant reductions in contention and achieve much quicker overall processing, which resolved its problems without a need for upgrades.

Job Scheduling has become a highly sophisticated activity, including any number of variables – such as time-sensitivity, critical and non-critical dependencies, workload balancing, failure and resubmission, etc. As a result, most operations rely on Job Scheduling tools that allow IT Operations to schedule jobs for the optimal use of technology to achieve Service Level Objectives.

The latest generation of scheduling tools allows for a single toolset to schedule and automate technical activities and Service Management process activities (such as Change Scheduling). While this is a good opportunity for improving efficiency, it also represents a greater single point of failure. Organizations using this type of tool therefore still use point solutions as agents and also as a backup in case the main toolset fails.

5.2.3 Backup and Restore

Backup and Restore is essentially a component of good IT Service Continuity Planning. As such, Service Design should ensure that there are solid backup strategies for each service and Service Transition should ensure that these are properly tested.

In addition, regulatory requirements specify that certain types of organization (such as Financial Services or listed companies) must have a formal Backup and Restore strategy in place and that this strategy is executed and audited. The exact requirements will vary from country to country and by industry sector. This should be determined during Service Design and built into the service functionality and documentation.

The only point of taking backups is that they may need to be restored at some point. For this reason it is not as important to define how to back a system up as it is to define what components are at risk and how to effectively mitigate that risk.

There are any number of tools available for Backup and Restore, but it is worth noting that features of storage technologies used for business data are being used for backup/restore (e.g. snapshots). There is therefore an increasing degree of integration between Backup and Restore activities and those of Storage and Archiving (see section 5.6).

5.2.3.1 Backup

The organization's data has to be protected and this will include backup (copying) and storage of data in remote locations where it can be protected – and used should it need to be restored due to loss, corruption or implementation of IT Service Continuity Plans.

An overall backup strategy must be agreed with the business, covering:

- What data has to be backed up and the frequency and intervals to be used.
- How many generations of data have to be retained – this may vary by the type of data being backed up, or what type of file (e.g. data file or application executable).
- The type of backup (full, partial, incremental) and checkpoints to be used.
- The locations to be used for storage (likely to include disaster recovery sites) and rotation schedules.
- Transportation methods (e.g. file transfer via the network, physical transportation on magnetic media).
- Testing/checks to be performed, such as test-reads, test restores, check-sums etc.
- **Recovery Point Objective**. This describes the point to which data will be restored after recovery of an IT Service. This may involve loss of data. For example, a Recovery Point Objective of one day may be

supported by daily backups, and up to 24 hours of data may be lost. Recovery Point Objectives for each IT service should be negotiated, agreed and documented in OLAs, SLAs and UCs.

■ **Recovery Time Objective**. This describes the maximum time allowed for recovery of an IT service following an interruption. The Service Level to be provided may be less than normal Service Level Targets. Recovery Time Objectives for each IT service should be negotiated, agreed and documented in OLAs, SLAs and UCs.

■ How to verify that the backups will work if they need to be restored. Even if there are no error codes generated, there may be several reasons why the backup cannot be restored. A good backup strategy and operations procedures will minimize the risk of this happening. Backup procedures should include a verification step to ensure that the backups are complete and that they will work if a restore is needed. Where any backup failures are detected, recovery actions must be initiated.

There is also a need to procure and manage the necessary media (disks, tapes, CDs, etc.) to be used for backups, so that there is no shortage of supply.

Where automated devices are being used, pre-loading of the required media will be needed in advance. When loading and clearing media returned from off-site storage it is important that there is a procedure for verifying that these are the right ones. This will prevent the most recent backup being overwritten with faulty data, and then having no valid data to restore. After successful backups have been taken, the media must be removed for storage.

The actual initiation of the backups might be automated, or carried out from the Operations Bridge.

Some organizations may utilize Operations staff to perform the physical transportation and racking of backup copies to/from remote locations, where in other cases this may be handed over to other groups such as internal security staff or external contractors.

If backups are being automated or performed remotely, then Event Monitoring capabilities should be considered so that any failures can be detected early and rectified before they cause problems. In such cases IT Operations has a role to play in defining alerts and escalation paths.

In all cases, IT Operations staff must be trained in backup (and restore) procedures – which must be well documented in the organization's IT Operations Procedures Manual. Any specific requirements or targets should be referenced in OLAs or UCs where appropriate,

while any user or customer requirements or activity should be specified in the appropriate SLA.

5.2.3.2 Restore

A restore can be initiated from a number of sources, ranging from an event that indicates data corruption, through to a Service Request from a user or customer logged at the Service Desk. A restore may be needed in the case of:

■ Corrupt data
■ Lost data
■ Disaster recovery/IT Service Continuity situation
■ Historical data required for forensic investigation.

The steps to be taken will include:

■ Location of the appropriate data/media
■ Transportation or transfer back to the physical recovery location
■ Agreement on the checkpoint recovery point and the specific location for the recovered data (disk, directory, folder etc)
■ Actual restoration of the file/data (copy-back and any roll-back/roll-forward needed to arrive at the agreed checkpoint
■ Checking to ensure successful completion of the restore – with further recovery action if needed until success has been achieved.
■ User/customer sign-off.

5.2.4 Print and Output

Many services consist of generating and delivering information in printed or electronic form. Ensuring the right information gets to the right people, with full integrity, requires formal control and management.

Print (physical) and Output (electronic) facilities and services need to be formally managed because:

■ They often represent the tangible output of a service. The ability to measure that this output has reached the appropriate destination is therefore very important (e.g. checking whether files with financial transaction data have actually reached a bank through an FTP service)
■ Physical and electronic output often contains sensitive or confidential information. It is vital that the appropriate levels of security are applied to both the generation and the delivery of this output.

Many organizations will have centralised bulk printing requirements which IT Operations must handle.

In addition to the physical loading and re-loading of paper and the operation and care of the printers, other activities may be needed, such as:

- Agreement and setting of pre-notification of large print runs and alerts to prevent excessive printing by rogue print jobs
- Physical control of high-value stationery such as company cheques or certificates, etc.
- Management of the physical and electronic storage required to generate the output. In many cases IT will be expected to provide archives for the printed and electronic materials
- Control of all printed material so as to adhere to data protection legislation and regulation e.g. HIPAA (Health Insurance Portability and Accountability Act) in the USA, or FSA (Financial Services Authority) in the UK.

Where print and output services are delivered directly to the users, it is important that the responsibility for maintaining the printers or storage devices is clearly defined. For example, most users assume that cleaning and maintenance of printers must be performed by IT. If this is not the case, this must be clearly stated in the SLA.

5.3 MAINFRAME MANAGEMENT

Mainframes are still widely in use and have well established and mature practices. Mainframes form the central component of many services and its performance will therefore set a baseline for service performance and user or customer expectations, although they may never know that they are using the mainframe.

The ways in which mainframe management teams are organized are quite diverse. In some organizations Mainframe Management is a single, highly specialized team that manages all aspects from daily operations through to system engineering. In other organizations, the activities are performed by several teams or departments, with engineering and third-level support being provided by one team and daily operations being combined with the rest of IT Operations (and very probably managed through the Operations Bridge).

Typically, the following activities are likely to be undertaken:

- Mainframe operating system maintenance and support
- Third-level support for any mainframe-related incidents/problems
- Writing job scripts
- System programming

- Interfacing to hardware (H/W) support; arranging maintenance, agreeing slots, identifying H/W failure, liaison with H/W engineering.
- Provision of information and assistance to Capacity Management to help achieve optimum throughput, utilization and performance from the mainframe.

5.4 SERVER MANAGEMENT AND SUPPORT

Servers are used in most organizations to provide flexible and accessible services from hosting applications or databases, running client/server services, Storage, Print and File Management. Successful management of servers is therefore essential for successful Service Operation.

The procedures and activities which must be undertaken by the Server Team(s) or department(s) – separate teams may be needed where different server-types are used (UNIX, Wintel etc) – include:

- **Operating system support**: Support and maintenance of the appropriate operating system(s) and related utility software (e.g. failover software) including patch management and involvement in defining backup and restore policies.
- **Licence management** for all server CIs, especially operating systems, utilities and any application software not managed by the Application Management teams.
- **Third-level support**: Third-level support for all server and/or server operating system-related incidents, including diagnosis and restoration activities. This will also include liaison with third-party hardware support contractors and/or manufacturers as needed to escalate hardware-related incidents.
- **Procurement advice**: Advice and guidance to the business on the selection, sizing, procurement and usage of servers and related utility software to meet business needs.
- **System security**: Control and maintenance of the access controls and permissions within the relevant server environment(s) as well as appropriate system and physical security measures. These include identification and application of security patches, Access Management (see section 4.5) and intrusion detection.
- **Definition and management of virtual servers**. This implies that any server that has been designed and built around a common standard can be used to process workloads from a range of applications or users. Server Management will be required to set these standards and then ensure that workloads are

appropriately balanced and distributed. They are also responsible for being able to track which workload is being processed by which server so that they are able to deal with incidents effectively.

■ **Capacity and Performance**: Provide information and assistance to Capacity Management to help achieve optimum throughput, utilization and performance from the available servers. This is discussed in more detail in Service Design, but includes providing guidance on, and installation and operation of, virtualization software so as to achieve value for money by obtaining the highest levels of performance and utilization from the minimal number of servers.

■ Other **routine activities** include:

● Defining standard builds for servers as part of the provisioning process. This is covered in more detail in Service Design and Service Transition

● Building and installing new servers as part of ongoing maintenance or for the provision of new services. This is discussed in more detail in Service Transition

● Setting up and managing clusters, which are aimed at building redundancy, improving service performance and making the infrastructure easier to manage.

■ **Ongoing maintenance**. This typically consists of replacing servers or 'blades' on a rolling schedule to ensure that equipment is replaced before it fails or becomes obsolete. This results in servers that are not only fully functional, but also capable of supporting evolving services.

■ **Decommissioning and disposal of old server equipment**. This is often done in conjunction with the organization's environmental policies for disposal.

5.5 NETWORK MANAGEMENT

As most IT services are dependent on connectivity, Network Management will be essential to deliver services and also to enable Service Operation staff to access and manage key service components.

Network Management will have overall responsibility for all of the organization's own Local Area Networks (LANs), Metropolitan Area Networks (MANs) and Wide Area Networks (WANs) – and will also be responsible for liaising with third-party network suppliers.

Their role will include the following activities:

■ Initial planning and installation of new networks/network components; maintenance and

upgrades to the physical network infrastructure. This is done through Service Design and Service Transition.

■ Third-level support for all network related activities, including investigation of network issues (e.g. pinging or trace route and/or use of network management software tools – although it should be noted that pinging a server does not necessarily mean that the service is available!) and liaison with third-parties as necessary. This also includes the installation and use of 'sniffer' tools, which analyse network traffic, to assist in incident and problem resolution.

■ Maintenance and support of network operating system and middleware software including patch management, upgrades, etc.

■ Monitoring of network traffic to identify failures or to spot potential performance or bottleneck issues.

■ Reconfiguring or rerouting of traffic to achieve improved throughput or batter balance – definition of rules for dynamic balancing/routing.

■ Network security (in liaison with the organization's Information Security Management) including firewall management, access rights, password protection etc.

■ Assigning and managing IP addresses, Domain Name Systems (DNSs – which convert the name of a service to its associated IP address) and Dynamic Host Configuration Protocol (DHCP) systems, which enable access and use of the DNS.

■ Managing Internet Service Providers (ISPs).

■ Implementing, monitoring and maintaining Intrusion Detection Systems on behalf of Information Security Management. They will also be responsible for ensuring that there is no denial of service to legitimate users of the network.

■ Updating Configuration Management as necessary by documenting CIs, status, relationships, etc.

Network Management is also often responsible, often in conjunction with Desktop Support, for remote connectivity issues such as dial-in, dial-back and VPN facilities provided to home-workers, remote workers or suppliers.

Some Network Management teams or departments will also have responsibility for voice/telephony, including the provision and support for exchanges, lines, ACD, statistical software packages etc. and for Voice over Internet Protocol (VoIP) and Remote Monitoring (RMon) systems.

At the same time, many organizations see VoIP and telephony as specialized areas and have teams dedicated to managing this technology. Their activities will be similar to those described above.

Note on managing VoIP as a service

Many organizations have experienced performance and availability problems with their VoIP solutions, in spite of the fact that there seems to be more than adequate bandwidth available. This results in dropped calls and poor sound quality. This is usually because of variations in bandwidth utilization during the call, which is often the result of utilization of the network by other users, applications or other web activity. This has led to the differentiation between measuring the bandwidth available to initiate a call (Service Access Bandwidth – or SAB) and the amount of bandwidth that must be continuously available during the call (Service Utilization Bandwidth – or SUB). Care should be taken in differentiating between these when designing, managing or measuring VoIP services.

5.6   STORAGE AND ARCHIVE

Many services require the storage of data for a specific time and also for that data to be available off-line for a certain period after it is no longer used. This is often due to regulatory or legislative requirements, but also because history and audit data are invaluable for a variety of purposes, including marketing, product development, forensic investigations, etc.

A separate team or department may be needed to manage the organization's data storage technology such as:

- Storage devices, such as disks, controllers, tapes, etc.
- Network Attached Storage (NAS), which is storage attached to a network and accessible by several clients
- Storage Area Networks (SANs) designed to attach computer storage devices such as disk array controllers and tape libraries. In addition to storage devices, a SAN will also require the management of several network components, such as hubs, cables, etc.
- Direct Attached Storage (DAS), which is a storage device directly attached to a server
- Content Addressable Storage (CAS) which is storage that is based on retrieving information based on its content rather than location. The focus in this type of system is on understanding the nature of the data and information stored, rather than on providing specific storage locations.

Regardless of what type of storage systems are being used, Storage and Archiving will require the management of the infrastructure components as well as the policies related to where data is stored, for how long, in what form

and who may access it. Specific responsibilities will include:

- Definition of data storage policies and procedures
- File storage naming conventions, hierarchy and placement decisions
- Design, sizing, selection, procurement, configuration and operation of all data storage infrastructure
- Maintenance and support for all utility and middleware data-storage software
- Liaison with Information Lifecycle Management team(s) or Governance teams to ensure compliance with freedom of information, data protection and IT governance regulations
- Involvement with definition and agreement of archiving policy
- Housekeeping of all data storage facilities
- Archiving data according to rules and schedules defined during Service Design. The Storage teams or departments will also provide input into the definition of these rules and will provide reports on their effectiveness as input into future design
- Retrieval of archived data as needed (e.g. for audit purposes, for forensic evidence, or to meet any other business requirements)
- Third-line support for storage- and archive-related incidents.

5.7 DATABASE ADMINISTRATION

Database Administration must work closely with key Application Management teams or departments – and in some organizations the functions may be combined or linked under a single management structure. Organizational options include:

- Database administration being performed by each Application Management team for all the applications under its control
- A dedicated department, which manages all databases, regardless of type or application
- Several departments, each managing one type of database, regardless of what application they are part of.

Database Administration works to ensure the optimal performance, security and functionality of databases that they manage. Database Administrators typically have the following responsibilities:

- Creation and maintenance of database standards and policies
- Initial database design, creation, testing

- Management of the database availability and performance; resilience, sizing, capacity volumetrics etc.
- Resilience may require database replication, which would be the responsibility of Database Administration
- Ongoing administration of database objects: indexes, tables, views, constraints, sequences snapshots and stored procedures; page locks – to achieve optimum utilization
- The definition of triggers that will generate events, which in turn will alert database administrators of potential performance or integrity issues with the database
- Performing database housekeeping – the routine tasks that ensure that the databases are functioning optimally and securely, e.g. tuning, indexing, etc.
- Monitoring of usage; transaction volumes, response times, concurrency levels, etc.
- Generating reports. These could be reports based on the data in the database, or reports related to the performance and integrity of the database
- Identification, reporting and management of database security issues; audit trails and forensics
- Assistance in designing database backup, archiving and storage strategy
- Assistance in designing database alerts and event management
- Provision of third-level support for all database-related incidents.

5.8 DIRECTORY SERVICES MANAGEMENT

A Directory Service is a specialized software application that manages information about the resources available on a network and which users have access to. It is the basis for providing access to those resources and for ensuring that unauthorized access is detected and prevented (see section 4.5 for detailed information on Access Management).

Directory Services views each resource as an object of the Directory Server and assigns it a name. Each name is linked to the resource's network address, so that users don't have to memorize confusing and complex addresses.

Directory Services is based on the OSI's X.500 standards and commonly uses protocols such as Directory Access Protocol (DAP) or Lightweight Directory Access Protocol (LDAP). LDAP is used to support user credentials for application login and often includes internal and external user/customer data which is especially good for extranet call logging. Since LDAP is a critical operational tool, and

generally kept up to date, it is also a good source of data and verification for the CMS.

Directory Services Management refers to the process that is used to manage Directory Services. Its activities include:

- Working as part of Service Design and Service Transition to ensure that new services are accessible and controlled when they are deployed
- Locating resources on a network (if these have not already been defined during Service Design)
- Tracking the status of those resources and providing the ability to manage those resources remotely
- Managing the rights of specific users or groups of users to access resources on a network
- Defining and maintaining naming conventions to be used for resources on a network
- Ensuring consistency of naming and access control on different networks in the organization
- Linking different Directory Services throughout the organization to form a distributed Directory Service, i.e. users will only see one logical set of network resources. This is called Distribution of Directory Services
- Monitoring Events on the Directory Services, such as unsuccessful attempts to access a resource, and taking the appropriate action where required
- Maintaining and updating the tools used to manage Directory Services.

5.9 DESKTOP SUPPORT

As most users access IT services using desktop or laptop computers, it is key that these are supported to ensure the agreed levels of availability and performance of services.

Desktop Support will have overall responsibility for all of the organization's desktop and laptop computer hardware, software and peripherals. Specific responsibilities will include:

- Desktop policies and procedures, for example licensing policies, use of laptops or desktops for personal purposes, USB lockdown, etc.
- Designing and agreeing standard desktop images
- Desktop service maintenance including deployment of releases, upgrades, patches and hot-fixes (in conjunction with Release Management (see Service Transition publication for further details)
- Design and implementation of desktop archiving/rebuild policy (including policy relating to cookies, favourites, templates, personal data, etc.)

- Third-level support of desktop-related incidents, including desk-side visits where necessary
- Support for connectivity issues (in conjunction with Network Management) to home-workers, mobile staff, etc.
- Configuration control and audit of all desktop equipment (in conjunction with Configuration Management and IT Audit).

5.10 MIDDLEWARE MANAGEMENT

Middleware is software that connects or integrates software components across distributed or disparate applications and systems. Middleware enables the effective transfer of data between applications, and is therefore key to services that are dependent on multiple applications or data sources.

A variety of technologies are currently used to support program-to-program communication, such as object request brokers, message-oriented middleware, remote procedure calls and point-to-point web services. Newer technologies are emerging all the time, for example Enterprise Service Bus (ESB), which enables programs, systems and services to communicate with each other regardless of the architecture and origin of the applications. This is especially being used in the context of deploying Service Oriented Architectures (SOAs).

Middleware Management can be performed as part of an Application Management function (where it is dedicated to a specific application) or as part of a Technical Management function (where it is viewed as an extension to the Operating System of a specific platform).

Functionality provided by middleware includes:

- Providing transfer mechanisms for data from various applications or data sources
- Sending work to another application or procedure for processing
- Transmitting data or information to other systems, such as sourcing data for publication on websites (e.g. publishing Incident status information)
- Releasing updated software modules across distributed environments
- Collation and distribution of system messages and instructions, for example Events or operational scripts that need to be run on remote devices
- Multicast setup with networks. Multicast is the delivery of information to a group of destinations simultaneously using the most efficient delivery route
- Managing queue sizes.

Middleware Management is the set of activities that are used to manage middleware. These include:

- Working as part of Service Design and Transition to ensure that the appropriate middleware solutions are chosen and that they can perform optimally when they are deployed
- Ensuring the correct operation of middleware through monitoring and control
- Detecting and resolving Incidents related to middleware
- Maintaining and updating middleware, including licensing, and installing new versions
- Defining and maintaining information about how applications are linked through Middleware. This should be part of the CMS (see Service Transition publication).

5.11 INTERNET/WEB MANAGEMENT

Many organizations conduct much of their business through the Internet and are therefore heavily dependent upon the availability and performance of their websites. In such cases a separate Internet/Web Support team or department will be desirable and justified.

The responsibilities of such a team or department incorporate both Intranet and Internet and are likely to include:

- Defining architectures for Internet and web services
- The specification of standards for development and management of web-based applications, content, websites and web pages. This will typically be done during Service Design
- Design, testing, implementation and maintenance of websites. This will include the architecture of websites and the mapping of content to be made available
- In many organizations, web management will include the editing of content to be posted onto the web
- Maintenance of all web development and management applications
- Liaison and advice to web-content teams within the business. Content may reside in applications or storage devices, which implies close liaison with Application Management and other Technical Management teams
- Liaison with and supplier management of ISPs, hosts, third-party monitoring or virtualization organizations etc. In many organizations the ISPs are managed as part of Network Management
- Third-level support for Internet-/web-related incidents

■ Support for interfaces with back-end and legacy systems. This will often mean working with members of the Application Development and Management teams to ensure secure access and consistency of functionality

■ Monitoring and management of website performance and including: heartbeat testing, user experience simulation, benchmarking, on-demand load balancing, virtualization

■ Website availability, resilience and security. This will form part of the overall Information Security Management of the organization.

5.12 FACILITIES AND DATA CENTRE MANAGEMENT

Facilities Management refers to the management of the physical environment of IT Operations, usually located in Data Centres or computer rooms. This is a vast and complex area and this publication will provide an overview of its key role and activities. A more detailed overview is contained in Appendix E.

In many respects Facilities Management could be viewed as a function in its own right. However, because this publication is focused on where IT Operations are housed, it will cover Facilities Management specifically as it relates to the management of Data Centres and as a subset of the IT Operations Management function.

The main components of Facilities Management are as follows:

■ **Building Management**, which refers to the maintenance and upkeep of the buildings that house the IT staff and Data Centre. Typical activities include cleaning, waste disposal, parking management and access control

■ **Equipment Hosting**, which ensures that all special requirements are provided for the physical housing of equipment and the teams that support them

■ **Power Management**, which refers to managing the sourcing and utilization of power sources that are used to keep the facility functional. This definition of Power Management has a number of implications, which are discussed in Appendix E. Note that information about power utilization is important for planning the capacity of both new services and new buildings

■ **Environmental Conditioning and Alert Systems**, which include the specification, maintenance and monitoring of systems such as smoke detection and

fire suppression, water, heating and cooling systems, etc.

■ **Safety** is concerned with compliance to all legislation, standards and policies relative to the safety of employees

■ **Physical Access Control** refers to ensuring that the facility is only accessed by authorized personnel and that any unauthorized access is detected and managed. This is discussed in more detail in Appendix F

■ **Shipping and Receiving** refers to the management of all equipment, furniture, mail, etc. that leaves or enters the building. It ensures that only appropriate items are entering or leaving the building and that they are routed to the correct party

■ Involvement in **Contract Management** of the various suppliers and service providers involved in the facility

■ **Maintenance** refers to regular, scheduled upkeep of the facility, as well as the detection and resolution of problems with the facility.

Important note regarding Data Centres

Data Centres are generally specialized facilities and, while they use and benefit from generic Facilities Management disciplines, they need to adapt these. For example layout, heating and conditioning, power planning and many other aspects are all managed uniquely in Data Centres.

This means that, although Data Centres may be facilities owned by an organization, they are better managed under the authority of IT Operations, although there may be a functional reporting line between IT and the department that manages other facilities for the organization.

5.12.1 Data Centre strategies

Managing a Data Centre is far more than hosting an open space where technical groups install and manage equipment, using their own approaches and procedures. It requires an integrated set of processes and procedures involving all IT groups at every stage of the ITSM Lifecycle. Data Centre operations are governed by strategic and design decisions for management and control and are executed by operators. This requires a number of key factors to be put in place:

■ **Data Centre Automation**. Specialized automation systems that reduce the need for manual operators and which monitor and track the status of the facility and all IT operations at all times

- **Policy-based management**, where the rules of automation and resource allocation are managed by policy, rather than having to go through complex change procedures every time processing is moved from one resource to another
- **Real time services** 24 hours a day, 7 days a week
- **Standardization of equipment**. This provides greater ease of management, more consistent levels of performance and a means of providing multiple services across similar technology. Standardization also reduces the variety of technical expertise required to manage equipment in the Data Centre and to provide services
- **SOAs**, where service components can be reused, interchanged and replaced very quickly and with no impact on the business. This will make it possible for the Data Centre to be highly responsive in meeting changing business demands without having to go through lengthy and involved re-engineering and re-architecting
- **Virtualization**. This means that IT Services are delivered using an ever-changing set of equipment, geared to meet current demand. For example, an application may run on a dedicated device together with its database during high-demand times, but shifted to a shared device with its database on a remote device during non-peak times – all automated and automatic. This will mean even greater savings of costs as any equipment can be used at any time, without any human intervention, except to perform maintenance and replace failed equipment. The IT Infrastructure is more resilient since any component is backed up by any number of similar components, any of which could take over a failed component's workload automatically.

  Remote monitoring, control and management equipment and systems will be essential to manage a virtualized environment, as many services will not be linked to any one specific piece of equipment.
- **Unified management systems** have become more important as services run across multiple locations and technologies. Today it is important to define what actions need to be taken and what systems will perform that action. This means investing in solutions that will allow Infrastructure managers to simply specify what outcome is required, and allowing the management system to calculate the best combination of tools and actions to achieve the outcome.

5.13 INFORMATION SECURITY MANAGEMENT AND SERVICE OPERATION

Information Security Management as a process is covered in the ITIL Service Design publication. Information Security Management has overall responsibility for setting policies, standards and procedures to ensure the protection of the organization's assets, data, information and IT services. Service Operation teams play a role in executing these policies, standards and procedures and will work closely with the teams or departments responsible for Information Security Management.

Service Operation teams cannot take ownership of Information Security Management, as this would represent a conflict. There needs to be segregation of roles between the groups defining and managing the process and the groups executing specific activities as part of ongoing operation. This will help protect against breaches to security measures, as no single individual should have control over two or more phases of a transaction or operation. Information Security Management should assign responsibilities to ensure a cross-check of duties.

The role of Service Operation teams is outlined next.

5.13.1 Policing and reporting

This will involve Operation staff performing specific policing activities such as the checking of system journals, logs, event/monitoring alerts etc, intrusion detection and/or reporting of actual or potential security breaches. This is done in conjunction with Information Security Management to provide a check and balance system to ensure effective detection and management of security issues.

Service Operation staff are often first to detect security events and are in the best position to be able to shut down and/or remove access to compromised systems.

Particular attention will be needed in the case of third-party organizations that require physical access into the organization. Service Operation staff may be required to escort visitors into sensitive areas and/or control their access.

They may also have a role to play in controlling network access to third parties, such as hardware maintainers dialling in for diagnostic purposes, etc.

5.13.2 Technical assistance

Some technical support may need to be provided to IT Security staff to assist in investigating security incidents and assist in production of reports or in gathering forensic evidence for use in disciplinary action or criminal prosecutions.

Technical advice and assistance may also be needed regarding potential security improvements (e.g. setting up appropriate firewalls or access/password controls).

The use of event, incident, problem and configuration management information can be relied on to provide accurate chronologies of security-related investigations.

5.13.3 Operational security control

For operational reasons, technical staff will often need to have privileged access to key technical areas (e.g. root system passwords, physical access to Data Centres or communications rooms etc). It is therefore essential that adequate controls and audit trails are kept of all such privileged activities so as to deter and detect any security events.

Physical controls need to be in place for all secure areas with logging in-out of all staff. Where third-party staff or visitors need access, it may be Service Operation staff that are responsible for escorting and managing the movement of such personnel.

In the case of privileged systems access, this needs to be restricted to only those people whose need to access the system has been verified – and withdrawn immediately when that need no longer exists. An audit trail must be maintained of who has had access and when, and of all activities performed using those access levels.

5.13.4 Screening and vetting

All Service Operation staff should be screened and vetted to a security level appropriate to the organization in question.

Suppliers and third-party contractors should also be screened and vetted – both the organizations and the specific personnel involved. Many organizations have started using police or government agency background checks, especially where contractors will be working with classified systems. Where necessary, appropriate non-disclosure and confidentiality agreements must be agreed.

5.13.5 Training and awareness

All Service Operation staff should be given regular and ongoing training and awareness of the organization's security policy and procedures. This should include details of disciplinary measures in place. In addition, any security requirements should be specified in the employee's contract of employment.

5.13.6 Documented policies and procedures

Service Operation documented procedures must include all relevant information relating to security issues – extracted from the organization's overall security policy documents. Consideration should be given to the use of handbooks to assist in getting the security messages out to all relevant staff.

5.14 IMPROVEMENT OF OPERATIONAL ACTIVITIES

All Service Operation staff should be constantly looking for areas in which process improvements can be made to give higher IT service quality and/or performed in a more cost-effective way. This might include some of the following activities.

5.14.1 Automation of manual tasks

Any tasks which have to be carried out manually, particularly those that have to be regularly repeated, are likely to be more time consuming, costly and error prone than those that can be systemised and automated. All tasks should be examined for potential automation to reduce effort and costs and to minimize potential errors.

A judgement must be made on the costs of the automation and the likely benefits that will occur.

5.14.2 Reviewing makeshift activities or procedures

Because of the pragmatic nature of Service Operation, it may sometimes arise that makeshift activities or processes are introduced to address short-term operational expediencies. There is a danger that such practices can be continued and become the 'norm' – leading to ongoing inefficiencies. Where any makeshift activities or procedures do have to be introduced it is important that these are reviewed as soon as the immediate expediency is overcome – and either dispensed with or replaced with efficient agreed processes for the longer term.

5.14.3 Operational Audits

Regular audits should be conducted of all Service Operation processes to ensure that they are working satisfactorily.

5.14.4 Using Incident and Problem Management

Problem and Incident Management provide a rich source of operational improvement opportunities. These processes are discussed in detail in Chapter 4 of this publication.

5.14.5 Communication

It should go without saying that good communication about changing requirements, technology and processes will result in improvement in Service Operation. However, communication is often neglected. Service Operation improvement is dependent on formal and regular communication between teams responsible for design, support and operation of services.

5.14.6 Education and training

Service Operation teams should understand the importance of what they do on a daily basis. Education is required to ensure that staff understand what business functions or services are supported by their activities. This will encourage greater care and attention to detail and will also help Service Operation teams to better identify business priorities.

Training programmes should ensure that all staff have the appropriate skills for the technology or applications that they are managing. Training should always be provided when new technology is introduced, or when existing technology is changed.

Organizing for
Service Operation

6 Organizing for Service Operation

6.1 FUNCTIONS

A function is a logical concept that refers to the people and automated measures that execute a defined process, an activity or a combination of processes or activities. In larger organizations a function may be broken up and performed by several departments, teams and groups, or it may be embodied within a single organizational unit.

The Service Operation functions given in Figure 6.1 are needed to manage the 'steady state' operational IT environment. These are logical functions and do not necessarily have to be performed by an equivalent organizational structure. This means that Technical and Application Management can be organized in any combination and into any number of departments. The second-level groupings in Figure 6.1 are examples of typical groups of activities performed by Technical Management (see Chapter 5) and are not a suggested organization structure.

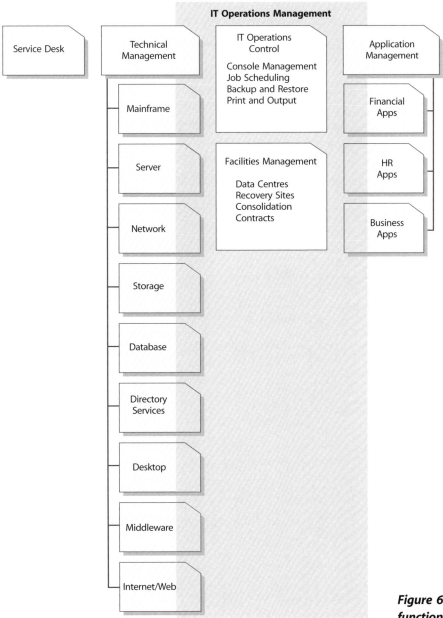

Figure 6.1 Service Operation functions

The following is an overview of the Service Operation functions in Figure 6.1:

■ The **Service Desk** is the primary point of contact for users when there is a service disruption, for service requests or even for some categories of Request for Change. The Service Desk provides a point of communication to the users and a point of coordination for several IT groups and processes. To enable them to perform these actions effectively the Service Desk is usually separate from the other Service Operation functions. In some cases, e.g. where detailed technical support is offered to users on the first call, it may be necessary for Technical or Application Management staff to be on the Service Desk. This does not mean that the Service Desk becomes part of the Technical Management function. In fact, while they are on the Service Desk, they cease to be a part of the Technical Management or Application Management functions and become part of the Service Desk, even if only temporarily.

■ **Technical Management** provides detailed technical skills and resources needed to support the ongoing operation of the IT Infrastructure. Technical Management also plays an important role in the design, testing, release and improvement of IT services. In small organizations, it is possible to manage this expertise in a single department, but larger organizations are typically split into a number of technically specialized departments (see later in this chapter). In many organizations, the Technical Management departments are also responsible for the daily operation of a subset of the IT Infrastructure. Figure 6.1 shows that, although they are part of a Technical Management department, staff who perform these activities are logically part of the IT Operations Management function.

■ **IT Operations Management** is the function responsible for the daily operational activities needed to manage the IT Infrastructure. This is done according to the Performance Standards defined during Service Design. In some organizations this is a single, centralized department, while in others some activities and staff are centralized and some are provided by distributed or specialized departments. This is illustrated in Figure 6.1 by the overlapping from the Technical and Application Management functions. IT Operations Management has two functions that are unique and which are generally formal organizational structures. These are:

● **IT Operations Control**, which is generally staffed by shifts of operators and which ensures that routine operational tasks are carried out. IT Operations Control will also provide centralized monitoring and control activities, usually using an Operations Bridge or Network Operations Centre.

● **Facilities Management** refers to the management of the physical IT environment, usually Data Centres or computer rooms. In many organizations Technical and Application Management are co-located with IT Operations in large Data Centres. In some organizations many physical components of the IT Infrastructure have been outsourced and Facilities Management may include the management of the outsourcing contracts.

■ **Application Management** is responsible for managing applications throughout their lifecycle. The Application Management function supports and maintains operational applications and also plays an important role in the design, testing and improvement of applications that form part of IT services. Application Management is usually divided into departments based on the application portfolio of the organization (see the examples in Figure 6.1), thus allowing easier specialization and more focused support. In many organizations Application Management departments have staff who perform daily operations for those applications. As with Technical Management, these staff logically form part of the IT Operations Management function.

Special note on Information Security Management

Although most would agree that Information Security Management is a function, it is highly specialized and spans several phases of the lifecycle. It is also responsible for the oversight of many activities within all Service Operation functions. For a more in-depth description of Information Security Management, please refer to the Service Design publication and to section 5.13 of this publication.

6.1.1 Functions and activities

Chapter 5 of this publication introduced a number of common Service Operation activities. Due to the technical nature and specialization of these activities, the teams, groups or departments that perform them are often given names that correspond to the particular activities. For example, Network Management could be performed by a 'Network Management Department'. This, however, is by no means a rule. There are a number of options available in mapping activities to a team or department, for example:

- One activity could be performed by several teams or departments, e.g. if an organization has five major Application Support departments, each supporting a different set of applications, each of these departments could perform Database Administration for 'its' applications
- One department could perform several activities, e.g. the Network Management Department could be responsible for managing the network, Directory Services Management and Server Management
- An activity could be performed by groups, e.g. Security Administration can be performed by any person with responsibility for managing an application, server, middleware or desktop.

These organizational decisions are influenced by a number of factors, such as:

- The size and location of the organization. Smaller, less distributed organizations will tend to combine these functions, whereas large, decentralized organizations may have several teams or departments performing the same activity (e.g. per region).
- The complexity of technology used in the organization. The higher the number of different technologies used, the more likely there are to be several different teams, each doing something similar, but in a different context (e.g. UNIX Server Management and Windows Server Management).
- The availability of skills. Where technical skills are scarce, it is common for organizations to use generalists to perform multiple groups of activities – although, in some cases, security considerations make this very difficult. For example, an organization working on classified or secret projects may have to hire expensive, specialized resources even when that means relocating them or contracting through security-cleared vendors.
- The culture of the organization. Some organizations prefer to work in highly specialized environments, while others tend to prefer the flexibility of generalist staff.
- The financial situation of the organization will determine how many people, with what type of skill, can be employed and how they will be organized.

As a result of these factors, it is impossible for this publication to prescribe an appropriate organizational structure that will fit every situation, however, the following sections list the required activities under the functional groups most likely to be involved in their operation. Please note that this does not mean that all organizations have to use these divisions. Smaller organizations will tend to combine these activities into single departments, or even individuals – if they are even needed at all.

> **Special note on outsourcing**
>
> These organizational considerations are likely to be most relevant to internal IT organizations. The situation becomes even more complex when some or all of a particular activity or function are outsourced. Prime opportunities for outsourcing have been the Service Desk and Network Operations. This will be covered in more detail in ITIL Complementary Guidance, but some of the key points to remember are:
>
> - Regardless of who is performing the activity, the company contracting the outsourcer is still responsible for ensuring that it is performed to a standard that will support the delivery of services to their customers and users.
>
> - Outsourcing to solve an organization's problems or as an alternative to good Service Management processes rarely works. The best results are obtained if these are in place before outsourcing.
>
> - Outsourcing works best when there is active involvement by both organizations. If the staff and managers of the customer organization disengage, the outsourcer is unlikely to be successful, simply because nobody understands the organization better than the people who work there.
>
> - The outsourcer should not determine their outputs or how they are measured. These are determined by understanding the business requirements of users and customers and ensuring that they can be met by the outsourcer's capabilities.
>
> - Although the outsourcer's services become an integral part of the organization, they are still a third-party organization, with a different set of business objectives, policies and practices. Security standards must be upheld and both parties must clearly understand their respective roles and contributions.

6.2 SERVICE DESK

A Service Desk is a functional unit made up of a dedicated number of staff responsible for dealing with a variety of service events, often made via telephone calls, web interface, or automatically reported infrastructure events.

The Service Desk is a vitally important part of an organization's IT Department and should be the single point of contact for IT users on a day-by-day basis – and will handle all incidents and service requests, usually using specialist software tools to log and manage all such events.

The value of an effective Service Desk should not be underrated – a good Service Desk can often compensate for deficiencies elsewhere in the IT organization, but a poor Service Desk (or the lack of a Service Desk) can give a poor impression of an otherwise very effective IT organization!

It is therefore very important that the correct calibre of staff is used on the Service Desk and that IT Managers do their best to make the desk an attractive place to work to improve staff retention.

The exact nature, type, size and location of a Service Desk will vary, depending upon the type of business, number of users, geography, complexity of calls, scope of services and many other factors.

In alignment to customer and business requirements, the IT organization's senior managers should decide the exact nature of its required Service Desk (and whether it should be internal or outsourced to a third party) as part of its overall ITSM strategy (see Service Strategy publication) – and then subsequent planning must be done to prepare for and then implement the appropriate Service Desk function (either when implementing a new function, or more likely these days when making necessary amendments to an existing function – see Service Design and Service Transition publications).

6.2.1 Justification and role of the Service Desk

Very little justification is needed today for a Service Desk, as many organizations have become convinced that this is by far the best approach for dealing with first-line IT support issues. One only needs ask the question 'What is the alternative?' to make a compelling case for the Service Desk concept. Where further justification is needed, the following benefits should be considered:

- Improved customer service, perception and satisfaction
- Increased accessibility through a single point of contact, communication and information
- Better-quality and faster turnaround of customer or user requests
- Improved teamwork and communication
- Enhanced focus and a proactive approach to service provision

- A reduced negative business impact
- Better-managed infrastructure and control
- Improved usage of IT Support resources and increased productivity of business personnel
- More meaningful management information for decision support
- It is common practice that the Service Desk provides 'entry-level' positions for ITSM staff. Working on the Service Desk is an excellent 'grounding' for anyone who wishes to pursue a career in Service Management. However, this could also present challenges with people who do not understand the business or technology. Users calling the Service Desk should be able to speak to someone who is able to address their needs, and Service Desk Analysts should not be burned out in less than a year because of undue stress. Care should be taken to select appropriately skilled individuals with a good understanding of the business and to provide adequate training – thus preventing reduction in levels of support due to a lack of knowledge at the first line.

6.2.2 Service Desk objectives

The primary aim of the Service Desk is to restore the 'normal service' to the users as quickly as possible. In this context 'restoration of service' is meant in the widest possible sense. While this could involve fixing a technical fault, it could equally involve fulfilling a service request or answering a query – anything that is needed to allow the users to return to working satisfactorily.

Specific responsibilities will include:

- Logging all relevant incident/service request details, allocating categorization and prioritization codes
- Providing first-line investigation and diagnosis
- Resolving those incidents/service requests they are able
- Escalating incidents/service requests that they cannot resolve within agreed timescales
- Keeping users informed of progress
- Closing all resolved incidents, requests and other calls
- Conducting customer/user satisfaction call-backs/surveys as agreed
- Communication with users – keeping them informed of incident progress, notifying them of impending changes or agreed outages, etc.
- Updating the CMS under the direction and approval of Configuration Management if so agreed.

Note: these activities are explained and set in context with the fuller Incident Management and Request Fulfilment process in sections 4.2 and 4.3 respectively.

6.2.3 Service Desk organizational structure

There are many ways of structuring Service Desks and locating them – and the correct solution will vary for different organizations. The primary options are detailed below, but in reality an organization may need to implement a structure that combines a number of these options in order to fully meet the business needs:

6.2.3.1 Local Service Desk

This is where a desk is co-located within or physically close to the user community it serves. This often aids communication and gives a clearly visible presence, which some users like, but can often be inefficient and expensive to resource as staff are tied up waiting to deal with incidents when the volume and arrival rate of calls may not justify this.

There may, however, be some valid reasons for maintaining a local desk, even where call volumes alone do not justify this. Reasons might include:

■ Language and cultural or political differences
■ Different time zones

■ Specialized groups of users
■ The existence of customized or specialized services that require specialist knowledge
■ VIP/criticality status of users.

6.2.3.2 Centralized Service Desk

It is possible to reduce the number of Service Desks by merging them into a single location (or into a smaller number of locations) by drawing the staff into one or more centralized Service Desk structures. This can be more efficient and cost-effective, allowing fewer overall staff to deal with a higher volume of calls, and can also lead to higher skill levels through great familiarization through more frequent occurrence of events. It might still be necessary to maintain some form of 'local presence' to handle physical support requirements, but such staff can be controlled and deployed from the central desk.

6.2.3.3 Virtual Service Desk

Through the use of technology, particularly the Internet, and the use of corporate support tools, it is possible to give the impression of a single, centralized Service Desk when in fact the personnel may be spread or located in any number or type of geographical or structural locations. This brings in the option of 'home working', secondary support group, off-shoring or outsourcing – or any

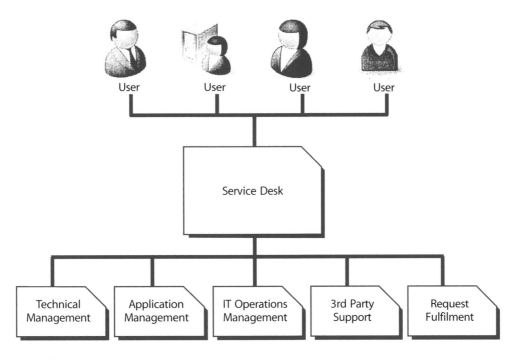

Figure 6.2 Local Service Desk

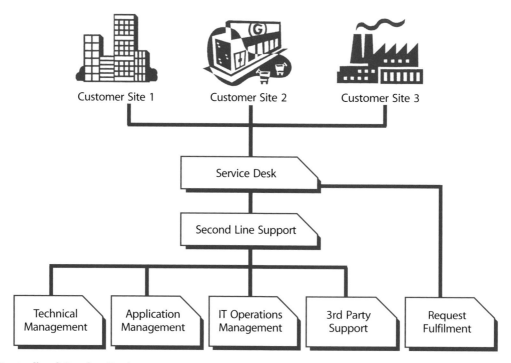

Figure 6.3 Centralized Service Desk

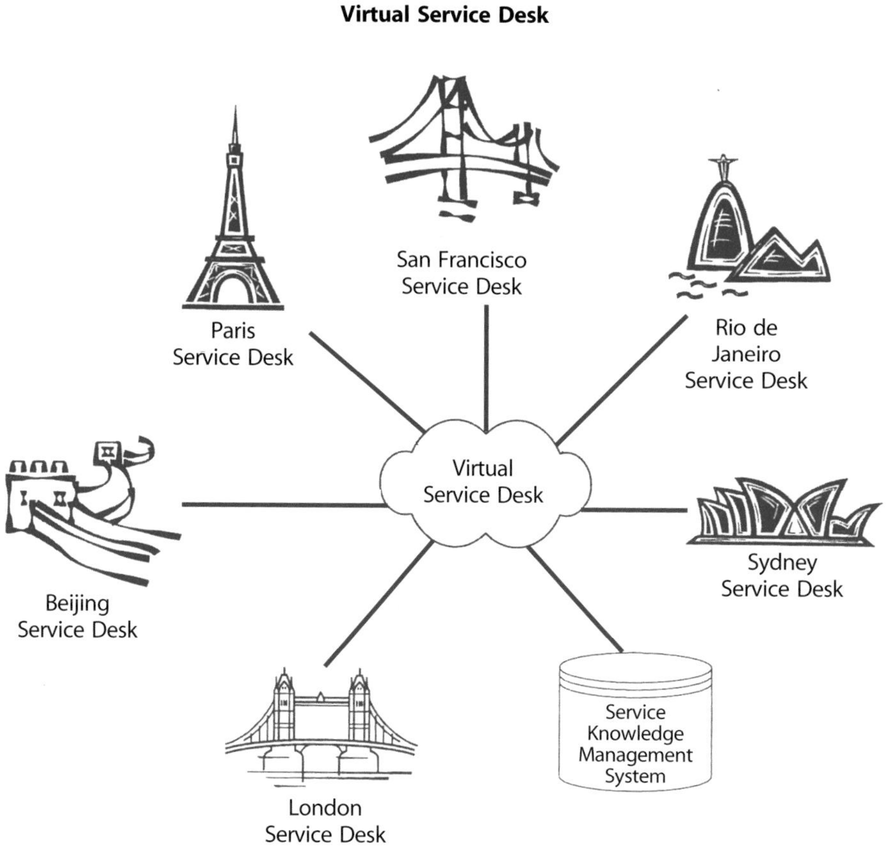

Virtual Service Desk

Figure 6.4 Virtual Service Desk

combination necessary to meet user demand. It is important to note, however, that safeguards are needed in all of these circumstances to ensure consistency and uniformity in service quality and cultural terms.

6.2.3.4 Follow the Sun

Some global or international organizations may wish to combine two or more of their geographically dispersed Service Desks to provide a 24-hour follow-the-sun service. For example, a Service Desk in Asia-Pacific may handle calls during its standard office hours and at the end of this period it may hand over responsibility for any open incidents to a European-based desk. That desk will handle these calls alongside its own incidents during its standard day and then hand over to a USA-based desk – which finally hands back responsibility to the Asia-Pacific desk to complete the cycle.

This can give 24-hour coverage at relatively low cost, as no desk has to work more than a single shift. However, the same safeguards of common processes, tools, shared database of information and culture must be addressed for this approach to proceed – and well-controlled escalation and handover processes are needed.

6.2.3.5 Specialized Service Desk groups

For some organizations it might be beneficial to create 'specialist groups' within the overall Service Desk structure, so that incidents relating to a particular IT service can be routed directly (normally via telephony selection or a web-based interface) to the specialist group. This can allow faster resolution of these incidents, through greater familiarity and specialist training.

The selection would be made using a script along the lines of 'If your call is about the X Service, please press 1 now, otherwise please hold for a Service Desk analyst'.

Care is needed not to over complicate the selection, so specialist groups should only be considered for a very small number of key services where these exist, and where call rates about that service justify a separate specialist group.

6.2.3.6 Environment

The environment where the Service Desk is to be located should be carefully chosen. Where possible, the following facilities should be provided:

- A location where the entire function can be positioned with sufficient natural light and overall space – to allow adequate desk and storage-space, and room to move around if necessary

- A quiet environment with adequate acoustic control so that one telephone conversation is not disrupted by another
- Pleasant surroundings and comfortable furniture so as to lighten the mood (the Service Desk can be a very stressful place to work, so every little helps!)
- A separate rest-room and refreshment area nearby so that staff can take short breaks as appropriate when necessary without being away for too long.

Anecdote

One company found that there was a 'them and us' culture existing between the Service Desk and the other support teams. The third-line teams often believed themselves to be better than the Service Desk. Hiding the Service Desk away in an isolated room helped to reinforce this culture. The company found that creating an open-plan office with the Service Desk in the middle encouraged closer working and helped to break down these barriers.

6.2.3.7 Building a single point of contact

Regardless of the combination of options chosen to fulfil an organization's overall Service Desk structure, individual users should be in no doubt about who to contact if they need assistance. A single telephone number (or a single number for each group if separate desks are chosen) should be provided and well publicized – as well as a single e-mail address and a single web Service Desk contact page.

Ideas that can be successfully used to help publicize the Service Desk telephone number and e-mail address, and making it available close to hand when users are likely to need them, are:

- Including the Service Desk telephone number on hardware CI labels, attached to the components the user is likely to be calling about
- Printing Service Desk contact details on telephones
- For PCs and laptops, using a customized background or desktop with the Service Desk contact details, together with information read from the system that will be needed when calling (such as IP address, OS build number, etc.) in one corner
- Printing the Service Desk number on 'freebies' (pens, pencils, mugs, mouse-mats, etc.)
- Prominently placing these details on Service Desk Internet/intranet sites

- Including them on any calling cards or satisfaction survey cards left with users when a desk visit has been necessary
- Repeating the details on all correspondence sent to the users (together with call reference numbers)
- Placing the details on notice boards or physical locations that users are likely to regularly visit (entrances, canteens, refreshment areas, etc.).

6.2.4 Service Desk staffing

The issues involved in, and criteria for, establishing the appropriate staffing model and levels are discussed in this section. Details about typical Service Desk roles and responsibilities can be found in paragraph 6.6.1 below. They include the Service Desk Manager, Supervisor, Analysts and, in some organizations, these roles are complemented by business users ('Super Users') who provide first-line support.

6.2.4.1 Staffing levels

An organization must ensure that the correct number of staff are available at any given time to match the demand being placed upon the desk by the business. Call rates can be very volatile and often in the same day the arrival rate may go from very high to very low and back again. An organization planning a new desk should attempt to predict the call arrival rate and profile – and to staff accordingly. Statistical analysis of call arrival rates under current support arrangements must be undertaken and then closely monitored and adjusted as necessary.

Many organizations will find that call rates peak during the start of the office day and then fall off quickly, perhaps with another burst in the early part of the afternoon – this obviously varies depending upon the organization's business but is an often occurring pattern for many organizations. In such circumstances it may be possible to utilize part-time staff, home-workers, second-line support staff or third parties to cover the peaks.

The following factors should be considered when deciding staffing levels:

- Customer service expectations
- Business requirements, such as budget, call response times, etc.
- Size, relative age, design and complexity of the IT Infrastructure and Service Catalogue – for example, the number and type of incidents, the extent of customised versus standard off-the-shelf software deployed, etc.
- The number of customers and users to support, and associated factors such as:

- Number of customers and users speaking a different language
- Skill level
- Incident and Service Request types (and types of RFC if appropriate):
  - Duration of time required for call types (e.g. simple queries, specialist application queries, hardware, etc.)
  - Local or external expertise required
  - The volume and types of incidents and Service Requests
- The period of support cover required, based on:
  - Hours covered
  - Out-of-hours support requirements
  - Time zones to be covered
  - Locations to be supported (particularly if Service Desk staff also conduct desk-side support)
  - Travel time between locations
  - Workload pattern of requests (e.g. daily, month end, etc.)
  - The service level targets in place (response levels etc.)
- The type of response required:
  - Telephone
  - E-mail/fax/voicemail/video
  - Physical attendance
  - Online access/control
- The level of training required
- The support technologies available (e.g. phone systems, remote support tools, etc.)
- The existing skill levels of staff
- The processes and procedures in use.

All these items should be carefully considered before making any decision on staffing levels. This should also be reflected in the levels of documentation required. Remember that the better the service, the more the business will use it.

A number of tools are available to help determine the appropriate number of staff for the Service Desk. These workload modelling tools are dependent on detailed 'local knowledge' of the organization such as call volumes and patterns, service and user profiles, etc.

6.2.4.2 Skill levels

An organization must decide on the level and range of skills it requires of its Service Desk staff – and then ensure that these skills are available at the appropriate times.

A range of skill options are possible, starting from a 'call-logging' service only – where staff need only very basic technical skills – right through to a 'technical' Service Desk where the organization's most technically skilled staff are used. In the case of the former, there will be a high handling but low resolution rate, while in the latter case this will be reversed.

The decision on the required skills level will often be driven by target resolution times (agreed with the business and captured in service level targets), the complexity of the systems supported and 'what the business is prepared to pay'.

There is a strong correlation between response and resolution targets and costs – generally speaking, the shorter the target times, the higher the cost because more resources are required.

While there may be instances when business dependency or criticality make a highly technically skilled desk an imperative, the optimum and most cost-effective approach is generally to have a 'call-logging' first line of support via the Service Desk, with quick and effective escalations to more skilled second-line and third-line resolution groups where skilled staff can be concentrated and more effectively utilised (see Incident Management, section 4.2, for more details and guidance on end-to-end support structures). However, this basic starting point can be improved over time by providing the first-line staff with an effective knowledge-base, diagnostic scripts and integrated support tools (including a CMS), as well as ongoing training and awareness, so that first-line resolution rates can gradually be increased.

This can also be achieved by locating second-level staff on the Service Desk, effectively creating a two-tier structure. This has advantages of making second-level staff available to help deal with peak call periods and to train more junior personnel, and it will often increase the first-call resolution rate. However, second-line staff often have duties outside of the Service Desk – resulting in rosters having to be managed or second-line staff positions being duplicated. In addition, having to deal with routine calls may be demotivating for more experienced staff. A further potential drawback is that the Service Desk becomes really good at resolving calls, whereas second-line staff should be focused on removing the root cause instead.

Another factor to consider when deciding on the skills requirements for Service Desk staff is the level of customization or specialization of the supported services. Standardized services require less specific knowledge to provide quality customer support. The more specialized the service, the more likely specialist knowledge will be required on the first call.

Note that first-line resolution rates can be reduced by effective Problem Management, which will reduce a number of the simpler, repetitive incidents. In such cases, although the resolution rates appear to be going down, the overall service quality will have improved by the complete removal of many incidents. While this is good, if Service Desk staff are paid incentives or bonuses for first-call resolution, it could prove disastrous for morale and process effectiveness unless the bonus threshold is reviewed.

Improvements in resolution times/rates should not be left to chance, but should instead be part of an ongoing Service Improvement Plan (see the Continual Service Improvement publication for fuller details).

Once the required skill levels have been identified, there is an ongoing task to ensure that the Service Desk is operated in such a way that the necessary staff obtain and maintain the necessary skills – and that staff with the correct balance of skills are on duty at appropriate times so that consistency is maintained.

This will involve an ongoing training and awareness programme which should cover:

- Interpersonal skills: such as telephony skills, communication skills, active listening and customer-care training.
- Business awareness: specific knowledge of the organization's business areas, drivers, structure, priorities, etc.
- Service awareness of all the organization's key IT services for which support is being provided
- Technical awareness (and deeper technical training to the appropriate level, depending upon the resolution rate sought)
- Depending on level of support provided, some diagnosis skills (e.g. Kepner and Tregoe)
- Support tools and techniques
- Awareness training and tutorials in new systems and technologies, prior to their introduction
- Processes and procedures (most particularly Incident, Change and Configuration Management – but an overview of all ITSM processes and procedures)
- Typing skills to ensure quick and accurate entry of incident or Service Request details.

For such a programme to be effective, skill requirements and levels should be evaluated periodically and training records maintained.

Careful formulation of staffing rotations or schedules should be maintained so that a consistent balance of staff experience and appropriate skill levels are present during all critical operational periods. It is not sufficient to have only the right number of staff on duty – the correct blend of skills should also be available.

6.2.4.3 Training

It is vital that all Service Desk staff are adequately trained before they are called upon to staff the Service Desk. A formal induction programme should be undertaken by all new staff, the exact content of which will vary depending upon the existing skill levels and experience of the new recruit, but is likely to include many of the required skills as described above.

Where possible, a business awareness programme, including short periods of secondment into key business areas, should be provided for new staff who do not already have this level of business awareness.

When starting on the Service Desk, new staff should initially 'shadow' experienced staff – sit with them and listen in on calls – before starting to take calls themselves with a mentor listening in and able to intervene and provide support where necessary. The mentor should initially review each call with the trainee after it concludes to learn any lessons. The frequency of such reviews should be gradually reduced as experience and confidence grows but the mentor should still be available to provide ongoing support even when the trainee has reached the stage of going solo.

Mentors may need to be trained on how to mentor. Service Desk experience and technical skills are not the only requirements for mentoring. Effective knowledge-transfer skills and the ability to teach without being condescending or threatening are equally important.

A programme will be necessary to keep Service Desk staff's knowledge up to date – and to make them aware of new developments, services and technologies. The timing of such events is critical so as not to impact upon the normal duties. Many Service Desks find that it is best to organize short 'tutorials' during quiet periods when staff are less likely to be needed for call handling.

Note: Investment should also be made in the professional development of Service Desk staff. Internal mentoring and shadowing second- and third-level support staff is a good start, but best-of-breed Service Desks benefit from a formalized programme of staff development. Organizational commitment to professional development helps instil a sense of accomplishment and opportunity to

staff. This often leads to innovation in Service Desk operation (such as specialized services) which in turn drive operational efficiencies at all tier levels of support. It helps to build skills that can be used in their current role as well as it jump-starts the training for a new role. While it is important to develop their core competencies in their current role, having a clear career path and recognising future requirement and development needs is also important.

6.2.4.4 Staff retention

It is very important that all IT Managers recognize the importance of the Service Desk and the staff who work on it, and give this special attention. Any significant loss of staff can be disruptive and lead to inconsistency of service – so efforts should be made to make the Service Desk an attractive place to work.

Ways in which this can be done include proper recognition of the role with reward packages recognizing this, team-building exercises, staff rotation onto other activities (projects, second-line support, etc.).

The Service Desk can often be used as a stepping stone into other more technical or supervisory/managerial roles. If this is done, care is needed to ensure that proper succession planning takes place so that the desk does not lose all of its key expertise in any area at one time. Also, good documentation and cross-training can mitigate this risk.

6.2.4.5 Super Users

Many organizations find it useful to appoint or designate a number of 'Super Users' throughout the user community, to act as liaison points with IT in general and the Service Desk in particular.

Super Users can be given some additional training and awareness and used as a conduit for communications flow in both directions. They can be asked to filter requests and issues raised by the user community (in some cases even going as far as to have incidents or requests raised by the Super User) – this can help prevent 'incident storms' when a key service or component fails, affecting many users.

They can also be used to cascade information from the Service Desk outwards throughout their local user community, which can be very useful in disseminating service details to all users very quickly.

It is important to note that Super Users should log all calls that they deal with, and not just those that they pass on to IT. This will mean access to, and training on how to use, the Incident logging tools. This will help to measure the activity of the Super User and also to ensure that their position is not abused. In addition, it will ensure that valuable history regarding incidents and service quality are not lost.

It may also be possible for Super Users to be involved in:

■ Staff training for users in their area
■ Providing support for minor incidents or simple request fulfilment
■ Involvement with new releases and rollouts.

Super Users do not necessarily provide support for the whole of IT. In many cases a Super User will only provide support for a specific application, module or business unit area. As a business user the Super User often has in-depth knowledge of how key business processes run and how services work in practice. This is very useful knowledge to share with the Service Desk, so that it can provide higher-quality services in future.

It should be noted that a firm commitment is needed from potential Super Users, and specifically their management, that they will have the time and interest to perform this role before selection and training commences.

A Super User, while a valuable interface to the business and the Service Desk, must be given proper training, accountability and expectation. Super Users can be vulnerable to misuse if their role, responsibilities and the process governing these are not clearly communicated to the users. It is imperative that a Super User is not seen as a replacement for, or a means to circumvent, the Service Desk.

6.2.5 Service Desk metrics

Metrics should be established so that performance of the Service Desk can be evaluated at regular intervals. This is important to assess the health, maturity, efficiency, effectiveness and any opportunities to improve Service Desk operations.

Metrics for Service Desk performance must be realistic and carefully chosen. It is common to select those metrics that are easily available and that may seem to be a possible indication of performance; however, this can be misleading. For example, the total number of calls received by the Service Desk is not in itself an indication of either good or bad performance and may in fact be caused by events completely outside the control of the Service Desk – for example a particularly busy period for the organization, or the release of a new version of a major corporate system.

An increase in the number of calls to the Service Desk can indicate less reliable services over that period of time – but may also indicate increased user confidence in a Service Desk that is maturing, resulting in a higher likelihood that users will seek assistance rather than try to cope alone. For this type of metric to be reliable for reaching either conclusion, further comparison of previous periods for any Service Desk improvements implemented since the last measurement baseline, or service reliability changes, problems, etc. to isolate the true cause for the increase is needed.

Further analysis and more detailed metrics are therefore needed and must be examined over a period of time. These will include the call-handling statistics previously mentioned under telephony, and additionally:

■ The first-line resolution rate: the percentage of calls resolved at first line, without the need for escalation to other support groups. This is the figure often quoted by organizations as the primary measure of the Service Desks performance – and used for comparison purposes with the performance of other desks – but care is needed when making any comparisons. For greater accuracy and more valid comparisons this can be broken down further as follows:
 ● The percentage of calls resolved during the first contact with the Service Desk, i.e. while the user is still on the telephone to report the call
 ● The percentage of calls resolved by the Service Desk staff themselves without having to seek deeper support from other groups. Note: some desks will choose to co-locate or embed more technically skilled second-line staff with the Service Desk (see Incident Management for further details). In such cases it is important when making comparisons to also separate out (i) the percentage resolved by the Service Desk staff alone; and (ii) the percentage resolved by the first-line Service Desk staff and second-line support staff combined.
■ Average time to resolve an incident (when resolved at first line)
■ Average time to escalate an incident (where first-line resolution is not possible)
■ Average Service Desk cost of handling an incident. Two metrics should be considered here:
 ● Total cost of the Service Desk divided by the number of calls. This will provide an average figure which is useful as an index and for planning purposes but does not accurately represent the relative costs of different types of calls

● By calculating the percentage of call duration time on the desk overall and working out a cost per minute (total costs for the period divided by total call duration minutes') this can be used to calculate the cost for individual calls and give a more accurate figure.

By evaluating the types of incidents with call duration, a more refined picture of cost per call by types arises and gives an indication of which incident types tend to cost more to resolve and possible targets for improvements.

■ Percentage of customer or user updates conducted within target times, as defined in SLA targets

■ Average time to review and close a resolved call

■ The number of calls broken down by time of day and day of week, combined with the average call-time metric, is critical in determining the number of staff required.

Further general details on metrics and how they should be used to drive forward service quality is included in the Continual Service Improvement publication.

6.2.5.1 Customer/user satisfaction surveys

As well as tracking the 'hard' measures of the Service Desk's performance (via the metrics described above), it is also important to assess 'soft' measures – such as how well the customers and users feel their calls have been answered, whether they feel the Service Desk operator was courteous and professional, whether they instilled confidence in the user.

This type of measure is best obtained from the users themselves. This can be done as part of a wider customer/user satisfaction survey covering all of IT or can be specifically targeted at Service Desk issues alone.

One effective way of achieving the latter is through a call-back telephone survey, where an independent Service Desk Operator or Supervisor rings back a small percentage of users shortly after their incident has been resolved, to ask the specific questions needed.

Care should be taken to keep the number of questions to a minimum (five to six at the most) so that the users will have the time to cooperate. Also survey questions should be designed so that the user or customer knows what area or subject questions are about and which incident or service they are referring to. The Service Desk must act on low satisfaction levels and any feedback received.

To allow adequate comparisons, the same percentage of calls should be selected in each period and they should be rigorously carried out despite any other time pressures.

Surveys are a complex and specialized area, requiring a good understanding of statistics and survey techniques. This publication will not attempt to provide an overview of all of these, but a summary of some of the more widely used techniques and tools is listed in Table 6.1.

Table 6.1 Survey techniques and tools

Technique/Tool	Advantages	Disadvantages
After-call survey Callers are asked to remain on the phone after the call and then asked to rate the service they were provided	■ High response rate since the caller is already on the phone ■ Caller is surveyed immediately after the call so their experience is recent	■ People may feel pressured into taking the survey, resulting in a negative service experience ■ The surveyor is seen as part of the Service Desk being surveyed, which may discourage open answers
Outbound telephone survey Customers and users who have previously used the Service Desk are contacted some time after their experience with the Service Desk	■ Higher response rate since the caller is interviewed directly ■ Specific categories of user or customer can be targeted for feedback (e.g. people who requested a specific service, or people experienced a disruption to a particular service)	■ This method could be seen as intrusive, if the call disrupts the user or customer from their work ■ The survey is conducted some time after the user or customer used the Service Desk, so their perception may have changed

(**continued overleaf**)

Table 6.1 Survey techniques and tools (*continued*)

Technique/Tool	Advantages	Disadvantages
Personal interviews Customers and users are interviewed personally by the person doing the survey. This is especially effective for customers or users who use the Service Desk extensively or who have had a very negative experience	■ The interviewer is able to observe non-verbal signals as well as listening to what the user or customer is saying ■ Users and customers feel a greater degree of personal attention and a sense that their answers are being taken seriously	■ Interviews are time-consuming for both the interviewer and the respondent ■ Users and customers could turn the interviews into complaint sessions
Group interviews Customers and users are interviewed in small groups. This is good for gathering general impressions and for determining whether there is a need to change certain aspects of the Service Desk, e.g. service hours or location	■ A larger number of users and customers can be interviewed ■ Questions are more generic and therefore more consistent between interviews	■ People may not express themselves freely in front of their peers or managers ■ People's opinions can easily be changed by others in the group during the interview
Postal/e-mail surveys Survey questionnaires are mailed to a target set of customers and users. They are asked to return their responses by e/mail	■ Specific or all customers or users can be targeted ■ Postal surveys can be anonymous, allowing people to express themselves more freely ■ E-mail surveys are not anonymous, but can be created using automated forms that make it convenient and easy for the user to reply and increase the likelihood it will be completed	■ Postal surveys are labour intensive to process ■ The percentage of people responding to postal surveys tends to be small ■ Misinterpretation of a question could affect the result
Online surveys Questionnaires are posted on a website and users and customers encouraged via e-mail or links from a popular site to participate in the survey	■ The potential audience of these surveys is fairly large ■ Respondents can complete the questionnaire in their own time ■ The links on popular websites are good reminders without being intrusive	The percentage of respondents cannot be predicted

6.2.6 Outsourcing the Service Desk

The decision to outsource is a strategic issue for senior managers – and is addressed in detail in the Service Strategy and Service Design publications. Many of the guidelines in this section are not unique to the Service Desk and can be applied to any function, support area or service being outsourced (or out-tasked).

Regardless of the reasons for, or the extent of, the outsourcing contract, it is vital that the organization retains responsibility for the activities and services provided by the Service Desk. The organization is ultimately responsible for the outcomes of the decision and must therefore determine what service the outsourcer provides, not the other way round.

If the outsourcing route is chosen, there are some safeguards that are needed to ensure that the outsourced Service Desk works effectively and efficiently with the organization's other IT teams and departments and that end-to-end Service Management control is maintained (this is particularly important for organizations seeking ISO/IEC 20000 certification as overall management control has to be demonstrated). Some of these safeguards are set out below.

6.2.6.1 Common tools and processes

The Service Desk does not have responsibility for all the processes and procedures that it initiates. For example, a Service Request is received by the Service Desk but the request is fulfilled by the internal IT Operational team.

If the Service Desk is outsourced, care must be taken that the tools are consistent with those still being used in the customer organization. Outsourcing is often seen as an opportunity to replace outdated or inadequate tools, only to find that there are severe integration problems between the new tool and the legacy tools and processes.

For this reason it is important to ensure that these issues are properly researched and the customer's requirements are adequately scoped and specified before the outsourcing contract. Service Desk tools must not only support the outsourced Service Desk, but they must support the customer organization's processes and business requirements as well.

Ideally the outsourced desk should use the same tools and processes (or, as a minimum, interfacing tools and processes) to allow smooth process flow between the Service Desk and second- and third-line support groups.

In addition, the outsourced Service Desk should have access to:

- All incident records and information
- Problem Records and information
- Known Error Data
- Change Schedule
- Sources of internal knowledge (especially technical or application experts)
- SKMS
- CMS
- Alerts from monitoring tools.

It is often a challenge integrating processes and tools in a less mature organization with those in a more mature organization. A common but incorrect assumption is that the maturity of the one organization will somehow result in higher maturity in the other. Active involvement to ensure alignment of processes and tools is essential to a smooth transition and ongoing management of services between the internal and external organizations. In fact, if this is not directly addressed, it could result in the failure of the contract.

It is also often incorrectly assumed that the proof of Service Management quality and maturity in an external outsource partner can be guaranteed by stating requirements in the procurement process for 'ITIL conformance' and / or 'ISO/IEC 20000 certification'. These statements may indicate that a potential supplier uses the ITIL Framework in its delivery of services to customers, or that they have achieved standards certification for their internal practices, but it is equally important to have the enabling technology in place and being used that demonstrates a service provider's capability to manage services and interface to internal practices harmoniously. There is no standard of compliance that ensures this and so procurement efforts should include specific queries to satisfy this requirement. More information on outsource provider acquisition can be found in the Service Design publication.

6.2.6.2 SLA targets

The SLA targets for overall incident-handling and resolution times need to be agreed with the customers and between all teams and departments – and OLA/UC targets need to be coordinated and agreed with individual support groups so that they underpin and support the SLA targets.

Examples of these can be seen in the section on metrics above (see section 6.2.5).

6.2.6.3 Good communications

The lines of communication between the outsourced Service Desk and the other support groups need to work very effectively. This can be assisted by some or all of the following steps:

- Close physical co-location
- Regular liaison/review meetings
- Cross-training tutorials between the teams and departments
- 'Partnership' arrangements when staff from both organizations are used jointly to staff the desk
- Communication Plans and performance targets are documented in a consistent manner in OLAs and UCs.

In cases where the Service Desk is located off-shore, not all of these measures will be possible. However, the need for training and communication of the Service Desk staff is still critical, even more so in cases where there are language and cultural differences.

This will be covered in more detail in ITIL complementary publications, but, as a rule, outsourcing companies who offer off-shore Service Desk solutions should take the following into account:

- Training programmes focused on cultural understanding of the customer market
- Language skills – especially the understanding of idiomatic use of the language in the customer market.

This is not so that the Service Desk staff sound like natives of the customer's country (that type of insincerity is very quickly detected by customers), but to facilitate better understanding of the customer and the better to appreciate their priorities

■ Regular visits by representatives of the customer organization to provide training and appropriate feedback directly to the Service Desk management and staff

■ Training in the use of the customer organizations tools and methods of work. This is especially effective if similar training materials are presented by the same instructors as those used by the customer organization.

6.2.6.4 Ownership of data

Clear ownership of the data collected by the outsourced Service Desk must be established. Ownership of all data relative to users, customers, affected CIs, services, incidents, Service Requests, changes, etc. must remain with the organization that is outsourcing the activity – but both organizations will require access to it.

Data that is related specifically to performance of employees of the outsourcing company will remain the property of that company, which is often legally prevented from sharing the data with the customer organization. This may also be true of other data that is used purely for the internal management of the Service Desk, such as head count, optimization activities, Service Desk cost information, etc.

All reporting requirements and issues around ownership of data must be specified in the underpinning contract with the company providing the outsourcing service.

6.3   TECHNICAL MANAGEMENT

Technical Management refers to the groups, departments or teams that provide technical expertise and overall management of the IT Infrastructure.

6.3.1 Technical Management role

Technical Management plays a dual role:

■ It is the custodian of technical knowledge and expertise related to managing the IT Infrastructure. In this role, Technical Management ensures that the knowledge required to design, test, manage and improve IT services is identified, developed and refined.

■ It provides the actual resources to support the ITSM Lifecycle. In this role Technical Management ensures that resources are effectively trained and deployed to design, build, transition, operate and improve the technology required to deliver and support IT services.

By performing these two roles, Technical Management is able to ensure that the organization has access to the right type and level of human resources to manage technology and, thus, to meet business objectives. Defining the requirements for these roles starts in Service Strategy and is expanded in Service Design, validated in Service Transition and refined in Continual Service Improvement (see other ITIL publications in this series).

Part of this role is also to ensure a balance between the skill level, utilization and the cost of these resources. For example, hiring a top-level resource at the higher end of the salary scale and then only using that skill for 10% of the time is not effective. A better Technical Management strategy would be to identify the times that the skill is needed and then hire a contractor for only those tasks.

Another strategy in larger organizations is to leverage specialist staff out of 'central' pools so that specialists can be well utilized and provide an economy of scale to the organization and minimize the need to hire in contractors. Specialized skills should be identified among resources in the IT organization, then leveraged for specific needs as they arise, analogous to a special tactical unit, whose members also perform regular duties but who are assigned to tasks needing their specialized skills. This type of resource utilization is particularly useful both for project teams and problem resolution.

An additional, but very important role played by Technical Management is to provide guidance to IT Operations about how best to carry out the ongoing operational management of technology. This role is partly carried out during the Service Design process, but it is also a part of everyday communication with IT Operations Management as they seek to achieve stability and optimum performance.

The objectives, activities and structures that enable Technical Management to perform these roles effectively are discussed below.

6.3.2 Technical Management objectives

The objectives of Technical Management are to help plan, implement and maintain a stable technical infrastructure to support the organization's business processes through:

■ Well designed and highly resilient, cost-effective technical topology

- The use of adequate technical skills to maintain the technical infrastructure in optimum condition
- Swift use of technical skills to speedily diagnose and resolve any technical failures that do occur.

6.3.3 Generic Technical Management activities

Technical Management is involved in two types of activity:

- Activities that are generic to the Technical Management function as a whole are discussed in this section as they enable Technical Management as a function to execute its role.
- A set of discrete activities and processes, which are performed by all three functions of Technical, Application and IT Operations Management, are covered in Chapter 5.

Generic Technical Management activities are highlighted as follows:

- Identifying the knowledge and expertise required to manage and operate the IT Infrastructure and to deliver IT services. This process starts during the Service Strategy phase, is expanded in detail in Service Design and is executed in Service Operation. Ongoing assessment and updating of these skills is done during Continual Service Improvement.
- Documentation of the skills that exist in the organization, as well as those skills that need to be developed. This will include the development of Skills Inventories and the performance of Training Needs Analyses.
- Initiating training programmes to develop and refine the skills in the appropriate technical resources and maintaining training records for all technical resources.
- Design and delivery of training for users, the Service Desk and other groups. Although training requirements must be defined in Service Design, they are executed in Service Operation. Where Technical Management does not deliver training, it is responsible for identifying organizations that can provide it.
- Recruiting or contracting resources with skills that cannot be developed internally, or where there are insufficient people to perform the required Technical Management activities.
- Procuring skills for specific activities where the required skills are not available internally or in the open market, or where it is more cost-efficient to do so.
- Definition of standards used in the design of new architectures and participation in the definition of technology architectures during the Service Strategy and Design phases.
- Research and development of solutions that can help expand the Service Portfolio or which can be used to simplify or automate IT Operations, reduce costs or increase levels of IT service.
- Involvement in the design and building of new services. Technical Management will contribute to the design of the Technical Architecture and Performance standards for IT services. In addition, it will also be responsible for specifying the operational activities required to manage the IT Infrastructure on an ongoing basis.
- Involvement in projects, not only during Service Design and Service Transition, but also for Continual Service Improvement or operational projects, such as Operating System upgrades, server consolidation projects or physical moves.
- Availability and Capacity Management are dependent on Technical Management for engineering IT services to meet the levels of service required by the business. This means that modelling and workload forecasting are often done with Technical Management resources.
- Assistance in assessing risk, identifying critical service and system dependencies and defining and implementing countermeasures.
- Designing and performing tests for the functionality, performance and manageability of IT services.
- Managing vendors. Many Technical Management departments or groups are the only ones who know exactly what is required of a vendor and how to measure and manage them. For this reason, many organizations rely on Technical Management departments to manage contracts with vendors of specific CIs. If this is the case it is important to ensure that these relationships are managed as part of the SLM process.
- Definition and management of Event Management standards and tools. Technical Management will also monitor and respond to many categories of events.
- Technical Management departments or groups are integral to the performance of Incident Management. They receive incidents through Functional Escalation and provide second- and higher-level support. They are also involved in maintaining categories and defining the escalation procedures that are executed in Incident Management.
- Technical Management as a function provides the resources that execute the Problem Management process. It is its technical expertise and knowledge that is used to diagnose and resolve problems. It is

also its relationship with the vendors that is used to escalate and follow up with vendor support teams.

■ Technical Management resources will be involved in defining coding systems that are used in Incident and Problem Management (e.g. Incident Categories).

■ Technical Management resources are used to support Problem Management in validating and maintaining the KEDB.

■ Change Management relies on the technical knowledge and expertise to evaluate changes, and many changes will be built by Technical Management.

■ Releases are frequently deployed using Technical Management resources.

■ Technical Management will provide information for, and operationally maintain, the Configuration Management system and its data. This will be done in cooperation with Application Management to ensure that the correct CI attributes and relationships are created from the deployment of services and the ongoing maintenance over the life of CIs.

■ Technical Management is involved in the Continual Service Improvement processes, particularly in identifying opportunities for improvement and then in helping to evaluate alternative solutions.

■ As a custodian of technical knowledge and expertise, Technical Management ensures that all system and operating documentation is up to date and properly utilized. This includes ensuring that all management, administration and user manuals are up to date and complete and that technical staff are familiar with their contents.

■ Updating and maintaining data used for reporting on technical and service capabilities, e.g. Capacity and Performance Management, Availability Management, Problem Management, etc.

■ Assisting IT Financial Management to identify the cost of technology and IT human resources used to manage IT services.

■ Involvement in defining the operational activities performed as part of IT Operations Management. Many Technical Management departments, groups or teams also perform the operational activities as part of an organization's IT Operations Management function.

6.3.4 Technical Management organization

Technical Management is not normally provided by a single department or group. One or more Technical Support teams or departments will be needed to provide technical management and support for the IT

Infrastructure. In all but the smallest organizations, where a single combined team or department may suffice, separate teams or departments will be needed for each type of infrastructure being used.

IT Operations Management consists of a number of technological areas. Each of these requires a specific set of skills to manage and operate it. Some skill sets are related and can be performed by generalists, whereas others are specific to a component, system or platform.

The primary criterion of Technical Management organizational structure is that of specialization or division of labour. The principle is that people are grouped according to their technical skill sets, and that these skill sets are determined by the technology that needs to be managed.

Sections 6.6 and 6.7 cover the organizational aspects of Technical Management in detail, but this list provides some examples of typical Technical Management teams or departments:

■ Mainframe team or department – if one or more mainframe types are still being used by the organization

■ Server team or department – often split again by technology types (e.g. Unix server, Wintel server)

■ Storage team or department, responsible for the management of all data storage devices and media

■ Network Support team or department, looking after the organization's internal WANs/LANs and managing any external network suppliers

■ Desktop team or department, responsible for all installed desktop equipment

■ Database team or department, responsible for the creation, maintenance and support of the organization's databases

■ Middleware team or department, responsible for the integration, testing and maintenance of all middleware in use in the organization

■ Directory Services team or department, responsible for maintaining access and rights to service elements in the infrastructure

■ Internet or Web team or department, responsible for managing the availability and security of access to servers and content by external customers, users and partners

■ Messaging team or department, responsible for e-mail services

■ IP-based Telephony team or department (e.g. VoIP).

6.3.5 Technical Design and Technical Maintenance and Support

Technical Management consists of specialist technical architects and designers (who are primarily involved during Service Design) and specialist maintenance and support staff (who are primarily involved during Service Operation).

In this publication, they are viewed as being part of the same function, but many organizations see them as two separate teams or even departments. The problem with this approach is that good design needs input from the people who are required to manage the solution – and good operation requires involvement from the people who designed the solution.

The problems that need to be overcome are similar to those faced in managing the Application Lifecycle (see section 6.5 for a more detailed discussion). The solution will include the following elements:

- Support staff should be involved during the design or architecture of a solution. Design staff should be involved in setting maintenance objectives and resolving support issues.
- A change in how both Design and Support staff are measured. Designers should be held partly accountable for design flaws that create operational outages. Support staff should be held partly accountable for contribution to the technical architecture.

6.3.6 Technical Management metrics

Metrics for Technical Management will largely depend on which technology is being managed, but some generic metrics include:

- **Measurement of agreed outputs.** These could include:
  - Contribution to achievement of services to the business. Although many of the Technical Management teams will not be in direct contact with the business, the technology they manage impacts the business. Metrics should reflect both negative (incidents traced to their team) and positive (system performance and availability) contributions
  - Transaction rates and availability for critical business transactions
  - Service Desk training
  - Recording problem resolutions into the KEDB
  - User measures of the quality of outputs as defined in the SLAs

- Installation and configuration of components under their control.
- **Process metrics.** Technical Management teams execute many Service Management process activities. Their ability to do so will be measured as part of the process metrics where appropriate (see section on each process for more details). Examples include:
  - Response time to events and event completion rates
  - Incident resolution times for second- and third-line support
  - Problem resolution statistics
  - Number of escalations and reason for those escalations
  - Number of changes implemented and backed out
  - Number of unauthorized changes detected
  - Number of releases deployed, total and successful
  - Security issues detected and resolved
  - Actual system utilization against Capacity Plan forecasts (where the team has contributed to the development of the plan)
  - Tracking against SIPs
  - Expenditure against budget.
- **Technology performance.** These metrics are based on Service Design specifications and technical performance standards set by vendors, and will typically be contained in OLAs or Standard Operation Procedures. Actual metrics will vary by technology, but are likely to include:
  - Utilization rates (e.g. memory or processor for server, bandwidth for networks, etc.)
  - Availability (of systems, network, devices, etc.), which is helpful for measuring team or system performance, but is not to be confused with Service Availability – which requires the ability to measure the overall availability of the service and may use the availability figures for a number of individual systems or components
  - Performance (e.g. response times, queuing rates, etc.).
- **Mean Time Between Failures of specified equipment.** This metric is used to ensure that good purchasing decisions are being made and, when compared with maintenance schedules, whether the equipment is being properly maintained
- **Measurement of maintenance activity,** including:
  - Maintenance performed per schedule
  - Number of maintenance windows exceeded
  - Maintenance objectives achieved (number and percentage).

■ **Training and skills development.** These metrics ensure that staff have the skills and training to manage the technology that is under their control, and will also identify areas where training is still required.

6.3.7 Technical Management documentation

Technical Management is involved in drafting and maintaining several documents as part of other processes (e.g. Capacity Planning, Change Management, Problem Management, etc.). These documents are discussed in some detail in the relevant process descriptions. However, there are some documents that are specific to the Technical Management groups or teams who will provide document management and control for documents relating to the technology under their control. Technical Management documentation includes the following.

6.3.7.1 Technical documentation

The sourcing and maintenance of technical documentation for all CIs is the responsibility of Technical Management. These include:

■ Technical manuals
■ Management and administration manuals
■ User manuals for CIs. These will typically exclude application user manuals, which are maintained by Application Management.

6.3.7.2 Maintenance Schedules

These schedules are drawn up and agreed during the Service Design phase related to Availability and Capacity Management, but they are essentially the property of the various Technical Management departments, groups or teams. This is because they have the technical expertise for specific technologies and are most likely to know what is needed to keep them in working order.

For more details on the definition of Maintenance Schedules and Service Maintenance Objectives, refer to the ITIL Service Design publication.

6.3.7.3 Skills Inventory

A Skills Inventory is a system or tool that identifies the skills required to deliver and support IT services and also the individuals who possess those skills. Skills Inventories are most effective if they are aligned with processes, architectures and performance standards.

In addition, Skills Inventories should identify the training available to cultivate each skill should existing staff leave the organization.

Skills Inventories can also be used as part of the Service Portfolio to assess whether a new service can be delivered with existing staff and skill sets, or whether an investment needs to be made in new staff or training. Skills Inventories can therefore contribute significantly to Capacity Planning.

The definition and maintenance of Skills Inventories requires a good interface with Human Resource processes and tools in the organization.

6.4 IT OPERATIONS MANAGEMENT

In business, the term 'Operations Management' is used to mean the department, group or team of people responsible for performing the organization's day-to-day operational activities – such as running the production line in a manufacturing environment or managing the distribution centres and fleet movements within a logistics organization.

Operations Management generally has the following characteristics:

■ There is work to ensure that a device, system or process is actually running or working (as opposed to strategy or planning)
■ This is where plans are turned into actions
■ The focus is on daily or shorter-term activities, although it should be noted that these activities will generally be performed and repeated over a relatively long period (as opposed to one-off project type activities)
■ These activities are executed by specialized technical staff, who often have to undergo technical training to learn how to perform each activity
■ There is a focus on building repeatable, consistent actions that – if repeated frequently enough at the right level of quality – will ensure the success of the operation
■ This is where the actual value of the organization is delivered and measured
■ There is a dependency on investment in equipment or human resources or both
■ The value generated, must exceed the cost of the investment and all other organizational overheads (such as management and marketing costs) if the business is to succeed.

In a similar way, IT Operations Management can be defined as the function responsible for the ongoing management and maintenance of an organization's IT Infrastructure to ensure delivery of the agreed level of IT services to the business.

IT Operations can be defined as the set of activities involved in the day-to-day running of the IT Infrastructure for the purpose of delivering IT services at agreed levels to meet stated business objectives.

6.4.1 IT Operations Management role

The role of Operations Management is to execute the ongoing activities and procedures required to manage and maintain the IT Infrastructure so as to deliver and support IT Services at the agreed levels. These have already been described in section 5, but are summarized here for completeness:

- **Operations Control**, which oversees the execution and monitoring of the operational activities and events in the IT Infrastructure. This can be done with the assistance of an Operations Bridge or Network Operations Centre. In addition to executing routine tasks from all technical areas, Operations Control also performs the following specific tasks:
  - **Console Management**, which refers to defining central observation and monitoring capability and then using those consoles to exercise monitoring and control activities
  - **Job Scheduling**, or the management of routine batch jobs or scripts
  - **Backup and Restore** on behalf of all Technical and Application Management teams and departments and often on behalf of users
  - **Print and Output management** for the collation and distribution of all centralized printing or electronic output
  - Performance of **maintenance activities** on behalf of Technical or Application Management teams or departments.
- **Facilities Management**, which refers to the management of the physical IT environment, typically a Data Centre or computer rooms and recovery sites together with all the power and cooling equipment. Facilities Management also includes the coordination of large-scale consolidation projects, e.g. Data Centre consolidation or server consolidation projects. In some cases the management of a data centre is outsourced, in which case Facilities Management refers to the management of the outsourcing contract.

As with many IT Service Management processes and functions, IT Operations Management plays a dual role.

- IT Operations Management is responsible for executing the activities and performance standards defined during Service Design and tested during Service Transition. In this sense IT Operations' role is primarily to maintain the status quo. The stability of the IT infrastructure and consistency of IT Services is a primary concern of IT Operations. Even operational improvements are aimed at finding simpler and better ways of doing the same thing.
- At the same time, IT Operations is part of the process of adding value to the different lines of business and to support the value network (see the ITIL Service Strategy publication). The ability of the business to meet its objectives and to remain competitive depends on the output and reliability of the day-to-day operation of IT. As such, IT Operations Management must be able to continually adapt to business requirements and demand. The Business does not care that IT Operations complied with a standard procedure or that a server performed optimally. As business demand and requirements change, IT Operations Management must be able to keep pace with them, often challenging the status quo.

IT Operations must achieve a balance between these roles, which will require the following:

- An understanding of how technology is used to provide IT services
- An understanding of the relative importance and impact of those services on the business
- Procedures and manuals that outline the role of IT Operations in both the management of technology and the delivery of IT services
- A clearly differentiated set of metrics to report to the business on the achievement of Service objectives; and to report to IT managers on the efficiency and effectiveness of IT Operations
- All IT Operations staff understand exactly how the performance of the technology affects the delivery of IT services
- A cost strategy aimed at balancing the requirements of different business units with the cost savings available through optimization of existing technology or investment in new technology
- A value, rather than cost, based Return on Investment strategy.

6.4.2 IT Operations Management objectives

The objectives of IT Operations Management include:

- Maintenance of the status quo to achieve stability of the organization's day-to-day processes and activities
- Regular scrutiny and improvements to achieve improved service at reduced costs, while maintaining stability
- Swift application of operational skills to diagnose and resolve any IT operations failures that occur.

6.4.3 IT Operations Management organization

Figure 6.1 in the introduction to Chapter 6 illustrated that IT Operations Management is seen as a function in its own right but that, in many cases, staff from Technical and Application Management groups form part of this function.

This means that some Technical and Application Management departments or groups will manage and execute their own operational activities. Others will delegate these activities to a dedicated IT Operations department.

There is no single method for assigning activities, as it depends on the maturity and stability of the infrastructure being managed. For example, Technical and Application Management areas that are fairly new and unstable tend to manage their own operations. Groups where the technology or application is stable, mature and well understood tend to have standardized their operations more and will therefore feel more comfortable delegating these activities.

Some options of how to structure IT Operations are discussed in detail in section 6.7 of this publication.

6.4.4 IT Operations Management metrics

IT Operations Management is measured in terms of its effective execution of specified activities and procedures, as well as its execution of process activities. Examples of these are as follows:

- Successful completion of scheduled jobs
- Number of exceptions to scheduled activities and jobs
- Number of data or system restores required
- Equipment installation statistics, including number of items installed by type, successful installations, etc.
- Process metrics. IT Operations Management executes many Service Management process activities. Their ability to do so will be measured as part of the process metrics where appropriate (see section on each process for more details). Examples include:
  - Response time to events
  - Incident resolution times for incidents
  - Number of security-related incidents
  - Number of escalations and reason for those escalations
  - Number of changes implemented and backed out
  - Number of unauthorized changes detected
  - Number of releases deployed, total and successful
  - Tracking against SIPs

- Expenditure against budget.
- If maintenance activities have been delegated, then metrics related to these activities will also be appropriate:
  - Maintenance performed per schedule
  - Number of maintenance windows exceeded
  - Maintenance objectives achieved (number and percentage).
- Metrics related to Facilities Management are extensive, but typically include:
  - Costs versus budget related to maintenance, construction, security, shipping, etc.
  - Incidents related to the building, e.g. repairs needed to the facility
  - Reports on access to the facility
  - Number of security events and Incidents and their resolution
  - Power usage statistics, especially as related to changes in layout and environmental conditioning strategies
  - Events or incidents related to shipping and distribution.

6.4.5 IT Operations Management documentation

A number of documents are produced and used during IT Operations Management. This list is a summary of some of the most important and does not include reports that are produced by IT Operations Management on behalf of other processes or functions.

6.4.5.1 Standard Operating Procedures

The SOPs are a set of documents containing detailed instructions and activity schedules for every IT Operations Management team, department or group.

These documents represent the routine work that needs to be done for every device, system or procedure. They also outline the procedures to be followed if an exception is detected or if a change is required.

SOP documents could also be used to define standard levels of performance for devices or procedures. In some organizations the SOP documents are referred to in the OLA. Instead of listing detailed performance measures in the OLA, a clause is inserted to refer to the performance standards in the SOP and how these will be measured and reported.

6.4.5.2 Operations Logs

Any activity that is conducted as part of IT Operations should be recorded for a number of reasons, including:

- They can be used to confirm the successful completion of specific jobs or activities
- They can be used to confirm that an IT service was delivered as agreed
- They can be used by Problem Management to research the root cause of incidents
- They are the basis for reports on the performance of the IT Operations Management teams and departments.

The format of these logs is as varied as the number of systems and Operations Management teams or departments. Examples of Operations Logs include the following:

- Operating System Logs stored on each device
- Application Activity Logs stored in a file on the application server
- Event Logs stored on the monitoring tool server
- Utilization Logs for key devices
- Physical access logs recording who accessed secure buildings and when
- Handwritten logs of actions performed by operators. This must be in a formal logbook or binder, numbered and stored in a secure environment. Checks should ensure that pages are not removed.

A policy needs to be established as part of the SOPs to state how long logs need to be kept, how they are archived and when they can be deleted. These policies will take into account statutory and compliance requirements. Policies should also specify the parameters for adequate storage and backup strategies to store and retrieve log files.

6.4.5.3 Shift Schedules and Reports

Shift Schedules are documents that outline the exact activities that need to be carried out during the shift. They will also list all dependencies and activity sequences. There will probably be more than one Shift Schedule, where each team will have a version for its own systems. It is important that all schedules are coordinated before the start of the shift. This is usually done by a person who is specialized in Shift Scheduling, with the help of scheduling tools.

A Shift Schedule could consist of a number of routine items that are included in the SOP. In this case the items

could simply be listed briefly with a reference to the section or page in the SOP.

Most Shift Schedules take the form of a checklist where operators can check off the item as it is completed, together with the time of completion. This makes it easy to see the progress of activities and also helps to identify any potential issues where jobs are taking too long.

Shift Reports are a form of Operations Log, but have the additional functions as follows:

- To record major events and actions that occurred during the shift
- To form part of the handover between shift leaders
- To report any exceptions to Service Maintenance Objectives
- To identify any uncompleted activity that could result in degraded performance on any service during the next service hours.

6.4.5.4 Operations Schedule

The Operations Schedules are similar to Shift Schedules but cover all aspects of IT Operations at a high level. This schedule will include an overview of all planned changes, maintenance, routine jobs and additional work, together with information about upcoming business or vendor events. The Operations Schedule is used as the basis for the Daily Operations Meeting and is the master reference for all IT Operations managers to track progress and detect exceptions.

6.5 APPLICATION MANAGEMENT

Application Management is responsible for managing applications throughout their lifecycle. The Application Management function is performed by any department, group or team involved in managing and supporting operational applications. Application Management also plays an important role in the design, testing and improvement of applications that form part of IT services. As such, it may be involved in development projects, but is not usually the same as the Applications Development teams.

6.5.1 Application Management role

Application Management is to applications what Technical Management is to the IT Infrastructure. Application Management plays a role in all applications, whether purchased or developed in-house. One of the key decisions that they contribute to is the decision of whether to buy an application or build it (this is discussed in detail in the Service Design publication). Once that decision is made, Application Management will play a dual role:

- It is the custodian of technical knowledge and expertise related to managing applications. In this role Application Management, working together with Technical Management, ensures that the knowledge required to design, test, manage and improve IT services is identified, developed and refined.
- It provides the actual resources to support the ITSM Lifecycle. In this role, Application Management ensures that resources are effectively trained and deployed to design, build, transition, operate and improve the technology required to deliver and support IT services.

By performing these two roles, Application Management is able to ensure that the organization has access to the right type and level of human resources to manage applications and thus to meet business objectives. This starts in Service Strategy and is expanded in Service Design, tested in Service Transition and refined in Continual Service Improvement (see other ITIL publications in this series).

Part of this role is to ensure a balance between the skill level and the cost of these resources.

In additional to these two high-level roles, Application Management also performs the following two specific roles:

- Providing guidance to IT Operations about how best to carry out the ongoing operational management of applications. This role is partly carried out during the Service Design process, but it is also a part of everyday communication with IT Operations Management as they seek to achieve stability and optimum performance.
- The integration of the Application Management Lifecycle into the ITSM Lifecycle. This is discussed below.

The objectives, activities and structures that enable Application Management to play these roles effectively are discussed below.

6.5.2 Application Management objectives

The objectives of Application Management are to support the organization's business processes by helping to identify functional and manageability requirements for application software, and then to assist in the design and deployment of those applications and the ongoing support and improvement of those applications.

These objectives are achieved through:

- Applications that are well designed, resilient and cost-effective
- Ensuring that the required functionality is available to achieve the required business outcome
- The organization of adequate technical skills to maintain operational applications in optimum condition
- Swift use of technical skills to speedily diagnose and resolve any technical failures that do occur.

6.5.3 Application Management principles

6.5.3.1 Build or buy?

One of the key decisions in Application Management is whether to buy an application that supports the required functionality, or whether to build the application specifically for the organization's requirements. These decisions are often made by a Chief Technical Officer (CTO) or Steering Committee, but they are dependent on information from a number of sources. These are discussed in detail in Service Design, but are summarized here from an Application Management function perspective.

Application Management will assist in this decision during Service Design as follows:

- Application sizing and workload forecasts (see section 4.6.4)
- Specification of manageability requirements
- Identification of ongoing operational costs
- Data access requirements for reporting or integration into other applications
- Investigating to what extent the required functionality can be met by existing tools – and how much customization will be required to achieve this
- Estimating the cost of customization
- Identifying what skills will be required to support the solution (e.g. if an application is purchased, will it require a new set of employees, or can existing employees be trained to support it?)
- Administration requirements
- Security requirements.

If the decision is to build the application, a further decision needs to be made on whether the development will be outsourced or built using employees. This is detailed in the Service Strategy and Service Design publications, but there are some important considerations affecting Service Operation, for example:

- How will manageability requirements be specified and agreed (e.g. designing application and transaction monitoring)? These are sometimes forgotten when the operational teams or departments are not represented in the project
- What are the Acceptance Criteria for operational performance; how and where will the solution be tested and who will perform the tests?
- Who will own and manage the Definitive Library for that application?
- Who will design and maintain the operational management and administration scripts for these applications?
- Who is responsible for environment set-up and owning and maintaining the different infrastructure components?
- How will the solution be instrumented so that it is capable of generating the required events?

6.5.3.2 Operational Models

An Operational Model is the specification of the operational environment in which the application will eventually run when it goes live. This will be used during testing and transition phases to simulate and evaluate the live environment. This is a way of ensuring that the application can be sized correctly and the required environmental conditions can be documented and understood by all. The Operational Model should be defined and used in testing during the Service Design and Service Transition phases respectively (see Service Design and Service Transition publications).

6.5.4 Application Management Lifecycle

The lifecycle followed to develop and manage applications has been referred to by many names, including the Software Lifecycle (SLC) and Software Development Lifecycle (SDLC). These are generally used by Applications Development teams and their Project Managers to define their involvement in designing, building, testing, deploying and supporting applications. Examples of these approaches are Structured Systems Analysis and Design Methodology (SSADM), Dynamic Systems Development Method (DSDM), Rapid Application Development (RAD), etc.

ITIL is primarily interested in the overall management of applications as part of IT Services, whether they are developed in-house or purchased from a third party. For this reason, the term Application Management Lifecycle has been used, as it implies a more holistic view.

This should not replace the SDLC, which is still a valid approach used by developers, especially by third-party software companies. However, it does mean that there should be greater alignment between the development view of applications and the 'live' management of those applications.

This is more difficult in large-scale purchased applications, such as e-mail, since the developers do not typically interact individually with their application's users. However, the basic lifecycle still holds true in that the application needs requirements, design, customization, operation and deployment. Optimization is achieved through better management, improvements to customization and upgrades.

The Application Management Lifecycle is illustrated as follows:

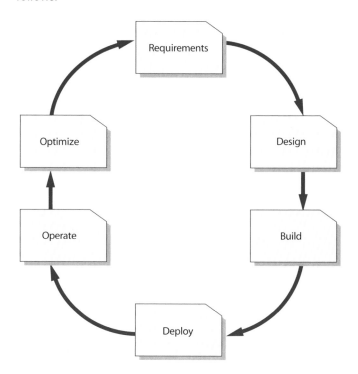

Figure 6.5 Application Management Lifecycle

ITSM processes and Applications Development processes have to be aligned as part of the overall strategy of delivering IT services in support of the business.

Applications Development and Operations are part of the same overall lifecycle and both should be involved at all stages, although their level of involvement will vary depending on the stage of the lifecycle.

Relationship between the Application Management and Service Management Lifecycles

The Application Management Lifecycle should not be seen as an alternative to the Service Management Lifecycle. Applications are part of services and have to be managed as such. Nevertheless, applications are a unique blend of technology and functionality and this requires a specialized focus at each stage of the Service Management Lifecycle.

Each stage of the Application Management Lifecycle has its own specific set of objectives, activities, deliverables and dedicated teams. Each stage also has a clear responsibility to ensure that their outputs match up to the specific objectives of the Service Management Lifecycle. Different aspects of Application Management are covered in detail in each of the ITIL publications, as follows:

■ **Service Strategy:** Defines the overall architecture of applications and infrastructure. This will include defining the criteria for developing in-house, outsourcing development, or purchasing and customizing applications. Service Strategy will also assist in defining the Service Portfolio (including applications) which also includes information about the Return on Investment of applications and the services they support. Thus high-level requirements are set during this phase.

■ **Service Design:** Helps to establish requirements for functionality and manageability of applications and works with Development teams to ensure that they meet these objectives. Service Design covers most of the Requirements phase and is involved during the Build phase of the Application Management Lifecycle.

■ **Service Transition:** Application Development and Management teams are involved in testing and validating what has been built and deploying it operationally.

■ **Service Operation:** This covers the Operate phase of the Application Management Lifecycle. These processes and structures are discussed in detail in this publication.

■ **Continual Service Improvement:** Covers the Optimize phase of the Application Management Lifecycle. Continual Service Improvement measures the quality and relevance of applications in operation and provides recommendations on how to improve applications if there is a clear Return on Investment for doing so.

6.5.4.1 Requirements

This is the phase during which the requirements for a new application are gathered, based on the business needs of the organization. This phase is active primarily during the Service Design phase of the ITSM Lifecycle.

There are six types of requirements for any application, whether being developed in-house, outsourced or purchased:

■ Functional requirements are those specifically required to support a particular business function

■ Manageability requirements, looked at from a Service Management perspective, address the need for a responsive, available and secure service, and deal with such issues as deployment, operations, system management and security

■ Usability requirements are those that address the needs of the end user, and result in features of the system that facilitate its ease of use

■ Architectural requirements, especially if this requires a change to existing architecture standards

■ Interface requirements, where there are dependencies between existing applications or tools and the new application

■ Service Level Requirements, which specify how the service should perform, the quality of its output and any other qualitative aspects measured by the user or customer.

6.5.4.2 Design

This is the phase during which requirements are translated into specifications. Design includes the design of the application itself, and the design of the environment, or operational model that the application has to run on. Architectural considerations are the most important aspect of this phase, since they can impact on the structure and content of both application and operational model. Architectural considerations for the application (design of the application architecture) and architectural considerations for the operation model (design of the system architecture) are strongly related and need to be aligned.

In the case of purchased software, most organizations will not be allowed direct input to the design of the software (which has already been built). However, it is important that Application Management is able to provide feedback to the software vendor about the functionality, manageability and performance of the software. This will, in turn, be taken up by the software vendor as part of the continual improvement of the software.

Part of the evaluation process for purchased software should include an evaluation of whether the vendor is responsive to such feedback. At the same time, they should ensure that there is a balance between being responsive and changing their software so much that it is disruptive or that it changes some basic functionality.

Design for purchased software will also include the design of any customization that is required. Of special importance here is an evaluation of whether future version of the software will support the customization.

6.5.4.3 Build

In the Build phase, both the application and the operational model are made ready for deployment. Application components are coded or acquired, integrated and tested.

Please note that Test is not a separate stage in the lifecycle, even though it is a discrete activity, and even though tests are conducted independently of both the development and operational activities. Without the Build and Deploy phases, there would be nothing to test and, without testing, there would be no control over what is developed and deployed.

Testing is an integral component of both the Build and Deploy phases as a validation of the activity and output of those phases – even if it uses different environments and staff. Testing in the Build phase focuses on whether the application meets its functionality and manageability specifications. Often the distinction is made between a development and test environment. The test environment allows for testing the combination of application and operational model. Testing is covered in the ITIL Service Transition publication.

For purchased software, this will involve the actual purchase of the application, any required middleware and the related hardware and networking equipment. Any customization that is required will need to be done here, as will the creation of tables, categories, etc. that will be used. This is often done as a pilot implementation by the relevant Application Management team or department.

6.5.4.4 Deploy

In this phase, both the operational model and the application are deployed. The operational model is incorporated in the existing IT environment and the application is installed on top of the operational model, using the Release and Deployment Management process described in the ITIL Service Transition publication.

Testing also takes place during this phase, although here the emphasis is on ensuring that the deployment process and mechanisms work effectively, e.g. testing whether the application still functions to specification after it has been downloaded and installed. This is known as Early Life Support and covers a pre-defined guarantee period that testing, validation and monitoring of a new application or service during that period occurs. Early Life Support is covered in detail in the Service Transition publication.

6.5.4.5 Operate

In the Operate phase, the IT services organization operates the application as part of delivering a service required by the business. The performance of the application in relation to the overall service is measured continually against the Service Levels and key business drivers. It is important to distinguish that applications themselves do not equate to a service. It is common in many organizations to refer to applications as 'services'; however, applications are but one component of many needed to provide a business service.

The Operate phase is not exclusive to applications and is discussed throughout this publication, with a more detailed list of activities given in section 6.5.5 below.

6.5.4.6 Optimize

In the Optimize phase, the results of the Service Level performance measurements are measured, analysed and acted upon. Possible improvements are discussed and developments initiated if necessary. The two main strategies in this phase are to maintain and/or improve the Service Levels and to lower cost. This could lead to iteration in the lifecycle or to justified retirement of an application.

One important thing to remember about the Application Management Lifecycle is that, because it is circular, the same application can reside in different phases of the lifecycle at the same time. For example, when the next version of an application is being designed, and the current version is being deployed, the previous version might still be in operation in parts of an organization. This obviously requires strong version, configuration and release control.

Particular phases might take longer or seem more significant than others, but they are all crucial. Every application must go through all of them at least once and, because of the circular nature of the lifecycle, will go through some more than once.

This approach also supports iterative development approaches, where software is continually being developed in incremental steps. Each step follows the lifecycle and the application is built in increments, using business priorities as a driver.

Good communication is the key as an application works its way through the phases of the lifecycle. It is critical that high-quality information is passed along by those handling the application in one phase of its existence to those handling it in the next phase. It is also important that an organization monitors the quality of the Application Management Lifecycle. Changes in the lifecycle, for example in the way an organization passes information between the different phases, will affect its quality. Understanding the characteristics of every phase in the Application Management Lifecycle is crucial to improving the quality of the whole. Methods and tools used in one phase might have an impact on others, while optimization of one phase might sub-optimize the whole.

6.5.5 Application Management generic activities

While most Application Management teams or departments are dedicated to specific applications or sets of applications, there are a number of activities which they have in common. These include:

- Identifying the knowledge and expertise required to manage and operate applications in the delivery of IT services. This process starts during the Service Strategy phase, is expanded in detail in Service Design and is executed in Service Operation. Ongoing assessment and updating of these skills are done during Continual Service Improvement.
- Initiating training programmes to develop and refine the skills in the appropriate Application Management resources and maintaining training records for these resources.
- Recruiting or contracting resources with skills that cannot be developed internally, or where there are insufficient people to perform the required Application Management activities.
- Design and delivery of end-user training. Training may be developed and delivered by either the Application Development or Application Management groups, or by a third party, but Application Management is responsible for ensuring that training is conducted as appropriate.
- Insourcing for specific activities where the required skills are not available internally or in the open market, or where it is more cost-efficient to do so.
- Definition of standards used in the design of new architectures and participation in the definition of

application architectures during the Service Strategy processes.

- Research and Development of solutions that can help expand the Service Portfolio or which can be used to simplify or automate IT Operations, reduce costs or increase levels of IT service.
- Involvement in the design and building of new services. All Application Management teams or departments will contribute to the design of the Technical Architecture and Performance standards for IT Services. In addition they will also be responsible for specifying the operational activities required to manage applications on an ongoing basis.
- Involvement in projects, not only during the Service Design process, but also for Continual Service Improvement or operational projects, such as Operating System upgrades, server consolidation projects or physical moves.
- Designing and performing tests for the functionality, performance and manageability of IT Services (bearing in mind that testing should be controlled and performed by an independent tester – see Service Transition publication).
- Availability and Capacity Management are dependent on Application Management for contributing to the design of applications to meet the levels of service required by the business. This means that modelling and workload forecasting are often done together with Technical and Application Management resources.
- Assistance in assessing risk, identifying critical service and system dependencies and defining and implementing countermeasures.
- Managing vendors. Many Application Management departments or groups are the only ones who know exactly what is required of a vendor and how to measure and manage them. For this reason, many organizations rely on Application Management to manage contracts with vendors of specific applications. If this is the case it is important to ensure that these relationships are managed as part of the SLM process.
- Involvement in definition of Event Management standards and especially in the instrumentation of applications for the generation of meaningful events.
- Application Management as a function provides the resources that execute the Problem Management process. It is their technical expertise and knowledge that is used to diagnose and resolve problems. It is also their relationship with the vendors that is used to escalate and follow up with vendor support teams or departments.

■ Application Management resources will be involved in defining coding systems that are used in Incident and Problem Management (e.g. Incident Categories).

■ Application Management resources are used to support Problem Management in validating and maintaining the KEDB together with the Application Development teams.

■ Change Management relies on the technical knowledge and expertise to evaluate changes and many changes will be built by Application Management teams.

■ Successful Release Management is dependent on involvement from Application Management staff. In fact they are frequently the drivers of the Release Management process for their applications.

■ Application Management will define, manage and maintain attributes and relationships of application CIs in the CMS.

■ Application Management is involved in the Continual Service Improvement processes, particularly in identifying opportunities for improvement and then in helping to evaluate alternative solutions.

■ Application Management ensures that all system and operating documentation is up to date and properly utilized. This includes ensuring that all design, management and user manuals are up to date and complete and that Application Management staff and users are familiar with their contents.

■ Collaboration with Technical Management on performing Training Needs Analysis and maintaining Skills Inventories.

■ Assisting IT Financial Management to identify the cost of the ongoing management of applications.

■ Involvement in defining the operational activities performed as part of IT Operations Management. Many Application Management departments, groups or teams also perform the operational activities as part of an organization's IT Operations Management function.

■ Input into, and maintenance of, software configuration policies.

■ Together with Software Development teams, the definition and maintenance of documentation related to applications. These will include user manuals, administration and management manuals, as well as any SOPs required to manage operational aspects of the application.

Application Management teams or departments will be needed for all key applications. The exact nature of the role will vary depending upon the applications being supported, but generic responsibilities are likely to include:

■ Third-level support for incidents related to the application(s) covered by that team or department

■ Involvement in operation testing plans and deployment issues

■ Application bug tracking and patch management (coding fixes for in-house code, transports/patches for third-party code)

■ Involvement in application operability and supportability issues such as error code design, error messaging, event management hooks

■ Application sizing and performance; volume metrics and load testing etc. This is in support of Capacity and Availability Management processes

■ Involvement in developing Release Policies

■ Identification of enhancements to existing software, both from a functionality and manageability perspective.

6.5.6 Application Management organization

Although all Application Management departments, groups or teams perform similar activities, each application or set of applications has a different set of management and operational requirements. Examples of these differences include:

■ **The purpose of the application**. Each application was developed to meet a specific set of objectives, usually business objectives. For effective support and improvement, the group that manages that application needs to have a comprehensive understanding of the business context and how the application is used to meet its objectives. This is often achieved by Business Analysts who are close to the business and responsible for ensuring that business requirements are effectively translated into application specifications. Business Analysts should recognize that business requirements must be translated into both functional and manageability specifications.

■ **The functionality of the application.** Each application is designed to work in a different way and to perform different functions at different times.

■ **The platform on which the application runs.** Although the platform is usually managed by a Technical Management team or department, each of them affects the way in which an application needs to be managed and operated.

■ **The type or brand of technology used.** Even applications that have similar functionality operate differently on different databases or platforms. These differences have to be understood in order to manage the application effectively.

Even though the activities to manage these applications are generic, the specific schedule of activities and the way they are performed will be different. For this reason, Application Management teams and departments tend to be organized according to the categories of applications that they support. Typical examples of Application Management organizations include:

- Financial applications. In larger organizations where a number of different applications are used for different aspects of Financial Management, there may be several department, groups or teams managing these applications, e.g. Debtors and Creditors, Age Analysis, General Ledger, etc.
- Messaging and collaboration applications
- HR applications
- Manufacturing support applications

- Sales force automation
- Sales order processing applications
- Call centre and marketing applications
- Business-specific applications (e.g. health care, insurance, banking, etc.)
- IT applications, such as Service Desk, Enterprise System Management, etc.
- Web portals
- Online shopping.

6.5.6.1 Organizational roles

Traditionally, Application Development and Management teams and departments have been autonomous units. Each one manages its own environment in its own way and each has a separate interface to the business. This is illustrated in Table 6.2.

Table 6.2 Organizational roles

	Application Development	Application Management
Primary focus	Building functionality for their customer. What the application does is more important to them than how it is operated	Focus on what the functionality is as well as how to deliver it. Manageability aspects of the application, i.e. how to ensure stability and performance of the application
Management mode	Most development work is done in projects where the focus is on delivering specific units of work to specification, on time and within budget. This means that it is often difficult for developers to understand and build for ongoing operations, especially since they are not available for support of the application once they have moved on to the next project	Most work is done as part of repeatable, ongoing processes. A relatively small number of people work in projects. This means that it is very difficult for operational staff to get involved in development projects, as that takes them away from their 'real jobs'
Measurement	Staff are rewarded for creativity and for completing one project so that they can move on to the next project	Staff are rewarded for consistency and for preventing unexpected events and unauthorized functionality (e.g. 'bells and whistles' added by developers)
Cost	Development projects are relatively easy to quantify since the resources are known and it is easy to link their expenses to a specific application or IT Service	Ongoing management costs are often mixed in with the costs of other IT services since resources are often shared across multiple IT services and applications
Lifecycles	Development staff focus on Software Development Lifecycles, which highlight the dependencies for successful operation, but do not assign accountability for these	Staff involved in ongoing management typically only control one or two phases of these lifecycles – Operation and Improvement

Over the last several years, these two worlds are being brought together by recent moves to Object Oriented and SOA approaches, together with growing pressure from the Business to be more responsive and easy to work with.

This means that Application Development will have greater accountability for the successful operation of applications they design, while Application Management will have greater involvement in the development of applications.

This does not change the fundamental role of each group, but it does require a more integrated approach to the SLC. It will also mean that the output of Application Development will be more commoditized and that Application Management will be more involved in Development projects.

This will require the following changes:

- A single interface to the business for all stages of the lifecycle and a common requirements and specification-setting process.
- A change in how both Development and Management staff are measured. Development teams should be held partly accountable for design flaws that create operational outages. Management staff should be held partly accountable for contribution to the technical architecture and manageability design of applications.
- A single Change Management process for both groups, with Change Control in each group being subordinate to the overall authority of Change Management (see Service Transition publication).
- A clear mapping of Development and Management activities in the lifecycle, which is illustrated at a high level in Figure 6.5. The exact activities and how they interact should be defined in each organization, although some generic guidelines are given in each of the ITIL publications.
- Greater focus on integrating functionality and manageability requirements early in the project.

Figure 6.6 shows a common Application Management Lifecycle with involvement from both groups. In this diagram it is clear that Application Development will be driving some phases with input from Application Management. In other cases Application Management will be driving the phase with input and support from Application Development. Both groups are subordinated to the IT Service Strategy of the organization and their efforts are coordinated through Service Transition mechanisms and processes.

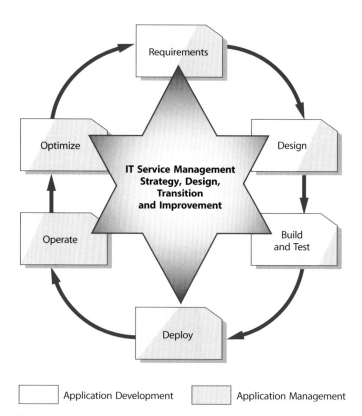

Figure 6.6 Role of teams in the Application Management Lifecycle

6.5.7 Application Management roles and responsibilities

6.5.7.1 Applications Managers/Team-leaders

An Applications Manager or Team-leader (depending upon the size and/or importance of the team or department and the application they support, and the organization's structure and culture) will be needed for each of the applications teams or departments. The role will:

- Take overall responsibility for leadership, control and decision-making for the applications team or department
- Provide technical knowledge and leadership in the specific applications support activities covered by the team or department
- Ensure necessary technical training, awareness and experience levels are maintained within the team or department relevant to the applications being supported and processes being used
- Involve ongoing communication with users and customers regarding application performance and evolving requirements of the business
- Report to senior management on all issues relevant to the applications being supported

■ Perform line-management for all team or department members.

6.5.7.2 Applications Analyst/Architect

Application Analysts and Architects are responsible for matching requirements to application specifications. Specific activities include:

■ Working with users, sponsors and all other stakeholders to determine their evolving needs

■ Working with Technical Management to determine the highest level of system requirements required to meet the business requirements within budget and technology constraints

■ Performing cost-benefit analyses to determine the most appropriate means to meet the stated requirement

■ Developing Operational Models that will ensure optimal use of resources and the appropriate level of performance

■ Ensuring that applications are designed to be effectively managed given the organization's technology architecture, available skills and tools

■ Developing and maintaining standards for application sizing, performance modelling, etc

■ Generating a set of acceptance test requirements, together with the designers, test engineers and the user, which determine that all of the high-level requirements have been met, both functional and with regard to manageability

■ Input into the design of configuration data required to manage and track the application effectively.

An appropriate number of Application Analysts will be needed for each of the Application Management teams or department to perform the generic activities described in paragraph 6.5.5.

The ways in which Application Management groups can be organized, and the options available, are discussed in some detail in section 6.7 below.

6.5.8 Application Management metrics

Metrics for Application Management will largely depend on which applications are being managed, but some generic metrics include:

■ **Measurement of agreed outputs.** These could include:
  ● Ability of users to access the application and its functionality
  ● Reports and files are transmitted to the users

  ● Transaction rates and availability for critical business transactions
  ● Service Desk training
  ● Recording problem resolutions into the KEDB
  ● User measures of the quality of outputs as defined in the SLAs.

■ **Process metrics.** Technical Management teams execute many Service Management process activities. Their ability to do so will be measured as part of the process metrics where appropriate (see section on each process for more details). Examples include:
  ● Response time to events and event completion rates
  ● Incident resolution times for second- and third-line support
  ● Problem resolution statistics
  ● Number of escalations and reason for those escalations
  ● Number of changes implemented and backed out
  ● Number of unauthorized changes detected
  ● Number of releases deployed, total and successful, including ensuring adherence to the Release Policies of the organization
  ● Security issues detected and resolved
  ● Actual system utilization against Capacity Plan forecasts (where the team has contributed to the development of the plan)
  ● Tracking against SIPs
  ● Expenditure against budget.

■ **Application performance.** These metrics are based on Service Design specifications and technical performance standards set by vendors and will typically be contained in OLAs or SOPs. Actual metrics will vary by application, but are likely to include:
  ● Response times
  ● Application availability, which is helpful for measuring team or application performance but is not to be confused with Service Availability – which requires the ability to measure the overall availability of the service, and may use the availability figures for a number of individual systems or components
  ● Integrity of data and reporting.

■ **Measurement of maintenance activity**, including:
  ● Maintenance performed per schedule
  ● Number of maintenance windows exceeded
  ● Maintenance objectives achieved (number and percentage).

- Application Management teams are likely to work closely with Application Development teams on **projects**, and appropriate metrics should be used to measure this, including:
  - Time spent on projects
  - Customer and user satisfaction with the output of the project
  - Cost of involvement in the project.
- **Training and skills development.** These metrics ensure that staff have the skills and training to manage the technology that is under their control, and will also identify areas where training is still required.

6.5.9 Application Management documentation

A number of documents are produced and used during Application Management. This list is a summary of some of the most important and does not include reports or documents that are produced by Application Management on behalf of other process or functions (e.g. RFC, Known Error documentation, Release Records, etc.). Note that documents should be controlled as CIs and related to the relevant applications or Application Management teams.

6.5.9.1 Application Portfolio

The Application Portfolio is used primarily as part of Service Strategy, but is referenced here for completeness. The Application Portfolio is a list (more accurately a system or database) of all applications in use within the organization, together with the following information:

Key attributes of the application

- Customers and users
- Business purpose
- Level of business criticality
- Architecture (including the IT Infrastructure dependencies)
- Developers, support groups, suppliers or vendors
- The investment made in the application to date. In this respect the Application Portfolio can be used as an asset register for applications,

The purpose of the Application Portfolio is to analyse the need for and use of applications in the organization. It can be used to link functionality and investment to business activity and is therefore an important part of ongoing IT planning and control. Another benefit of the Application Portfolio is that it can be used to identify duplication and excessive licensing of applications.

The Application Portfolio forms part of the overall IT Service Portfolio, which is discussed in detail in the Service Strategy publication.

> **The Application Portfolio and the Service Catalogue**
>
> The Application Portfolio should not be mistaken for the Service Catalogue and should not be advertised as a list of services to customers or users. Applications are one of the components used to provide IT services, usually not the service itself.
>
> The Application Portfolio should therefore be used as a planning document only by those managers and staff who are involved with the development and management of the organization's IT Strategy, as well as IT staff who are tasked with managing the applications or the platforms on which the applications run.
>
> The Service Catalogue should focus on listing the services that are available, rather than simply listing applications and assuming that users and customers can make the link. Having said that, there are times when the application is synonymous with the service, e.g. word-processing applications are typically known by their name; an application hosting service will mention the names of the application hosted, etc.

6.5.9.2 Application Requirements

There are two sets of documents containing requirements for applications:

- **Business Requirements** outline the Business Case for the required application, in other words what the business will do with the application. This will include the Return on Investment for the application as well as all related improvements to the business. Business requirements will also include the Service Level Requirements as defined by the service customers and users.
- **Application Requirements** documents are based on the Business Requirements and specify exactly how the application will meet those requirements. In short, Application Requirements documents gather information that will be used to commission new applications or changes to existing applications, for example:
  - To design the architecture of the application (specification of the different components of the system, how they relate to one another and how they will be managed)

- To specify a Request for Proposal (RFP) for a Commercial, Off the Shelf (COTS) application
- To initiate the design and building of an application in-house.

Requirements documents are normally owned by a project leader, either of a development project team, or for a team drawing up specifications for an RFP. Requirements documents are subject to document control for the project as they form part of the overall scope of the project.

Four different types of Application Requirements need to be defined (for more detailed information, please refer to the ITIL Service Design and Service Transition publications):

- **Functional Requirements** describe the things an application is intended to do, and can be expressed as services, tasks or functions the application is required to perform.
- **Manageability Requirements** are used to define what is needed to manage the application or to ensure that it performs the required functions consistently and at the right level. Manageability requirements also identify constraints on the IT system. These requirements serve as a basis for early system sizing and estimates of cost, and can support the assessment of the viability of the proposed IT system. Most importantly, they drive design of the operational models and performance standards used in IT Operations Management.
- **Usability Requirements** are normally specified by the users of the application and refer to its ease of use. Any special requirements for handicapped users also need to be specified here.
- **Test Requirements** specify what is required to ensure that the test environment is representative of the operational environment and that the test is valid (i.e. that it actually tests what it is supposed to).

6.5.9.3 Use and Change Cases

Use and Change Cases are managed as part of the Service Design and Continual Service Improvement processes, but are maintained by Application Management. For purchased software, it is common for the team that develops the functional specifications to maintain the Use Case for that application.

- **Use Cases** document the intended use of the application with real-life scenarios to demonstrate its boundaries and its full functionality. Use Cases can also be used as modelling and sizing scenarios and for

facilitating communication between users, Developers and Application Management staff.

- **Change Cases** use scenarios to predict the impact of potential changes to utilization, architecture or functionality, and project the impact of specific change scenarios. Change Cases are used to clarify scope and direction with the sponsor. Extra architecture and design work will be needed at this point to ensure the Change Cases can be met in the future at reasonable cost. The sponsor must be prepared to pay the extra cost. If not, the Change Cases should be reduced to what the sponsor is prepared to pay for. Change Cases are also used to evaluate the architecture. They influence the development process enabling the design of appropriate architectural features to minimize the impact of future changes.

For more information, refer to the ITIL Service Design and Continual Service Improvement publications.

6.5.9.4 Design documentation

This is not one specific document, but refers to any document produced by Application Development or Management staff that specifies how an application will be built. As these documents are generally owned and managed by the Development teams, this publication will not cover them in detail. However, to ensure successful operation, Application Management must ensure that design documentation contains:

- Sizing specifications
- Workload profiles and utilization forecasts
- Technical Architecture
- Data models
- Coding standards
- Performance standards
- Software Configuration Management definitions
- Environment definitions and building considerations (if appropriate).

For COTS applications, these documents take the form of Application Specifications that are used as input into the writing of RFPs. In these cases the documents are owned and managed by Application Management.

For more information on Design Documentation, refer to the ITIL Service Design publication.

6.5.9.5 Manuals

Application Management is responsible for the management of manuals for all applications. Although these are normally developed by the Application

Development teams or third party suppliers, Application Management is responsible for ensuring that the manuals are relevant to the operational versions of the applications.

Three types of manuals are generally maintained by Application Management:

- **Design manuals** contain information about the structure and architecture of the application. These are helpful for creating reports or defining event correlation rules. They could also help in diagnosing problems.
- **Administration or management manuals** describe the activities required to maintain and operate the application at the levels of performance specified in the Design phase. These manuals will also provide detailed troubleshooting, Known Error and Fault descriptions, and step-by-step instructions for common maintenance tasks.
- **User manuals** describe the application functionality as it is used by an end-user. These manuals contain step-by-step instructions on how to use the application, as well as descriptions of what should typically be entered into certain fields, or what to do if there is an error.

Manuals and Standard Operating Procedures

Manuals should not be seen as a replacement for SOPs, but as input into the SOPs.

SOPs should contain all aspects of applications that need to be managed as part of standard operations. If they are not extracted from the manuals, there is a high likelihood that they will be ignored or performed in a non-standard manner. Application Management should ensure that any such instructions are extracted from the manuals and inserted into separate SOP documentation for Operations. It is also responsible for ensuring that these instructions are updated with every change or new release of the software.

6.6 SERVICE OPERATION ROLES AND RESPONSIBILITIES

The key to effective ITSM is ensuring that there is clear accountability and roles defined to carry out the practice of Service Operation. A role is often tied to a job description or work group description but does not necessarily need to be filled by one individual. The size of an organization, how it is structured, the existence of external partners and other factors will influence how roles are assigned. Whether a particular role is filled by a single individual or shared between two or more, the importance is the consistency of accountability and execution, along with the interaction with other roles in the organization.

6.6.1 Service Desk roles

The following roles are needed for the Service Desk.

6.6.1.1 Service Desk Manager

In larger organizations where the Service Desk is of a significant size, a Service Desk Manager role may be justified with the Service Desk Supervisor(s) reporting to him or her. In such cases this role may take responsibility for some of the activities listed above and may additionally perform the following activities:

- Manage the overall desk activities, including the supervisors
- Act as a further escalation point for the supervisor(s)
- Take on a wider customer-services role
- Report to senior managers on any issue that could significantly impact the business
- Attend Change Advisory Board meetings
- Take overall responsibility for incident and Service Request handling on the Service Desk. This could also be expanded to any other activity taken on by the Service Desk – e.g. monitoring certain classes of event.

Note: In all cases, clearly defined job descriptions should be drafted and agreed so that specific responsibilities are known.

6.6.1.2 Service Desk Supervisor

In very small desks it is possible that the senior Service Desk Analyst will also act as the Supervisor – but in larger desks it is likely that a dedicated Service Desk Supervisor role will be needed. Where shift hours dictate it, there may be two or more post-holders who fulfil the role, usually on an overlapping basis. The Supervisor's role is likely to include:

- Ensuring that staffing and skill levels are maintained throughout operational hours by managing shift staffing schedules, etc.
- Undertaking HR activities as needed
- Acting as an escalation point where difficult or controversial calls are received
- Production of statistics and management reports
- Representing the Service Desk at meetings
- Arranging staff training and awareness sessions
- Liaising with senior management
- Liaising with Change Management

- Performing briefings to Service Desk staff on changes or deployments that may affect volumes at the Service Desk
- Assisting analysts in providing first-line support when workloads are high, or where additional experience is required.

6.6.1.3 Service Desk Analysts

The primary Service Desk Analyst role is that of providing first-level support through taking calls and handling the resulting incidents or Service Requests using the Incident Reporting and Request Fulfilment processes, in line with the objectives described earlier. The exact number of staff required is discussed in paragraph 6.2.4.1.

6.6.1.4 Super Users

Super Users are discussed in detail in the section on Service Desk staffing in paragraph 6.2.4. In summary, this role will consist of business users who act as liaison points with IT in general and the Service Desk in particular. The role of the Super User can be summarized as follows:

- To facilitate communication between IT and the business at an operational level
- To reinforce expectations of users regarding what Service Levels have been agreed
- Staff training for users in their area
- Providing support for minor incidents or simple request fulfilment
- Involvement with new releases and rollouts.

6.6.2 Technical Management roles

The following roles are needed in the Technical Management areas

6.6.2.1 Technical Managers/Team-leaders

A Technical Manager or Team-leader (depending upon the size and/or importance of the team and the organization's structure and culture) may be needed for each of the technical teams or departments. The role will:

- Take overall responsibility for leadership, control and decision-making for the technical team or department
- Provide technical knowledge and leadership in the specific technical areas covered by the team or department
- Ensure necessary technical training, awareness and experience levels are maintained within the team or department
- Report to senior management on all technical issues relevant to their area of responsibility

- Perform line-management for all team or department members.

6.6.2.2 Technical Analysts/Architects

This term refers to any staff member in Technical Management who performs the activities listed in paragraph 6.3.3, excluding the daily operational actions, which are performed by Operators in either Technical or IT Operations Management. Based on the list of generic activities in paragraph 6.3.3, the role of Technical Analysts and Architects includes:

- Working with users, sponsors, Application Management and all other stakeholders to determine their evolving needs
- Working with Application Management and other areas in Technical Management to determine the highest level of system requirements required to meet the requirements within budget and technology constraints
- Defining and maintaining knowledge about how systems are related and ensuring that dependencies are understood and managed accordingly
- Performing cost-benefit analyses to determine the most appropriate means to meet the stated requirements
- Developing Operational Models that will ensure optimal use of resources and the appropriate level of performance
- Ensuring that the infrastructure is configured to be effectively managed given the organization's technology architecture, available skills and tools
- Ensuring the consistent and reliable performance of the infrastructure to deliver the required level of service to the business
- Defining all tasks required to manage the infrastructure and ensuring that these tasks are performed appropriately
- Input into the design of configuration data required to manage and track the application effectively.

The ways in which Technical Management can be organized, and the options available, are discussed in some detail in section 6.7.

6.6.2.3 Technical Operator

This term is used to refer to any staff who performs day-to-day operational tasks in Technical Management. Usually, these tasks are delegated to a dedicated IT Operations team, and this role is therefore discussed in paragraph 6.6.3.4 on IT Operators.

6.6.3 IT Operations Management roles

The following roles and needed in the IT Operations Management area:

6.6.3.1 IT Operations Manager

An IT Operations Manager will be needed to take overall responsibility for all of the IT Operations Management activities, which include:

- **Operations Control**, which oversees the execution and monitoring of the operational activities in the IT Infrastructure. This can be done with the assistance of an Operations Bridge or Network Operations Centre. In addition to executing routine tasks from all technical areas, Operations Control also performs the following specific tasks:
  - **Console Management**, which refers to defining central observation and monitoring capability and then using those consoles to exercise monitoring and control activities
  - **Job Scheduling**, or the management of routine batch jobs or scripts
  - **Backup and Restore** on behalf of all Technical and Application Management teams or department and often on behalf of users
  - **Print and Output management** for the collation and distribution of all centralized printing or electronic output.
- **Facilities Management**, which refers to the management of the physical IT environment, typically a Data Centre or computer rooms and recovery sites together with all the power and cooling equipment. Facilities Management also includes the coordination of large-scale consolidation projects, e.g. data centre consolidation or server consolidation projects. In some cases the management of a Data Centre is outsourced, in which case Facilities Management refers to the management of the outsourcing contract.

The role of the IT Operations Manager is to:

- Provide overall leadership, control and decision-making and take responsibility for the IT Operations Management teams and department
- Report to senior management on all IT Operations issues
- Perform line-management for all IT Operations team or department managers/supervisors.

6.6.3.2 Shift Leaders

Many IT Operations areas will work extended hours – on either a two- or three-shift basis. In such cases a shift

leader will be needed on each of the shifts, to perform the following activities:

- Take overall responsibility for leadership, control and decision-making during the shift period
- Ensure that all operational activities are satisfactorily performed within agreed timescales and in accordance with company policies and procedures
- Liaise with the other shift leader(s) to ensure handover, continuity and consistency between the shifts
- Act as line-manager for all Operations Analysts on his/her shift
- Assume overall health and safety, and security responsibility for the shift (unless specifically designated to other staff members).

6.6.3.3 IT Operations Analysts

IT Operations Analysts are senior IT Operations staff who are able to determine the most effective and efficient way to conduct a series of operations, usually in high-volume, diverse environments.

This role is normally performed as part of Technical Management, but large organizations may find that the volume and diversity of operational activities requires some more in-depth planning and execution. Examples include Job Scheduling and the definition of a Backup strategy and schedule.

6.6.3.4 IT Operators

IT Operators are the staff who perform the day-to-day operational activities that are defined in Technical or Application Management and, in some cases, IT Operations Analysts. Typical Operator roles include:

- Performing backups
- Console operations, i.e. monitoring the status of specific systems, job queues, etc. and providing first-level intervention if appropriate
- Managing print devices, restocking with paper, toner, etc.
- Ensuring that batch jobs, archiving, etc. are performed
- Running scheduled housekeeping jobs, such as database maintenance, file clean-up, etc.
- Burning images for distribution and installation on new servers, desktops or laptops
- Physical installation of standard equipment in the Data Centre.

6.6.4 Application Management roles

6.6.4.1 Applications Managers/Team-leaders

An Applications Manager or Team-leader should be considered for each of the applications teams or departments. The role will:

- Take overall responsibility for leadership, control and decision-making for the applications team or department
- Provide technical knowledge and leadership in the specific applications support activities covered by the team or department
- Ensure necessary technical training, awareness and experience levels are maintained within the team or department relevant to the applications being supported and processes being used
- Involve ongoing communication with users and customers regarding application performance and evolving requirements of the business
- Report to senior management on all issues relevant to the applications being supported
- Perform line-management for all team or department members.

6.6.4.2 Applications Analyst/Architect

Application Analysts and Architects are responsible for matching requirements to application specifications. Specific activities include:

- Working with users, sponsors and all other stakeholders to determine their evolving needs
- Working with Technical Management to determine the highest level of system requirements required to meet the requirements within budget and technology constraints
- Performing cost-benefit analyses to determine the most appropriate means to meet the stated requirement
- Developing Operational Models that will ensure optimal use of resources and the appropriate level of performance
- Ensuring that applications are designed to be effectively managed given the organization's technology architecture, available skills and tools
- Developing and maintaining standards for application sizing, performance modelling, etc.
- Generating a set of acceptance test requirements, together with the designers, test engineers and the user, which determine that all of the high-level

requirements have been met, both functional and with regard to manageability
- Input into the design of configuration data required to manage and track the application effectively.

An appropriate number of Application Analysts will be needed for each of the Application Management teams or department to perform the activities described elsewhere in this publication, primarily in paragraph 6.5.5.

The ways in which Application Management groups can be organized, and the options available, are discussed in some detail in section 6.7.

6.6.5 Event Management roles

It is unusual for an organization to appoint an 'Event Manager', as events tend to occur in multiple contexts and for many different reasons. However, it is important that Event Management procedures are coordinated to prevent duplication of effort and tools. The roles of the Service Operation functions in Event Management are as follows.

6.6.5.1 The role of the Service Desk

The Service Desk is not typically involved in Event Management as such, unless an event requires some response that is within the scope of the Service Desk's defined activity, for example notifying a user that a report is ready. Generally, though, this type of activity is performed by the Operations Bridge, unless the Service Desk and Operations Bridge have been combined.

The investigation and resolution of events that have been identified as being Incidents will initially be undertaken by the Service Desk and then escalated to the appropriate Service Operation team(s)

The Service Desk is also responsible for communicating information about this type of incident to the relevant Technical or Application Management team and, where appropriate, the user.

6.6.5.2 The role of Technical and Application Management

Technical and Application Management plays several important roles as follows:

- During **Service Design**, they will participate in the instrumentation of the service, classify events, update correlation engines and ensure that any auto responses are defined
- During **Service Transition** they will test the service to ensure that events are properly generated and that the defined responses are appropriate

- During **Service Operation** these teams will typically perform Event Management for the systems under their control. It is unusual for teams to have a dedicated person to manage Event Management, but each manager or team leader will ensure that the appropriate procedures are defined and executed according to the process and policy requirements
- **Technical and Application Management** will also be involved in dealing with incidents and problems related to events
- If **Event Management** activities are delegated to the Service Desk or IT Operations Management, Technical and Application Management must ensure that the staff are adequately trained and that they have access to the appropriate tools to enable them to perform these tasks.

6.6.5.3 The role of IT Operations Management

Where IT Operations is separated from Technical or Application Management, it is common for Event Monitoring and first-line response to be delegated to IT Operations Management. Operators for each area will be tasked with monitoring events, responding as required, or ensuring that Incidents are created as appropriate. The instructions for how to do so must be included in the SOPs for those teams.

Event Monitoring is commonly delegated to the Operations Bridge where it exists. The Operations Bridge can initiate and coordinate, or even perform, the responses required by the service, or provide first-level support for those events which generate an incident.

6.6.6 Incident Management roles

The following roles are needed for the Incident Management process.

6.6.6.1 Incident Manager

An Incident Manager has the responsibility for:

- Driving the efficiency and effectiveness of the Incident Management process
- Producing management information
- Managing the work of incident support staff (first- and second-line)
- Monitoring the effectiveness of Incident Management and making recommendations for improvement
- Developing and maintaining the Incident Management systems
- Managing Major Incidents

- Developing and maintaining the Incident Management process and procedures.

In many organizations the role of Incident Manager is assigned to the Service Desk Supervisor – though in larger organizations with high volumes a separate role may be necessary. In either case it is important that the Incident Manager is given the authority to manage incidents effectively through first, second and third line.

6.6.6.2 First line

This is covered in detail under the Service Desk (section 6.1) and will not be repeated here.

6.6.6.3 Second line

Many organizations will choose to have a second-line support group, made up of staff with greater (though still general) technical skills than the Service Desk – and with additional time to devote to incident diagnosis and resolution without interference from telephone interruptions.

Such a group can handle many of the less complicated incidents, leaving more specialist (third-line) support groups to concentrate on dealing with more deep-rooted incidents and/or new developments etc.

Where a second-line group is used, there are often advantages of locating this group close to the Service Desk to aid with good communications and to ease movement of staff between the groups, which may be helpful for training/awareness and during busy periods or staff shortages. A second-line support manager (or supervisor if just a small group) will normally head this group.

It is conceivable that this group may be outsourced – and this is more likely and practical if the Service Desk itself has been outsourced.

6.6.6.4 Third line

Third-line support will be provided by a number of internal technical groups and/or third-party suppliers/maintainers. The list will vary from organization to organization but is likely to include:

- Network Support
- Voice Support (if separate)
- Server Support
- Desktop Support
- Application Management – likely that there may be separate teams for different applications or application types – some of which may be external

supplier/maintainers. In many cases the same team will be responsible for Application Developments as well as support – and it is therefore important that resources are prioritized so that support is given adequate prominence

- Database Support
- Hardware Maintenance Engineers
- Environmental Equipment Maintainers/Suppliers.

Note: Depending upon where an organization decides to source its support services, any of the above groups could be internal or external groups.

6.6.7 Request Fulfilment roles

Initial handling of Service Requests will be undertaken by the Service Desk and Incident Management staff.

Eventual fulfilment of the request will be undertaken by the appropriate Service Operation team(s) or departments and/or by external suppliers, as appropriate. Often, Facilities Management, Procurement and other business areas aid in the fulfilment of the Service Request. In most cases there will be no need for additional roles or posts to be created.

In exceptional cases where a very high number of Service Requests are handled, or where the requests are of critical importance to the organization, it may be appropriate to have one or more of the Incident Management team dedicated to handling and managing Service Requests.

6.6.8 Problem Management roles

The following roles are needed for the Problem Management process.

6.6.8.1 Problem Manager

There should be a designated person (or, in larger organizations, a team) responsible for Problem Management. Smaller organizations may not be able to justify a full-time resource for this role, and it can be combined with other roles in such cases, but it is essential that it not just left to technical resources to perform. There needs to be a single point of coordination and an owner of the Problem Management process. This role will coordinate all Problem Management activities and will have specific responsibility for:

- Liaison with all problem resolution groups to ensure swift resolution of problems within SLA targets
- Ownership and protection of the KEDB
- Gatekeeper for the inclusion of all Known Errors and management of search algorithms
- Formal closure of all Problem Records

- Liaison with suppliers, contractors, etc. to ensure that third parties fulfil their contractual obligations, especially with regard to resolving problems and providing problem-related information and data
- Arranging, running, documenting and all follow-up activities relating to Major Problem Reviews.

6.6.8.2 Problem-Solving Groups

The actual solving of problems is likely to be undertaken by one or more technical support groups and/or suppliers or support contractors – under the coordination of the Problem Manager.

Where an individual problem is serious enough to warrant it, a dedicated problem management team should be formulated to work together in overcoming that particular problem. The Problem Manager has a role to play in making sure that the correct number and level of resources is available in the team and for escalation and communication up the management chain of all organizations concerned.

6.6.9 Access Management roles

Since Access Management is an execution of Security and Availability Management, these two areas will be responsible for defining the appropriate roles. It is unusual for an organization to appoint an 'Access Manager', although it is important that there is a single Access Management process and a single set of policies related to managing rights and access. This process and the related policies are likely to be defined and maintained by Information Security Management and executed by the various Service Operation functions. Their activities can be summarized as follows:

6.6.9.1 The role of the Service Desk

The Service Desk is typically used as a means to request access to a service. This is normally done using a Service Request. The Service Desk will validate the request by checking that the request has been approved at the appropriate level of authority, that the user is a legitimate employee, contractor or customer and that they qualify for access.

Once it has performed these checks (usually by accessing the relevant databases and Service Level Management documents) it will pass the request to the appropriate team to provide access. It is quite common for the Service Desk to be delegated responsibility for providing access for simple services during the call.

The Service Desk will also be responsible for communicating with the user to ensure that they know when access has been granted and to ensure that they receive any other required support.

The Service Desk is also well situated to detect and report incidents related to access. For example, users attempting to access services without authority; or users reporting incidents that indicate that a system or service has been used inappropriately, i.e. by a former employee who used an old username to gain access and make unauthorized changes.

6.6.9.2 The role of Technical and Application Management

Technical and Application Management play several important roles as follows:

- During **Service Design**, they will ensure that mechanisms are created to simplify and control Access Management on each service that is designed. They will also specify ways in which abuse of rights can be detected and stopped
- During **Service Transition** they will test the service to ensure that access can be granted, controlled and prevented as designed
- During **Service Operation** these teams will typically perform Access Management for the systems under their control. It is unusual for teams to have a dedicated person to manage Access Management, but each manager or team leader will ensure that the appropriate procedures are defined and executed according to the process and policy requirements
- Technical and Application Management will also be involved in dealing with Incidents and Problems related to **Access Management**
- If **Access Management** activities are delegated to the Service Desk or IT Operations Management, Technical and Application Management must ensure that the staff are adequately trained and that they have access to the appropriate tools to enable them to perform these tasks.

6.6.9.3 The role of IT Operations Management

Where IT Operations is separated from Technical or Application Management, it is common for operational Access Management tasks to be delegated to IT Operations Management. Operators for each area will be tasked with providing or revoking access to key systems or resources. The circumstances under which they may do so, and the instructions for how to do so, must be included in the SOPs for those teams.

The Operations Bridge, if it exists, can be used to monitor events related to Access Management and can even provide first-line support and coordination in the resolution of those events where appropriate.

6.7 SERVICE OPERATION ORGANIZATION STRUCTURES

Some general information has already been provided about organizational considerations for each function (see paragraphs 6.2.3, 6.3.4 and 6.5.6.). This section considers some specific organizational structures for all functions. There are a number of ways of organizing Service Operation functions, and each organization will have to make it own decisions, based upon its scale, geography, culture and business environment. Some options are discussed in the rest of this section.

6.7.1 Organization by technical specialization

In this type of organization, departments are created according to technology and the skills and activities needed to manage that technology. IT Operations will follow the structure of the Technical and Application Management departments. The implication of this is that IT Operations is geared toward the operational agendas of the Technical and Application Management departments.

This structure can work well, provided that these groups are fully represented in the Service Design, Testing and Improvement processes, which will ensure that their agendas are aligned with the requirements of the business.

This structure also assumes that all Technical and Application Management departments have clearly distinguished between their Management activity and operations activity. It also requires that they have standardized these operational activities so that they can be effectively managed by the IT Operations Manager without undue interference from the Technical and Application Management teams or departments.

An example of an IT Operations organization structure based on technical expertise is given in Figure 6.7

The advantages of this type of organizational structure include:

- It is easier to set internal performance objectives since all staff in a single department have a similar set of tasks on a similar technology

■ Individual devices, systems or platforms can be managed more effectively since people with the appropriate skills are dedicated to manage these and measured according to their performance

■ Managing training programmes is easier since skill sets are clearly defined and separated into specific groups.

The disadvantages of this type of organizational structure include the following:

■ When people are divided into separate departments the priorities of their own group tend to override the priorities of other departments. An example of this is when departments refuse to accept ownership of an incident, each one blaming the other while the business continues to be disrupted.

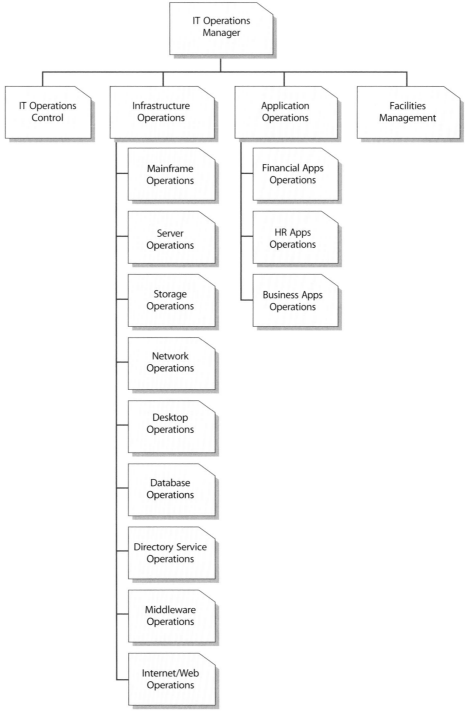

Figure 6.7 IT Operations organized according to technical specialization (sample)

■ Knowledge about the infrastructure and relationships between components is difficult to collect and fragmented. Individual groups tend to collect and maintain only the data that is required to support their own function, and do not give access to it very easily.

■ Each technology managed by a group is seen as a separate entity. This becomes a problem on systems that consist of components managed by different teams, e.g. an application, managed by the Application Management team, runs on a server managed by the Server Management department, using a network segment managed by the Local Area Networking department. If a change is made by one team or department without consulting the others, this could be disastrous for the service.

■ It is more difficult to understand the impact of a single department's poor performance on the IT Service since there are many different groups contributing to the same service, each with its own set of performance objectives.

■ It is more difficult to track overall IT Service performance since each group is being measured on an individual basis.

■ Coordinating Change Assessments and Schedules is more difficult since many different departments have to provide input for each change.

■ Work requiring knowledge of multiple technologies is difficult since most resources are only trained for and concerned with the management of a single technology. Projects therefore have to include cross-training, which is time-consuming and expensive.

6.7.2 Organization by activity

This type of organization structure focuses on the fact that similar activities have to be performed on all technologies in the organization. This means that people who perform similar activities, regardless of the technology, should be grouped together, although within each department there may be teams focusing on a specific technology, application, etc.

In this type of organization, there is no clear differentiation between the different Technical and Application Management areas. Similar activities from many different areas can be grouped into a single department.

Examples of departments that have been set up to perform a specific set of activities across multiple technologies include:

■ Maintenance (this implies that one team will coordinate and perform all maintenance across all technologies)

■ Contract Management or Third Party Management

■ Monitoring and Control

■ Operations Bridge

■ Network Operations Centre

■ Operations Strategy and Planning (which, as part of the Service Design processes, normally defines the standards to be used in IT Operations) – this department can set strategy or standards for every type of Technical and Application Management area.

The Operations Strategy and Planning department is used to illustrate this type of structure in Figure 6.8.

The advantages of this type of organizational structure include the following:

■ It is easier to manage groups of related activities since all the people involved in these activities report to the same manager

■ Measurement of teams or departments is based more on output than on isolated activities. This helps to build higher levels of assurance that a service can be delivered.

The disadvantages of this type of organizational structure include the following:

■ Resources with similar skills may be duplicated across different functions, which results in higher costs

■ Although measurement is more output-based, it is still focused on the performance of internal activities rather than driven by the experience of the customer or end user.

6.7.3 Organizing to manage processes

It is not a good idea to structure the whole organization according to processes. Processes are used to overcome the 'silo effect' of departments, not to create silos. However, there are a number of processes that will need a dedicated organization structure to support and manage it. For example, it will be very difficult for Financial Management to be successful without a dedicated Finance department – even if that department consists of a small number of staff.

In process-based organizations people are organized into groups or departments that perform or manage a specific process. This is similar to the activity-based structure, except that its departments focus on end-to-end sets of activities rather than on one individual type of activity.

Organization by Activity

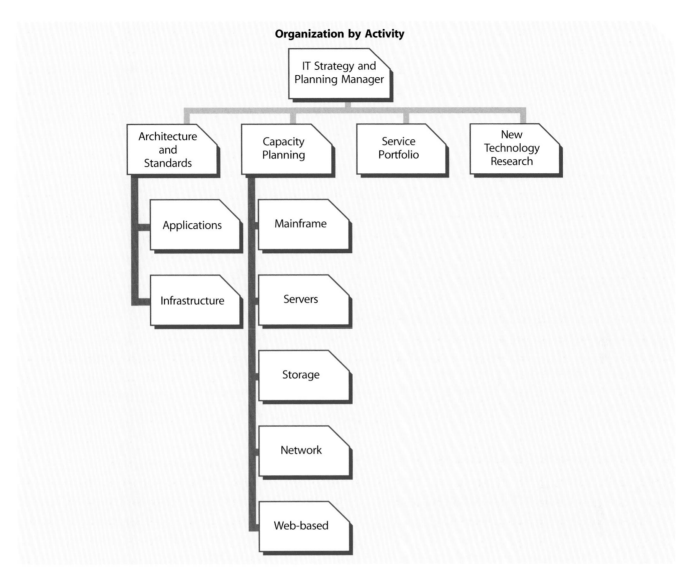

Figure 6.8 A department based on executing a set of activities

It should be noted that this type of organization structure should only be used if IT Operations Management is responsible for more than just IT Operations. In some organizations, for example, IT Operations is responsible for defining SLAs and negotiating UCs.

In addition, processes specifically exist to link the activities of different groups to achieve a specific outcome. Using processes as the basis to create departments can defeat the purpose of having processes in the first place. Process-based departments are really only effective when they are able to coordinate the execution of the process through the entire organization.

This means that process-based departments should only be considered if IT Operations Management is to play the role of Process Owner for a specific process.

Examples of process-based groups or departments include:

- Capacity Operations
- Availability Monitoring and Control
- IT Financial Management
- Security Administration
- Asset and Configuration Management (including equipment installation and deployment).

The advantages of this type of organizational structure include the following:

- Processes are easier to define
- There is less role conflict as job descriptions and process role descriptions are the same. In other structures a single job description will typically include activities for several roles

■ Metrics of team or department performance and process performance are the same, effectively aligning 'internal' and 'external' metrics.

The disadvantages of this type of organizational structure include the following:

■ A basic principle of processes is that they are a means of linking the activities of various departments and groups. By using processes as a basis for organizational design, additional processes need to be defined to ensure that the departments work together.

■ Even if a department is responsible for executing a process, there will still be external dependencies. Groups may not view process activities outside of their own process as being important, resulting in processes that cannot be fully executed because dependencies cannot be met.

■ While some aspects of a process can be centralized, there will always be a number of activities that will have to be performed by other groups. The relationship between the dedicated team or department and the people performing the decentralized activities is often difficult to define and manage.

6.7.4 Organizing IT Operations by geography

IT Operations can be physically distributed and in some cases each location needs to be organized according to its own particular context.

This structure is typically used in the following circumstances:

■ Data Centres are geographically distributed

■ Different regions or countries have different technologies or provide a different set of services

■ There are different business models or organizational structures in the different regions, i.e. the business is decentralized by geography and each Business Unit is fairly autonomous

■ Different legislation applies to different countries or regions (e.g. safety regulations)

■ Different standards apply to different countries or regions

■ Cultural or language differences exist between staff managing IT.

An example of this type of structure is given in Figure 6.9. Note that in this example each geographical department is structured internally using Technical Specialization. This could be different in each region. For example one region

may be structured in this way, while another region uses a process- or activity-based structure.

Figure 6.9 also illustrates that one location could perform centralized operations for all regions if they are similar enough. In this example, the American Server Operations Department manages all server operations in all locations, Brussels manages all database operations and Singapore manages all storage operations.

The advantages of this type of organizational structure include the following:

■ Organization structure can be customized to meet local conditions

■ IT Operations can be customized to meet differing levels of IT service from region to region.

The disadvantages of this type of organizational structure include the following:

■ Reporting lines and authority structures can be confusing. For example, does Network Operations report into the local Data Centre Manager or to a centralized Network Operations Manager?

■ Operational standards are difficult to impose, resulting in inconsistent and duplicated activities and tools, resulting in reduced economies of scale, which in turn increases the overall cost of operations.

■ Duplication of roles, activities, tools and facilities across multiple locations could be very costly.

■ Shared services, such as e-mail, are more difficult to deliver as each regional organization operates differently.

■ Communication with customers and inside IT will be more difficult as they are not co-located and it may be difficult for staff in one location to understand the priorities of customers or staff in another location.

6.7.5 Hybrid organization structures

It is unlikely that IT Operations Management will be structured using only one type of organization structure. Most organizations use a technical specialization, with some additional activity- or process-based departments.

The type of structure used and the exact combination of technical specialization, activity-based and process-based departments will depend on a number of organizational variables.

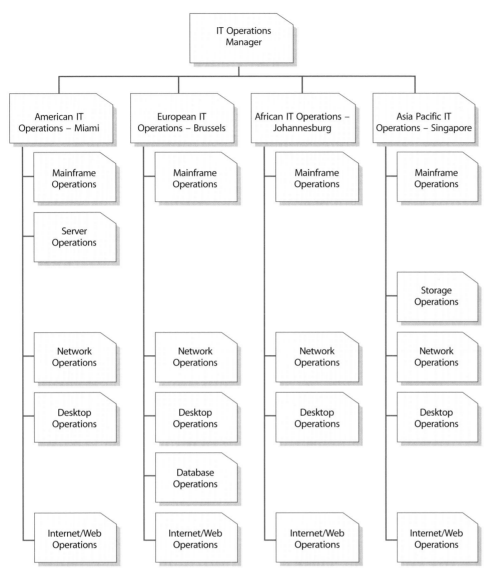

Figure 6.9 IT Operations organized according to geography

Organizational structure variables

The exact criteria chosen and the resulting organizational structure will depend on a number of variables, which may include:

- The nature of the business

- Business requirements and expectations

- The technological and technical architecture

- The stability of the current IT Infrastructure and the availability of skills to manage it

- The governance of the organization (i.e. the way in which authority is assigned and decisions are made – as well as any formal governance framework that is used, such as COBIT or SOX)

- The legislative, political and socio-economic environment of the organization

- The type and level of skills available to the organization

- The size, age and maturity of the organization

- The management style of the organization

- Dependence on IT for business-critical activities, processes and functions

- The way in which IT participates in the value network (i.e. the way IT interacts with the business and its partners, suppliers and customers)

- The relationship between IT and its vendors.

For a more complete description of how these factors influence organizational design, please refer to the 'Organizational Development' section of the Service Strategy publication.

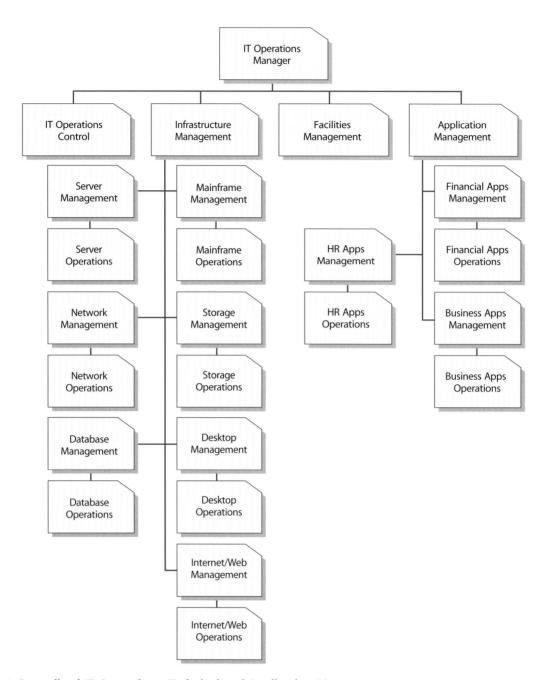

Figure 6.10 Centralized IT Operations, Technical and Application Management structure

6.7.5.1 Combined functions

One last type of organization should be discussed. This structure incorporates IT Operations, Technical and Application Management departments into a single structure. This is sometimes the case where all groups are co-located in a single data centre. Here, the Data Centre Manager takes responsibility for all Technical, Application and IT Operations Management.

This type of organization structure is illustrated in Figure 6.10.

In this structure, IT Operations Management is responsible for the Technical and Application Management functions, which in turn are responsible for managing their own operational activities. Each department is able to delegate some of these activities to the Operations Control department.

The advantages of this organization structure are:

■ There is greater consistency and control between the more tactical and more operational Technical Management activities

- It is easier to enforce the performance standards and technical architectures that are created in Service Design, since the people who were involved in design are managing the activities of the people who are executing those activities
- As there is no duplication between location or activity, this structure is often more cost-effective.

The disadvantage of this organization structure is:

- The scope of this structure makes it very difficult to manage effectively in large organizations or in organizations with multiple Data Centres.

6.7.5.2 Organizing Application and Technical Management

Technical and Application Management organizations tend to be fairly straightforward. As stated in paragraphs 6.3.4 and 6.5.6, Technical Management departments are usually based on the technology they manage and Application Management departments on the applications and sets of applications they manage.

However, there are some alternative organization structures and variations, which are discussed in this section.

6.7.5.3 Geography

In organizations with multiple locations, it is common for the Technical and Application Management departments to be represented in each physical location. However, this does not mean that each location will have all the same departments, or that they are all responsible for the same actions.

As support and management tools mature more and more IT Infrastructure and application CIs can be managed remotely. This means that each department will have a strong, centralized Technical or Application Management team, with local members to provide specialized, on-site activities or support.

For example, in Server Management, the central team will help to create standards for server configuration, they will monitor and control remote devices, perform backups, perform Operating System upgrades, etc. The local teams will provide basic on-site support, hardware maintenance and repair and configuration and installation of new servers.

In Application Management, the central team could participate in ongoing design and testing of the application, monitoring and control; perform backups, data integrity checks, etc. The local team could provide on-site support and education to end users and work with the local Technical Management team to resolve more complex problems involving local equipment.

There is one potential issue that needs to be resolved however, and that is who the local team reports to. In some organizations they report to the manager of the centralized team. This has the added advantage of consistent performance and management across the whole enterprise.

In other organizations the local teams report to the most senior IT Manager at that site. This has the added advantage that IT Services can be customized to meet local conditions, but it creates a lot of confusion about who the local teams should take direction from.

The advantages of this type of organizational structure include the following:

- Organization structure can be customized to meet local conditions
- Technical and Application Management can be customized to meet differing levels of IT service from region to region.

The disadvantages of this type of organizational structure include the following:

- Reporting lines and authority structures can be confusing
- Standards are difficult to impose, resulting in inconsistent and duplicated activities and tools, resulting in reduced economies of scale, which in turn increases the overall cost of operations
- Duplication of roles, activities, tools and facilities across multiple locations could be very costly.

6.7.5.4 Combined Technical and Application Management structure

Some organizations organize their Technical and Application Management functions according to systems. This means that each department will consist of application specialists and IT Infrastructure technical specialists, all geared towards managing the services based on that set of systems. Components that are shared across all these systems, such as the network, will be managed by dedicated Technical Management departments.

The advantage of this organization structure is:

- It is easier to produce high-quality output to the end user because all department members are focused on the success of the system as a whole, rather than the performance of an individual technology component or application.

The disadvantages of this organization structure are:

- Duplication of skills and resources across several departments will increase the cost of the organization. For example, each group is likely to have an individual or team dedicated to managing servers – each of which will be doing very similar tasks.

- Communication between staff who are managing similar technology is reduced. This reduces the amount of learning by experience and increases reliance on collaborative knowledge management tools.

- When people with similar skills are in the same department, the department will compensate for members with lower skill and competency levels. When there is only one person with Server Management skills on a system-based department, and their competency is minimal, it will affect the performance of the entire department.

Technology considerations

7

7   Technology considerations

Each function and process is defined in the relevant section in Chapters 4 and 6. This chapter brings all technology requirements together to define the overall requirement of an integrated set of Service Management technology for Service Operation.

The same technology, with some possible additions, should be used for the other phases of ITSM – Service Strategy, Service Design, Service Transition and Continual Service Improvement – to give consistency and allow an effective ITSM Lifecycle to be properly managed.

The main requirements for Service Operation are as set out in this chapter.

7.1   GENERIC REQUIREMENTS

An integrated ITSM technology (or toolset, as some suppliers sell their technology as 'modules' whereas some organizations may choose to integrate products from alternative suppliers) is needed that includes the following core functionality.

7.1.1   Self-Help

Many organizations find it beneficial to offer 'Self-Help' capabilities to their users. The technology should therefore support this capability with some form of web front-end allowing web pages to be defined offering a menu-driven range of Self-Help and Service Requests – with a direct interface into the back-end process-handling software.

7.1.2   Workflow or process engine

A workflow or process control engine is needed to allow the pre-definition and control of defined processes such as an Incident Lifecycle, Request Fulfilment Lifecycle, Problem Lifecycle, Change Model, etc.

This should allow responsibilities, activities, timescales, escalation paths and alerting to be pre-defined and then automatically managed.

7.1.3   Integrated CMS

The tool should have an integrated CMS to allow the organization's IT infrastructure assets, components, services and any ancillary CIs (such as contracts, locations, licences, suppliers etc. – anything that the IT organization wishes to control) to be held, together with all relevant attributes, in a centralised location – and to allow relationships between each to be stored and maintained,

and linked to Incident, Problem, Known Error and Change Records as appropriate.

7.1.4   Discovery/Deployment/Licensing technology

In order to populate or verify the CMS data and to assist in Licence Management, discovery or automated audit tools will be required. Such tools should be capable of being run from any location on the network and allow interrogation and recovery of information relating to all components that make up, or are connected to, the IT Infrastructure.

Such technology should allow 'filtering' so that the data being carried forward can be vetted and only required data extracted. It is also very helpful if 'changes only' since the last audit can be extracted and reported upon.

The same technology can often be used to deploy new software to target locations – this is an essential requirement for all Service Operation teams or departments, to allow patches, transports etc. to be distributed to the correct users.

An interface to 'Self Help' capabilities is desirable to allow approved software downloads to be requested in this way but automatically handled by the deployment software.

Tools that allow automatic comparison of software licences' details held (in the CMS, ideally) and actual licence numbers deployed – with reporting of any discrepancies – are extremely desirable.

7.1.5   Remote control

It is often helpful for the Service Desk Analysts and other support groups to be able to take control of the user's desk-top (under properly controlled security conditions) so as to allow them to conduct investigations or correct settings, etc. Facilities to allow this level of remote control will be needed.

7.1.6   Diagnostic utilities

It could be extremely useful for the Service Desk and other support groups if the technology incorporated the capability to create and use diagnostic scripts and other diagnostic utilities (such as, for example, case-based reasoning tools) to assist with earlier diagnosis of incidents. Ideally, these should be 'context sensitive' and presentation of the scripts automated so far as possible.

7.1.7 Reporting

There is no use in storing data unless it can be easily retrieved and used to meet the organization's purposes. The technology should therefore incorporate good reporting capabilities, as well as allow standard interfaces which can be used to input data to industry-standard reporting packages, dashboards, etc. Ideally, instant, on-screen as well as printed reporting can be provided through the use of context-sensitive 'top ten' reports.

7.1.8 Dashboards

Dashboard-type technology is useful to allow 'see at a glance' visibility of overall IT service performance and availability levels. Such displays can be included in management-level reports to users and customers – but can also give real-time information for inclusion in IT web pages to give dynamic reporting, and can be used for support and investigation purposes. Capabilities to support customized views of information to meet specific levels of interest can be particularly useful.

However, they sometimes represent a technical rather than service view of the infrastructure and in such cases they may be of less interest to customers and users.

7.1.9 Integration with Business Service Management

There is a trend within the IT industry to try to bring together business-related IT with the processes and disciplines of IT Service Management – some call this Business Service Management. To facilitate this, business applications and tools need to be interfaced with ITSM support tools to give the required functionality. This can be illustrated by this example:

An Eastern European telecoms company was able to interface its telephone cell-net monitoring and billing system to its Event Management, Incident Management and Configuration Management processes. In this way it was able to detect any unusual usage/billing patterns and interpret these such that it could identify, with a high degree of certainly, that a telephone had been stolen and was being used to make illicit calls.

It was able to raise events for such patterns and automate actions to suspend usage of the mobile phone devices and, in parallel, identify the exact location of the illicit user (using GPRS technology) and raise incidents so that the police had the capability of finding the suspected thief and recovering the device.

More advanced tools integration capabilities are needed to allow greater exploitation of this sort of business and IT integration.

7.2 EVENT MANAGEMENT

The following features are desirable for any Event Management technology:

- Multi-environmental, open interface to allow monitoring and alerting across heterogeneous services and an organization's entire IT Infrastructure.
- Easy to deploy, with minimal set up costs.
- 'Standard' agents to monitor most common environments/components/systems.
- Open interfaces to accept any standard (e.g. SNMP) event input and generation of multiple alerting.
- Centralized routing of all events to a single location, programmable to allow different location(s) at various times.
- Support for design/test phases – so that new applications/services can be monitored during design/test phases and results fed back into the design and transition.
- Programmable assessment and handling of alerts depending upon symptoms and impact.
- The ability to allow an operator to acknowledge an alert, and if no response is entered within a defined timeframe, to escalate the alert.
- Good reporting functionality to allow feed-back into design and transition phases as well a meaningful management information and business user 'dashboard'.

Such technology should allow a direct interface into the organization's Incident Management processes (via entry into the Incident Log), as well as the capability to escalate to support staff, third-party suppliers, engineers etc. via e-mail, SMS messaging, etc.

Specialist facilities, or perhaps separate specialist tools, will be required for website monitoring. Such facilities must be able to simulate customer traffic onto the website and to report on availability and performance in relation to the 'customer experience'.

7.3 INCIDENT MANAGEMENT

7.3.1 Integrated ITSM technology

Integrated ITSM technology is required that has the following functionality:

- An integral CMS to allow automated relationships to be made and maintained between incidents, service requests, problems, Known Errors and all other configuration items.
- The CMS that can be used to assist in determining priority and aid in investigation and diagnosis.
- A process flow engine to allow processes to be pre-defined (including pre-defined incident models, see paragraph 3.2.1.5) and automatically controlled – with flexible internal routing to all relevant support groups and external e-mail/SMS interfaces.
- Automated alerting and escalation capabilities to prevent an incident being overlooked or delayed.
- Open interfacing to Event Management tools, so that any failures can be automatically raised as incidents.
- A web interface to allow self-help and service requests to be input via Internet/Intranet screens.
- An integrated KEDB so that diagnosed and/or resolved incident/problems can be recorded and searched to help in speeding future incident resolution.
- Easy-to-use reporting facilities to allow incident metrics to be produced and to facilitate incident analysis for Problem Management and Availability Management purposes.
- Diagnostic tools (either integrated or interfaces to separate products), as already mentioned under Service Desk.

7.3.2 Workflow and automated escalation

The target times should be included in support tools, which should be used to automate the workflow control and escalation paths.

If for example a second-line support group has not resolved an incident within a 60-minute agreed target, the incident must be automatically routed to the appropriate (determined by incident categorization) third-line support group – and any necessary hierarchic escalation should be automatically undertaken (e.g. SMS message to the Service Desk Manager, Incident Manager and/or IT Services Manager and perhaps to the user, if appropriate). The second-line support group must be informed of the escalation action as part of the automated process.

7.4 REQUEST FULFILMENT

Integrated ITSM technology is needed so that Service Requests can be linked to incidents or events that have initiated them (and been stored in the same CMS, which can be interrogated to report against SLAs). Some organizations will be content to use the Incident Management element of such tools and to treat Service Requests as a subset and defined category of incidents. Where an organization chooses to raise separate Service Requests, it will require a tool which allows this capability.

Front-end Self-Help capabilities will be needed to allow users to submit requests via some form of web-based, menu-driven selection process.

In all other respects the facilities needed to manage Service Requests are very similar to those for managing incidents: pre-defined workflow control of Request Models, priority levels, automated escalation, effective reporting, etc.

7.5 PROBLEM MANAGEMENT

7.5.1 Integrated Service Management Technology

An integrated ITSM tool is needed that differentiates between incidents and problems – so that separate Problem Records can be raised to deal with the underlying causes of incidents, but linked to the related incidents. The functionality of Problem Records should be similar to those needed for Incident Records and also allow for multiple incident matching against Problem Records.

7.5.2 Change Management

Integration with Change Management is very important, so that Request, Event, Incident and Problem Records can be related to RFCs that have caused problems. This is to evaluate the success of the Change Management process – as well as Incident and Known Error Records – and so that RFCs can be readily raised to control the activities needed to overcome problems that have been identified through Root-Cause Analysis or Proactive Trend Analysis.

7.5.3 Integrated CMS

It is also important to have an integrated CMS which allows Problem Records to be linked to the components affected and the services impacted – and to any other relevant CIs.

Configuration Management forms part of a larger SKMS which includes linkages to many of the data repositories used in Service Operations. The process and practices of

Configuration Management and its underlying technologies requirements are included in the Service Transition publication.

7.5.4 Known Error Database

An effective KEDB will be as essential requirement, which should allow easy storage and retrieval of Known Error data.

Good reporting facilities are needed to ease the production of management reports, allowing the data to be incorporated automatically without the need for re-keying of data – and to allow drill-down capabilities for Incident and Problem Analysis.

Note: In some cases, components or systems being investigated by Problem Management may be provided by third-party vendors or manufacturers. To address this, vendors' support tools and/or KEDBs may also need to be used.

7.6 ACCESS MANAGEMENT

Access Management uses a variety of technologies, mainly:

- Human Resource Management technology, to validate the identity of users and to track their status
- Directory Services Technology (see section 5.8 for a description of Directory Services). This technology enables technology managers to assign names to resources on a network and then provide access to those resources based on the profile of the user. Directory Services tools also enable Access Management to create roles and groups and to link these to both users and resources
- Access Management features in Applications, Middleware, Operating Systems and Network Operating Systems
- Change Management systems
- Request Fulfilment technology (see section 7.4).

7.7 SERVICE DESK

Adequate tools and technology support should be provided to enable Service Desk staff to perform their roles as efficiently and effectively as possible. This will include the following.

7.7.1 Telephony

Because a high percentage of incidents are likely to be raised by telephone calls from users, the Service Desk should be provided with good, modern telephony services. This should include:

- An automated call distribution (ACD) system to allow a single telephone number (or numbers if a distributed or segmented Service Desk is the preferred option) and group pick-up capabilities. Warning: If options are offered via the ACD, via keyboard or Interactive Voice Recognition (IVR) selection, do not use too many levels of options or offer ambiguous options. Also do not include any 'dead ends' or options which, once chosen, do not allow the caller to go back to previous menus.
- Computer Telephony Interface (CTI) software to allow caller recognition (via the linked ACD) and automated population of the users' details into the incident record from the CMS.
- VoIP – use of this technology can significantly reduce telephony costs when dealing with remote and international users
- Statistical software to allow telephony statistics to be gathered and easily interrogated/printed for analysis – this should allow the following information to be obtained for any selected period:
  - Number of calls received, in total and broken down by any 'splits' – where any call-routing has been chosen and being provided by an IVR system/keypad response
  - Call arrival profiles and answer times
  - Call abandon rates
  - Call handling rates by individual Service Desk call handlers
  - Average call durations
- Hands-free headsets, with dual-user access capabilities (on at least some of the headsets) for use during training of new staff, etc.

7.7.2 Support tools

There are a range of free-standing Service Desk support tools available in the marketplace – and some organizations may choose to produce their own simple incident logging/management systems. If an organization seriously intends to implement ITSM then a fully integrated ITSM toolset will be required that has a CMS at the centre and provides integrated support for all the ITIL-defined processes.

Specific elements of such a tool that will be particularly beneficial for the Service Desk include the following.

7.7.2.1 Known Error Database

An integrated KEDB should be used to store details of previous incidents/problems and their resolutions – so that any recurrences can be more quickly diagnosed and fixed.

To facilitate this, functionality is needed to categorize and quickly retrieve previous Known Errors, using pattern matching and key word searching against symptoms. Management of the KEDB is the responsibility of Problem Management, but the Service Desk will use to help speed incident handling.

7.7.2.2 Diagnostic scripts

Multi-level diagnostic scripts should be developed, stored and managed to allow Service Desk staff to pinpoint the cause of failures. Specialist support groups and suppliers should be asked to provide details of the likely failures and the key questions to be asked to identify exactly what has gone wrong – and for details of the resolution actions to be taken.

These details should then be included in context-sensitive scripts that should appear on-screen, dependent upon the multi-level categorization of the incident, and should be driven by the user's answers to diagnostic questions.

7.7.2.3 Self-Help web Interface

It is often cost effective and expedient to provide some form of automated 'Self-Help' functionality, so users can seek and obtain assistance which will enable them to resolve their own difficulties. Ideally this should be via a 24/7 web interface that is driven by menu selection and might include, as appropriate:

- Frequently asked questions (FAQs) and solutions.
- 'How to do' search capabilities – to guide users through a context-sensitive list of tasks or activities.
- A bulletin-type service containing details of outstanding service issues/problems together with anticipated restoration times.
- Password change capabilities – using secure password protection software to check identities, perform authorization and change passwords without the need for Service Desk intervention.
- Software fix downloads (patches, service packs, bug fixes etc. where it is determined that the user has the wrong version or a fix is needed) – tools are available to automate the checking process, to compare the actual desktop image with the agreed 'standard' builds and to allow upgrades to be offered and accepted where necessary.
- Software repairs – where it is detected that a corruption may have occurred, to allow software fixes, removal and/or re-installation.
- Software removal requests – automatically completed with any licence being returned to the pool.

- Downloads of additional software packages – tools are available to check a pre-defined software policy and to allow the download of additional software packages, if covered by the policy. This can include automated software licence checks and financial approvals as well as CMS updating.
- Advanced notice of any planned downtime or services outages or degradations.

The self-help solution should include the capability for users to log incidents themselves, which can be used during periods that the Service Desk is closed (if not operating 24/7) and attended to by Service Desk staff at the start of the next shift.

Some care has to be exercised to ensure that the Self-Help activities selected for inclusion are not too advanced for the average user, and that safeguards are included to prevent a 'little knowledge being a dangerous thing'! It may be possible to offer slightly more advanced Self-Help facilities to 'Super Users' who have had extra training. It is also necessary to be very careful about assumptions made when staffing a Service Desk about the amount of use that users will make of Self-Help facilities.

Note: As already covered in the list above, it is possible to combine some simpler Request Fulfilment activities as part of an overall Self-Help system – which can also be of significant benefit in reducing calls to the Service Desk (see paragraph 7.1.1 for further details).

7.7.2.4 Remote control

As already stated, but repeated here for completeness, it is often helpful for the Service Desk Analysts to be able to take control of the user's desktop so as to allow them to conduct investigations or correct settings, etc. Facilities to allow this level of remote control will be needed.

7.7.3 IT Service Continuity Planning for ITSM support tools

Organizations are likely to become quickly dependent upon their ITSM tools and will find it difficult to work without them. A full Business Impact Analysis and Risk Analysis should be performed and plans then developed to ensure appropriate IT Service Continuity and resilience levels.

Implementing Service Operation

8 Implementing Service Operation

It should be noted that Service Operation is a phase in a lifecycle and not an entity in its own right. By the time a service, process, organization structure or technology is operating, it has already been implemented. However, there are a number of processes and functions described in this publication, and it is therefore important to address the implementation considerations which should have been addressed by the time they come into operation.

A number of these have been covered in the relevant section – for example guidance is given about organization structures and roles in Chapter 6. This will not be repeated here. Rather, this section will focus on some generic implementation guidance for Service Operation as a whole.

8.1 MANAGING CHANGE IN SERVICE OPERATION

Service Operation should strive to achieve stability – but not stagnation! There are many valid and advantageous reasons why 'change is a good thing' – but Service Operation staff must ensure that any changes are absorbed without adverse impact upon the stability of the IT services being offered.

8.1.1 Change triggers

There are many things that may trigger a change in the Service Operation environment. These include:

- New or upgraded hardware or network components
- New or upgraded applications software
- New or upgraded system software (operating systems, utilities, middleware etc. including patches and bug fixes
- Legislative, conformance or governance changes
- Obsolescence – some components may become obsolete and require replacement or cease to be supported by the supplier/maintainer
- Business imperative – you have to be flexible to work in ITSM, particularly during Service Operation, and there will be many occasions when the business needs IT changes to meet dynamic business requirements
- Enhancements to processes, procedures and/or underpinning tools to improve IT delivery or reduce financial costs

- Changes of management or personnel (ranging from loss or transfer of individuals right through to major take-overs or acquisitions)
- Change of service levels or in service provision – outsourcing, in-sourcing, partnerships, etc.

8.1.2 Change assessment

Service Operation staff must be involved in the assessment of all changes to ensure that operational issues are fully taken into account. This involvement should commence as soon as possible (see paragraph 4.6.1) not just at the later stages of change – i.e. CAB and ECAB membership – by which time many fundamental decisions will have been made and influence is likely to be very limited. The Change Manager should inform all affected parties of the change being assessed so input can be prepared and available prior to CAB meetings.

However, it is important that Service Operation staff are involved at these latter stages as they may be involved in the actual implementation and they will wish to ensure that careful scheduling takes place to avoid potential contentions or particularly sensitive periods.

8.1.3 Measurement of successful change

The ultimate measure of success in respect of changes made to Service Operation is that customers and users do not experience any variation or outage of service. So far as possible, the effects of changes should be invisible, apart from any enhanced functionality, quality or financial savings resulting from the change.

8.2 SERVICE OPERATION AND PROJECT MANAGEMENT

Because Service Operation is generally viewed as 'business as usual' and often focused on executing defined procedures in a standard way, there is a tendency not to use Project Management processes when they would in fact be appropriate. For example, major infrastructure upgrades, or the deployment of new or changed procedures, are significant tasks where formal Project Management can be used to improve control and manage costs/resources.

Using Project Management to manage these types of activity would have the following benefits:

- The project benefits are clearly stated and agreed
- There is more visibility of what is being done and how it is being managed, which makes it easier for other IT groups and the business to quantify the contributions made by operational teams
- This in turn makes it easier to obtain funding for projects that have traditionally been difficult to cost justify
- Greater consistency and improved quality
- Achievement of objectives results in higher credibility for operational groups.

8.3 ASSESSING AND MANAGING RISK IN SERVICE OPERATION

There will be a number of occasions where it is imperative that risk assessment to Service Operation is quickly undertaken and acted upon.

The most obvious area is in assessing the risk of potential changes or Known Errors (already covered elsewhere) but in addition Service Operation staff may need to be involved in assessing the risk and impact of:

- Failures, or potential failures – either reported by Event Management or Incident/Problem Management, or warnings raised by manufacturers, suppliers or contractors
- New projects that will ultimately result in delivery into the live environment
- Environmental risk (encompassing IT Service Continuity-type risks to the physical environment and locale as well as political, commercial or industrial-relations related risks)
- Suppliers, particularly where new suppliers are involved or where key service components are under the control of third parties
- Security risks – both theoretical or actual arising from security related incidents or events
- New customers/services to be supported.

8.4 OPERATIONAL STAFF IN SERVICE DESIGN AND TRANSITION

All IT groups will be involved during Service Design and Service transition to ensure that new components or service are designed, tested and implemented to provide the correct levels of functionality, usability, availability, capacity, etc.

Additionally, Service Operation staff must be involved during the early stages of Service Design and Service

Transition to ensure that when new services reach the live environment they are fit for purpose, from a Service Operation perspective, and are 'supportable' in the future.

In this context, 'supportable' means:

- Capable of being supported from a technical and operational viewpoint from within existing, or pre-agreed additional resources and skills levels
- Without adverse impact on other existing technical or operational working practices, processes or schedules
- Without any unexpected operational costs or ongoing or escalating support expenditure
- Without any unexpected contractual or legal complications
- No complex support paths between multiple support departments of third-party organizations.

Note: Change is not just about technology. It also requires training, awareness, cultural change, motivational issues and a lot more. Further details regarding wider management of change are covered in the Service Transition publication.

8.5 PLANNING AND IMPLEMENTING SERVICE MANAGEMENT TECHNOLOGIES

There are a number of factors that organizations need to plan for in readiness for, and during deployment and implementation of, ITSM support tools. These include the following.

8.5.1 Licences

The overall cost of ITSM tools, particularly the integrated tool that will form the heart of the required toolset, is usually determined by the number and type of user licences that the organization needs.

Such tools are often sold in modular format, so the exact functionality of each module needs to be well understood and some initial sizing must be conducted to determine how many – and what type – of users will need access to each module.

Licences are often available in the following types (the exact terminology may vary depending upon the software supplier).

8.5.1.1 Dedicated licences

For use by those staff that requires frequent and prolonged use of the module (e.g. Service Desk staff would need a dedicated licence to use an Incident Management module).

8.5.1.2 Shared licences

For staff who make fairly regular use of the module, but with significant intervals in between, so can usually manage with a shared licence (e.g. third-line support staff may need regular access to an Incident Management module – but only at times when they are actively updating an incident record). The ratio of required licences to users needs to be estimated, so the correct number of licences can be purchased – this will depend upon the number of potential users, the length of periods of use and the expected frequency between usages to give an estimated concurrency level.

The cost of a shared licence is usually more expensive than that of dedicated licences – but the overall cost is less as users are sharing and fewer licences are therefore needed in total.

8.5.1.3 Web licences

Usually allowing some form of 'light interface' via web access to the tool's capabilities, this is usually suitable for staff requiring remote access, only occasional access, or usage of just a small subset of the functionality (e.g. engineering staff wishing to log details of actions taken on incidents or users just wanting to log an incident directly). Web licences usually cost a lot less than other licences (may even be free with other licences!) and the ratio of use is also often lower – so overall costs are reduced further.

Note that some staff may require access to multiple licences (e.g. support staff may require a dedicated or shared licence when in the office during the day, but may require a web licence when providing out of hours support from home). Keep in mind that licences may be required for customers/users/suppliers using the same tool to input, view or update records or reports.

Note: Some licence agreements (of any of the types mentioned above) may restrict the usage of the software to an individual device or CPU!

8.5.1.4 Service on demand

There has been a trend within the IT industry for suppliers to offer IT applications 'on demand', where access is given to the application for a period of demand and then severed when it is no longer needed – and charged on the basis of the time spent using the application. This type of offering may be offered by some ITSM tool suppliers – which could be attractive to smaller organizations or if the tools in question are very specialised and used relatively infrequently.

An alternative to this is where the use of a tool is offered as part of a specific consultancy assignment (e.g. a specialist Capacity Management consultancy, say, who may offer a regular but relatively infrequent Capacity Planning consultancy package and provide use of the tools for the duration of the assignment). In such cases the licence fees are likely to be included as part of, or as an addendum to, the consultancy fee.

A further variation is where software is licensed and charged on an agent/activity basis. An example of this is interrogation/monitoring and/or simulation software (e.g. agent software that can simulate pre-defined customer paths through an organization's website, to assess and report upon performance and availability). Such software is typically charged on the basis of the number of agents, their location and/or the amount of activity generated.

In all cases, full investigations of the licensing structure must be investigated and well understood during the procurement investigations and well before tools are deployed – so that the ultimate costs do not come as any sort of surprise.

8.5.2 Deployment

Many ITSM tools, particularly Discovery and Event Monitoring tools, will require some client/agent software deploying to all target locations before they can be used. This will need careful planning and execution – and should be handled through formal Release and Deployment Management (see Service Transition publication).

Even where network deployment is possible, this needs careful scheduling and testing – and records must be maintained throughout the rollout so that support staff have knowledge of who has been upgraded and who has not. Some form of interim Change Management may be necessary and the CMS should be updated as the rollout progresses.

It is often necessary for a reboot of the devices for the client software to be recognized – and this needs to be arranged in advance, otherwise long delays can occur if staff do not generally switch off their desktops overnight.

There may be particular problems deploying to laptops and other portable equipment and special arrangements may be necessary for staff to log on and receive the new software.

8.5.3 Capacity checks

Some Capacity Management may be necessary in advance to ensure that all of the target locations have sufficient storage and processing capacity to host and run the new software – any that cannot will need upgrading or replacing, and lead times for these actions need to be included in the plans.

The capacity of the network should also be checked to establish whether it can handle the transmission of management information, the transmission of log files and the distribution of clients' and also possibly software and configuration files.

8.5.4 Timing of technology deployment

Care is needed to ensure that tools are deployed at the appropriate time in relation to the organization's level of ITSM sophistication and knowledge. If tools are deployed too soon, they may be seen as an immediate panacea and any necessary action to change processes, working practices or attitudes may be hindered or overlooked.

A tool alone is usually not enough to make things work better. There is an old adage: 'A fool with a tool is still a fool!'

The organization must first examine the processes that the tool is seeking to address and also ensure that staff are 'bought in' to the new processes and way of working and have a adopted a 'service culture'.

However, tools can and often do make things a reality for many people – they are tangible and technical staff can immediately see how the new processes can work and how they may improve their way of working.

Some processes just cannot be done without adequate tooling, so there is a careful balance to be made to ensure tools are introduced when they are needed – but not before!

Similarly, care is needed to ensure that training in any tools is provided at the correct point – not too early or knowledge will diminish or be lost, but early enough so that staff can be formally trained and fully familiarize themselves with the operation of the tools well in advance of live deployment. Additional training should be planned

for an additional period when the tools go live and into the future, as needed.

8.5.5 Type of introduction

A decision is needed on what type of introduction is needed – whether to go for a 'Big Bang' introduction or some sort of phased approach. As most organizations will not start from a 'green field' situation, and will have live services to keep running during the introduction, a phased approach is more likely to be necessary.

In many cases a new tool will be replacing an older, probably less sophisticated, tool and the switchover between the two is another factor to be planned.

This will often involve deciding what data needs to be carried forward from the old tool to the new one – and this may require significant reformatting to achieve the required results. Ideally this transfer should be done electronically – but in some cases a small amount of re-keying of live data may be inevitable and should be factored into the plans.

Caution: older tools generally relied on more manual entry and maintenance of data so if electronic data migration is being used, an audit should be performed to verify data quality.

Where data transfer is complicated or time consuming to achieve, an alternative might be to allow a period of parallel running – with the old tool being available for an initial period alongside the new one, so that historical data can be referenced if needed. In such cases it will be prudent to make the old tool 'read-only' so that no mistakes can be made by logging new data in the old tool.

Complete details on the Release and Deployment Management process can be found in the Service Transition publication.

Challenges, Critical Success Factors and risks

9

9 Challenges, Critical Success Factors and risks

9.1 CHALLENGES

There are a number of challenges faced within Service Operation that need to be overcome. These include those set out in this section.

9.1.1 Lack of engagement with development and project staff

Traditionally, there has been a separation between Service Operation staff and those staff involved in developing new applications or running projects that will eventually deliver new functionality into the operational environment.

This separation was originally deliberate and driven by the desire to prevent collusion and avoid potential security risks (in some organizations it is still a legislative requirement). However, instead of using this separation of duties to create positive contributions, in many organizations it is a source of rivalry and political manoeuvring.

All too often, ITSM is seen as something that has been initiated in the operational areas and is nothing to do with development or projects.

This view is very damaging as the appropriate time to be thinking of Service Operation issues is at the outset of new developments or projects – when there is still time to include these factors in the planning stages.

The Service Design and Service Transition publications describe the steps needed to ensure that IT Operations issues are considered from the outset of new developments and projects.

Anecdotes

One organization uses an 'Operation Transition-In Policy' to ensure that services being deployed have had the appropriate level of input from the operational teams. This is basically a policy that clearly shows under what circumstances an application is 'ready' to transition into Operations. This helped with communication to development and project teams and also provided a clear set of guidelines on how to work with the operational teams.

Another organization uses Operations Use Cases to get development teams to include requirements that should be fulfilled by the application to be run in production under the control of Operations personnel.

9.1.2 Justifying funding

It is often difficult to justify expenditure in the area of Service Operation, as money spent in this sphere is often regarded as 'infrastructure costs' – with nothing new to show for the investment.

The Service Strategy publication discusses how to ensure a Return on Investment and eliminate the perception of investment as a purely Infrastructure 'overhead'. Good guidance is offered on how to justify investment.

In reality, many investments in ITSM, particularly in the Service Operation areas, can save money and show a positive Return on Investment – as well as resulting improvement in service quality. Some examples of potential areas of savings include:

- Reduced software licence costs through the better management of licences and deployed copies
- Reduced support costs due to fewer incidents and problems and reduced resolution times
- Reduced headcount through workforce rationalization, supporting roles and accountability structures
- Less 'lost business' due to poor IT service quality
- Better utilization of existing infrastructure equipment and deferral of further expenditure due to better capacity management
- Better-aligned processes, leading to less duplication of activities and better usage of existing resources.

9.1.3 Challenges for Service Operation Managers

The following is a list of some of the challenges that Managers in Service Operation should expect to face. There is no easy solution to these challenges, mainly because they are by-products of the organization culture and the decisions made during the process of deciding the organizational structure. The purpose of including the list is to ensure that Service Operation Managers are conscious of them and can create a plan to deal with them.

The differences between Design activities and Operational activities will continue to present challenges. This is for a number of reasons, including the following:

- Service Design may tend to focus on an individual service at a time, whereas Service Operation tends to focus on delivering and supporting all services at the same time. Operation Managers should work closely with Service Design and Service Transition to provide the Operation perspective to ensure that design and transition outcomes support the overall operational needs.

- Service Design will often be conducted in projects, while Service Operation focuses on ongoing, repeatable management processes and activities. The result of this is that operational staff are often not available to participate in Service Design project activities, which in turn results in IT services that are difficult to operate, or which do not include adequate manageability design elements. In addition, once project staff have finished the design of one IT Service they could move onto the next project and not be available to support difficulties in the operational environment. Overcoming this challenge requires Service Operation to plan for its staff to be actively involved in design projects, to resource the transition activities and participate in Early Life Support of services introduced in the operational environment.

- The two stages in the lifecycle have different metrics, which encourages Service Design to complete the project on time, to specification and in budget. In many cases it is difficult to forecast what the service will look like and how much it will cost after it has been deployed and operated for some time. When it does not run as expected, IT Operations Management is held responsible. While this challenge will always be a reality in Service Management, this can be addressed by active involvement in the Service Transition stage of the lifecycle. The objective of Service Transition is to ensure that designed services will operate as expected and the Operations Manager can provide the knowledge needed to Service Transition to assess, and remedy, issues before they become issues in the operational environment.

- Service Transition that is not used effectively to manage the transition between the Design and Operation phases. For example, some organizations may only use Change Management to schedule the deployment of changes that have already been made – rather than testing to see whether the change will successfully make the transition between Design and Operation. It is imperative that the practices of Service Transition are followed and organization policies to prevent poorly managed Change practices are in place. Operation, Change and Transition Managers must have the authority to deny any changes into the operational environment, without exception, that are not thoroughly tested.

These challenges can only be dealt with if Service Operation staff are involved in Service Design and Transition, and this will require that they are formally tasked and measured to do this. Roles identified in the Service Design processes should be included in Technical and IT Application Management staff job descriptions and their time allocated on a project-by-project basis.

Another set of challenges relates to measurement. Each alternative structure will introduce different combinations of items that are easy or difficult to measure. For example measuring the performance of a device or team could be relatively easy, but determining whether that performance is good or bad for the overall IT Service is another matter altogether. A good Service Level Management process will help to resolve this, but this means that Service Operation teams must be an integral part of that process (see Continual Service Improvement publication).

A third set of challenges relates to the use of Virtual Teams. Traditional, hierarchical management structures are becoming inadequate because of the complexity and diversity of most organizations. A management paradigm (Matrix Management) has emerged where employees report to different sources for different tasks. This has resulted in a complex web of accountability and an increased risk of activities falling through the cracks. On the other hand, it also enables the organization to make skills and knowledge available where they are most needed to support the business. Knowledge Management and the mapping of authority structures will become increasingly important as organizations expand and diversify. This is discussed in the ITIL Service Strategy publication.

One of the most significant challenges faced by Service Operation Managers is the balancing of many internal and external relationships. Most IT organizations today are complex and as services become more commoditized there is an increased use of value networks, partnerships and shared services models. While a significant advantage to dynamically evolving business needs, this increases the complexity of managing services cohesively, efficiently and providing the invisible seam between the customer and the intricate web of how services are actually delivered. A Service Operation Manager should invest in relationship management knowledge and skills to help deal with the complexity of this challenge.

9.2 CRITICAL SUCCESS FACTORS

9.2.1 Management support

Senior and Middle Management support is needed for all ITSM activities and processes, particularly in Service Operation.

Senior Management support is critical for obtaining and maintaining adequate funding and resourcing. Rather than seeing Service Operation as a 'black hole' for investment, Senior Management should quantify and champion the benefits of good Service Operation. They should also be fully informed of the dire results that can occur because of poor Service Operation.

Senior Management must provide visible support during the launch of new Service Operation initiatives (such as through appearances at seminars, signatories to memos and announcements, etc.) and their ongoing support must be equally well demonstrated. Entirely the wrong messaging can be given if a senior manager fails to turn up to an important project meeting or launch seminar. Even worse are senior managers who support the initiative verbally, but abuse their authority to encourage circumvention of the Service Operation practice.

Senior Managers should also empower the Middle Managers who will be directly responsible for Service Operation. Supporting the initiative publicly, but then overriding budget requirements or necessary changes, will harm both the implementation and ongoing Service Operation initiative.

Middle Managers must also provide the necessary support – and in particular this should be demonstrated by their actions. If a Middle Manager is seen to be circumventing or overriding an agreed procedure (e.g. implementing a change that has not been through the Change Management process) then this gives the clear message that others can do the same – and that the procedure is worthless and can be ignored by all. Middle Managers

should go out of their way to make their support known, not just by their words but also by their actions and adherence to the organization's agreed processes and procedures.

Middle Managers should also give their full support to hiring staff to support the process, instead of accepting the need for formalized Service Operation and then simply increasing the workload of existing staff to get it done.

9.2.2 Business support

It is important that the Business Units also support Service Operation. This level of support can be far better achieved if the Service Operation staff involve the business in all of their activities and are open in their reporting of both successes and failures – and their efforts to improve.

It is equally important that the Business Units understand, accept and carry out the role they play in Service Operation. Good service requires good customers! Adhering to the policies, processes and procedures, such as using the Service Desk for logging all requests, is a direct responsibility of the customer to support and promote within the business.

Regular communications with the business to understand their concerns and aspirations and to give feedback on efforts to meet their needs are essential in building the correct relationships and ensuring ongoing support.

Also the business should agree to the costs for implementing Service Operation and understand the return on the investment, unless this has already been agreed as part of the Design process.

9.2.3 Champions

ITSM projects and the resulting ongoing practice (performed by Service Operation staff) are often more successful if one or more 'champions' are forthcoming who can lead others through their enthusiasm and commitment for ITSM.

In some cases these champions may be senior managers who are leading from the top. But champions can also be successful if they come from other tiers of the organization. One or two junior staff can still have a significant beneficial influence on a successful conclusion.

Champions are often created or heavily influenced through formal Service Management training, particularly at more advanced levels where the potential benefits to an organization, and to the individuals who make a career path in Service Management, can be fully explored.

It should be noted that champions emerge over time. They cannot be created or appointed. Often it is users or customers who provide the most help in creating good Service Management processes as they are acutely aware of needed improvements from a business perspective. It is important to recognize that these are usually highly motivated staff who often voluntarily take on the greatest workloads. If their input is to be most effective they must be given time to work as the champion.

9.2.4 Staffing and retention

Having the appropriate number of staff with the appropriate skills is critical to the success of Service Operation. Some challenges that need to be overcome include the following:

- Projects for new services are usually quite good about specifying required new skills, but often underestimate the number of staff required and how to retain the new skills. See paragraph 9.2.1 for some ideas on how to facilitate better communication about requirements.

- Scarcity of resources who have a good understanding of Service Management. Having good technical people is necessary, but there needs to be a number of key people who are able to move between technology issues and service issues.

- Since these resources are fairly scarce it is quite common to train them, only to have them resign and join another company for a better salary. Clear career paths and good incentives should be part of every Service Management initiative.

- Attempting to assign too much, too soon, to existing staff. Achieving efficient Service Operation will take time, but if approached correctly it will be achieved. Unfortunately, some managers try to expedite the savings by assigning the interim work of implementing the new processes and tools to existing, very busy, staff. Invariably either the project fails, or service suffers and sometimes valuable staff will leave. Successful Service Management projects often require a short-term investment in either temporary staff or contractors, and this should not be underestimated.

9.2.5 Service Management training

Adequate training and awareness can have much wider overall benefits. As well as creating champions of a few, it can be used to win the 'hearts and minds' of many. Service Operation staff must all be aware of the consequences of their actions, both good and bad, on the

organization – and all must be instilled with a 'Service Management culture'.

It is possible to have the finest Service Operation practice and tools in the world – but Service Management will not be successful unless the people are also attuned to the overall Service Management objectives. Buy-in and support of all staff are therefore very important – and the role of training and awareness, and even formal qualifications that benefit the individual, should not be underestimated.

Training required for successful Service Management includes:

- Training IT staff on the processes that have been implemented. This will include generic training so that they understand the concepts fully, as well as training specially targeted at the organization's own processes

- Training on 'soft' or 'people' skills, especially for those staff in customer-facing positions

- Training about understanding the business, and the importance of achieving a service culture

- Where tools have been implemented, training on how to use and manage those tools

- Also, customers and users need appropriate training on how to work with IT – access services, request changes, submit requests, use tools, etc.

9.2.6 Suitable tools

Many Service Operation processes and activities cannot be performed effectively without adequate support tools (as outlined in Chapter 7). Senior management must ensure that funding for such tools is included in ongoing budgets and support their procurement, deployment and ongoing maintenance.

9.2.7 Validity of testing

The quality of IT services that can be provided in Service Operation is dependent upon the quality of systems and components delivered into the operational environment.

The quality level will be significantly enhanced if adequate and complete testing of new components and releases is carried out in good time. Documentation should also be tested for completeness and quality.

This requires a comprehensive and realistic testing environment to be in place for all systems/components – which mirrors the operational environment in terms of volume as well as characteristics. There should be independent testers wherever possible. Funding for such testing environments is essential if high-quality services are to be achieved.

Additionally, sufficient time and effort are needed to ensure that testing is properly planned and designed – and adequate time is included for testing, and re-testing should some parts fail! The best way to ensure this is by following the guidance in the Service Transition publication.

9.2.8 Measurement and reporting

A clear definition is needed of how things will be measured and reported (as outlined in Appendix B) so that all staff have clear targets to aim for and IT and Business Managers are able to quickly and easily review progress and pinpoint any areas for attention.

9.3 RISKS

Failure to meet the challenges already described in section 9.1 or to address the Critical Success Factors outlined in section 9.2 are obvious risks – but others are described as set out below.

9.3.1 Service loss

The ultimate risk to the business of weaknesses in Service Operation is the loss of critical IT services with subsequent adverse impact on its employees, customers and finances. In extreme cases there may be potential loss to life and limb where the IT services affected are used for critical health or safety purposes – such as emergency vehicle deployment or health scanning, etc.

9.3.2 Risks to successful Service Operation

The risks to achieving successful Service Operation are numerous – and in many cases are the opposite of the Critical Success Factors as described earlier – but also include:

- **Inadequate funding and resources**: Funding must be justified, allocated and held in reserve for its original purpose.
- **Loss of momentum**: Where staff see Service Management as 'flavour of the month' rather than permanently changing the way they work for the future, any impetus is lost as a result: it must be made clear from the outset that a new way of working is required. Also, mechanisms should be in place to ensure that the initiative survives organizational changes.

- **Loss of key personnel**: Sometimes the loss of one or two key personnel can have a severe impact: to try to minimize this effect, organizations should seek to cross-train staff and reduce dependencies upon individuals. This is especially true in less mature organizations where knowledge has still not been formalised into processes, documents and tools. These organizations tend to be dependent on 'heroic' efforts of a few knowledgeable people, and are devastated when they leave.
- **Resistance to change**: Sometimes people object to new things and are reluctant to take them on board. Education, training, communication and highlighting benefits will help.
- **Lack of management support**: This often occurs among Middle Managers, who may not see the overall vision or gain the hands-on benefits that more junior staff may gain. See paragraph 9.2.1 for more information on this, but managers need to support Service Management and participate in the appropriate phases and processes of Service Design, Transition and Operation to provide tangible support.
- If the initial **design is faulty**, a successful implementation will never give the required results – and redesign will ultimately be necessary.
- In some organizations Service Management can be viewed with **suspicion** by both IT and the business. IT staff see it as an attempt to control them, while the business perceives it as an attempt by IT to gain more funding without actually improving anything. The benefits of Service Management should be clearly articulated for all stakeholders.
- **Differing customer expectations**. While operational staff are encouraged to execute against standards, customer and user expectations sometimes differ. In other cases one customer may have paid more for a superior service, but when a user from a different area sees the superior service, they feel cheated. This problem should be resolved through clear SLM and careful communication during Service Design. Complaints of this nature should be taken up through Continual Service Improvement processes and should not simply involve Service Operation automatically increasing service upon request.

Afterword

Afterword

A simple truth must guide us all in Service Operation. Business and technology will continue to evolve into the future. What was innovative last year is common this year. What is best practice today will be common tomorrow. Achieving excellence in Service Operation requires flexibility, balance and good judgement in the use of ITIL practices. The guidance in this publication is a key to achieving knowledge, wisdom, future vision and the ability to balance today's business needs and tomorrow's demand.

Common, good, best and future practices all contribute to the goal of service excellence. ITIL provides these as the basis for guiding you toward this goal.

Stability in a changing world is the reality for Service Providers. Those who excel, and remain the best of breed, understand this and know that the way to achieve is to adapt, learn, innovate and lead.

The Service Operation publication is an integral part of an overall ITSM Lifecycle practice, Used together, the ITIL Practice for Service Management forms a powerful tool in the hands of any Service Provider.

Appendix A: Complementary industry guidance

A

Appendix A: Complementary industry guidance

When ITIL was first introduced in the 1980s, there was little else available in terms of non-proprietary guidance on ITSM best practice.

Today, there are other frameworks or methodologies that have valid contributions to make in this area, that complement and have synergy with ITIL and which can be of assistance to Service Operation.

A1   COBIT

The COBIT framework, produced by the Information Systems Audit and Control Association (ISACA) and managed by the IT Governance Institute, provides a very useful framework of guidance for IT audit and security personnel.

The current version of COBIT, edition 4, includes 34 High Level Control Objectives, 13 of which are grouped under the 'Deliver and Support Domain', which maps quite closely onto ITIL's Service Operation phase. These are entitled:

- DS1 Define and manage service levels.
- DS2 Manage third-party services.
- DS3 Manage performance and capacity.
- DS4 Ensure continuous service.
- DS5 Ensure systems security.
- DS6 Identify and allocate costs.
- DS7 Educate and train users.
- DS8 Manage service desk and incidents.
- DS9 Manage the configuration.
- DS10 Manage problems.
- DS11 Manage data.
- DS12 Manage the physical environment.
- DS13 Manage operations.

Some aspects of Service Operation are also touched upon in some of the control objectives within other domains – but the vast majority of what COBIT has to say about the 'live operation' phase of IT is contained in the abovementioned control objectives.

COBIT is primarily aimed at auditors, so has an emphasis on what should be audited and how, rather than including detailed guidance for those who are operating the

processes that will be audited – but it has a lot of valid material which organizations may find useful.

It should be noted that COBIT and ITIL are not 'competitive' nor are they mutually exclusive – on the contrary, they can be used in conjunction as part of an organization's overall managerial and governance framework. ITIL provides an organization with best-practice guidance on how to manage and improve its process to deliver high-quality, cost-effective IT services. COBIT provides guidance on how these processes should be audited and assessed to determine whether they are operating as intended and giving optimum benefit for the organization.

For a more complete overall picture, organizations may wish to read and become familiar with what COBIT has to say alongside their reading and understanding of ITIL. Further details of the standard can be found via ISACA at www.isaca.org

A2   ISO/IEC 20000

In December 2005 the International Standards Organization launched a formal international standard, ISO/ISE 20000, against which organizations can seek independent accreditation for ITSM. This was preceded by a British Standard, BS15000, which was originally introduced in 2000 and under which some organizations became accredited, but was superseded by ISO/ISE 20000 and accreditations were carried over.

While ISO/IEC 20000 initially mapped to the prior Service Support and Service Delivery publications of ITIL, the standard continues to map well to ITIL today and also covers IT Security, Business Relationship Management and Supplier Management.

For organizations seeking formal accreditation to ISO/IEC 20000, so as to get external, international recognition for the success of their ITSM processes, there will be a significant involvement by Service Operation staff in preparing for and undergoing the formal surveillance necessary to achieve the standard.

Further details of the standard can be found via the itSMF at www.itsmf.com or the ISO at www.iso.org

A3 CMMI

The Capability Maturity Model® Integration (CMMI) is a process improvement approach developed by the Software Engineering Institute (SEI) of Carnegie Mellon University. CMMI provides organizations with the essential elements of effective processes. It can be used to guide process improvement across a project, a division, or an entire organization. CMMI helps integrate traditionally separate organizational functions, set process improvement goals and priorities, provide guidance for quality processes and provide a point of reference for appraising current processes. For more information, see http://www.sei.cmu.edu/cmmi/

A number of IT consultancy organizations have built the maturity model into their ITSM assessment services as a way of assisting organizations prepare for and judge process improvements – including those in the Service Operation area. Organizations may wish to use some form of the model to help drive their path towards independent ISO/ISE 20000 accreditation.

A4 BALANCED SCORECARD

A new approach to strategic management was developed in the early 1990s by Drs. Robert Kaplan (Harvard Business School) and David Norton. They named this system the 'Balanced Scorecard'. Recognizing some of the weaknesses and vagueness of previous management approaches, the balanced scorecard approach provides a clear prescription as to what companies should measure in order to 'balance' the financial perspective. The Balanced Scorecard suggests that the organization is viewed from four perspectives, and it is valuable to develop metrics, collect data and analyse it relative to each of these perspectives:

- The Learning and Growth Perspective
- The Business Process Perspective
- The Customer Perspective
- The Financial Perspective.

Some organizations may choose to use the Balanced Scorecard method as a way of assessing and reporting their IT quality performance in general and their Service Operation performance in particular.

Further details are available through the Balanced Scorecard User Community at www.scorecardsupport.com

A5 QUALITY MANAGEMENT

There are distinct advantages of tying an organization's ITSM processes, and Service Operation processes in particular, to its quality management system. If an organization has a formal quality management system such as ISO9000, Six Sigma, TQM etc. then this can be used to assess progress regularly and drive forward agreed service improvement initiatives through regular reviews and reporting.

Many organizations have used a regular annual audit or external assessment as a way of determining the required improvements – and then their Quality Management system to drive through the specific programmes of work.

A6 ITIL AND THE OSI FRAMEWORK

At around the time that ITIL v1 was being written, the International Standards Organization launched an initiative that resulted in the Open Systems Interconnection (OSI) framework. Since this initiative covered many of the same areas as did the ITIL team, it is not surprising that they covered much of the same ground.

However, it is also not surprising that they classified their processes differently, used different terminology, or used the same terminology in different ways. To confuse matters even more, it is common for different groups in an organization to use terminology from both ITIL and the OSI framework.

Although it is not in the scope of this publication to explore the OSI framework, it has made significant contributions to the definition and execution of ITSM programmes and projects around the world. It has also caused a great deal of debate between teams that do not realize the origins of the terminology that they are using.

For example, some organizations have two Change Management departments – one following the ITIL Change Management process and the other using the OSI's Installation, Moves, Additions and Changes (IMAC) model. Each department is convinced that it is completely different from the other, and that they perform different roles. Closer examination will reveal that there are several areas of commonality.

In Service Operation, the management of Known Errors may be mapped to Fault Management. There is also a section related to Operational Capacity Management, which can be related to the OSI's concept of Performance Management.

Appendix B: Communication in Service Operation

B

Appendix B: Communication in Service Operation

B1 ROUTINE OPERATIONAL COMMUNICATION

Most communication in Service Operation has to do with ensuring that all teams and departments are able to execute the standard activities involved in delivering IT services and managing the IT infrastructure.

Serious consideration should be given during Service Design to defining the content, type and format of communication that is required to operate IT services.

Table B.1 Communication requirements in IT services

Purpose	■ To coordinate the regular activities of Service Operation at all levels.
	■ To ensure that all staff are aware of the scheduled activity at all times and that they are aware of any changes or initiatives that may affect the normal operation of the IT environment
Frequency	This type of communication is regular and is communicated in daily, weekly and monthly cycles
Role Players	■ All managers and staff involved in Service Operation
	■ All process managers for processes executed by Service Operation staff – especially Change, Incident and Problem Management
	■ Customers and users
	■ Vendor staff involved in Service Operation
Content	■ Summarize events since the previous communication to ensure that everyone is aware of any follow-up that needs to occur. Also to ensure that all batches have completed and the teams or departments are ready for standard operational activity
	■ A report on the health of major systems
	■ Inform Operations Management staff of any news or events that may effect operations that period
	■ Discuss any outstanding problems or incidents and ensure that an action plan is in place for each
	■ Discuss the schedule of changes that are expected to be made during the day, together with a briefing of potential incidents that may occur as a result and the appropriate action to be taken. This should not be confused with the CAB meeting. This is an opportunity to check whether changes that were agreed and scheduled by the CAB, or through a Change Model, are still on track
	■ Any planned maintenance or other outages that have been scheduled for the next operational period
	■ Announcement of the results of any Post Mortem or Crisis meetings that were held since the previous communication
	■ Announcement or reminder of training that may be available over the next week or month to give staff and their supervisors time to schedule the training into the Operations Schedule
Context/sources	■ Operations Logs
	■ Incident Reports
	■ Problem Reports
	■ Maintenance Schedules
	■ Change Schedule

B2 COMMUNICATION BETWEEN SHIFTS

Not all organizations work in shifts, but for those who do, Table B.2 will summarize the communication that needs to take place between shifts.

Table B.2 Communication requirements between shifts

Purpose	This communication ensures that the handover between outgoing and incoming shifts is smooth and also makes the new shift aware of any potential difficulties. They also ensure that the new shift is aware of any tasks that need to be completed.
Frequency	At the handover of every shift
Role Players	■ Shift leaders of each shift ■ Staff from each shift who perform similar tasks ·
Content	■ A summary report on operations undertaken during the previous shift ■ A summary of all exceptions and alerts that were resolved during the shift ■ Details of any outstanding exceptions and alerts, with information about all actions taken to the current point and any information about anticipated future actions (e.g. a vendor is expected to be on site to provide support during the next four hours)·
Context/sources	Communication between shifts will usually be based on the following sources:· ■ Shift logs ■ Shift Leader's report ■ Interpersonal verbal or electronic 'chat' communication where shift personnel are in different facilities

B3 PERFORMANCE REPORTING

Performance Reporting in the context of communication refers to three main areas, as set out below.

IT Service Performance

This category of Performance Reporting is generally done as part of SLM and is covered in the Continual Service Improvement publication. However, there is a very important aspect of Service Reporting that concerns Service Operation, namely that it is the Service Operation teams or departments that are required to record and communicate the information that goes into these reports.

However, Service Operation staff are not in the best position to decide on the content, format and frequency of Service Performance Reporting. The requirements for this type of communication have to be to be clearly defined during Service Design and refined during Continual Service Improvement.

Service Operation team or department performance

This is an 'internal' communication in that it takes place between the members of a team or department and their manager, or a process manager and the team that executes the process. People outside of these teams or departments should not be involved in this type of communication as it is aimed at managing people rather than measuring the quality of a service.

However, it is a common mistake for IT departments to communicate this type of information to customers as if it were the same as reporting on Service Quality. For example, a manager might report that their department solves 80% of all problems. As far as the average user is concerned, however, this information is irrelevant. They are more concerned with whether their IT Service performed as agreed. In addition, disclosing internal information to customers and users could be embarrassing for the Service Operation teams and departments and could result in high levels of interference from the business to 'correct' perceived problems.

Table B.3   Performance Reporting requirements: IT service

Purpose	To provide information to the groups responsible for IT Service reporting to customers and users, which they can use to demonstrate the achievement of service targets and as input to Service Level Review meetings The information can also be used as a basis for charging for IT services
Frequency	As defined in the SLAs and OLAs. This information is usually communicated regularly on a daily, monthly and quarterly basis.
Role Players	■ Service Operation teams and departments, usually IT Operations staff ■ SLM staff ■ Service Design teams (who help to define performance standards and refine these through Continual Service Improvement) ■ Continual Service Improvement teams, especially those tasked with Service Reporting
Content	Examples of the type of Service Performance information that needs to be communicated to enable reporting on Service Performance are: ■ Achievement of specific activities as defined in OLAs ■ Achievement of targets for delivery of specified outputs ■ Service or system availability achievements ■ Ability to meet Service Maintenance Objectives within targeted times and impact levels
Context/sources	■ Monitoring and reporting tools ■ Event Logs ■ Shift Logs

Table B.4   Performance Reporting requirements: Service Operation team or department

Purpose	There are three main purposes of Service Operation team or department Performance communication: ■ Proactively, to ensure that Service Operation staff are executing the activities required to deliver IT services and to support the IT Infrastructure ■ To detect potential issues with resource levels, capability and circumvention of procedures ■ To ensure that corrective action has been correctly implemented and adhered to
Frequency	There is no set frequency for this type of communication. Although some Performance Reports may be produced daily, weekly or monthly, most managers are involved in ongoing communication with their teams or departments as the situation requires. Under normal operating situations, this communication will tend to be less frequent than in situations where there is a high degree of change or where the organization is experiencing high numbers and severity of incidents
Role Players	■ Service Operation Managers ■ Service Operation staff ■ Performance issues may be escalated to the Service Manager or CIO
Content	■ Comparison between required and actual performance ■ Trends of performance over time ■ Specific reports of misconduct or failure to perform a required action
Context/sources	■ Regular performance reports, e.g. Incident Logs, maintenance records, process metrics ■ Interpersonal and verbal communication during working situations ■ Team or department meetings ■ Coaching by a team leader or manager ■ Investigation following a poor Service Report may initiate a series of communications in Service Operation ■ Individual Performance Appraisals, usually using (KPIs) documented in the individual's job description

Infrastructure or process performance

As with team or department performance, this is an 'internal' communication that takes place between the members of a team or department who are responsible for managing an infrastructure component or system, or the members of a process team. People outside of these teams should not be involved in this type of communication as it is aimed at managing people rather than measuring the quality of a service.

Table B.5   Performance Reporting requirements: infrastructure or process

Purpose	There are at least three purposes of this type of communication:· ■ To ensure normal operation of the infrastructure or a process ■ To detect potential issues with the infrastructure or process concerned ■ To ensure that corrective action has been taken and that it was effective
Frequency	The frequency of this type of communication will vary depending on the nature of the system(s) being managed or the process being executed. Some components of the infrastructure are more volatile and will require frequent communications and even meetings to ensure that it performs predictably. More stable components will simply require a confirmation that everything is still working as expected. Some processes have a requirement of frequent reporting and communication. For example, Incident Management may require updates every five minutes for a high-impact incident. Other processes do not need to communicate that frequently. For example Capacity Planning needs to communicate changes on a monthly or even quarterly basis.
Role Players	■ Staff who manage key CIs ■ Staff who execute processes ■ Process owners and technology managers ■ Potential escalation to more senior managers, the Service Manager
Content	■ Comparison between required and actual performance ■ Trends of performance over time ■ Specific reports of missed targets or unexpected levels of performance
Context/sources	■ Event Logs ■ System Performance Records ■ Process Performance Reports ■ Incident and Problem Records ■ Exception Reports and Audit Reports ■ Review with vendor ■ Service reporting may indicate a problem with one or more technology areas or processes

B4   COMMUNICATION IN PROJECTS

Service Operation staff are often involved in projects. This may be to provide input to a new design, or to assist in verifying utilization or throughput rates, or to assist in conducting tests of new or changed services. In other cases the projects may affect existing OLAs and their feedback will be required. It must be recognized that this involvement will add to the level of communication that these individuals will be receiving and transmitting. This will require additional time and focus, which should be allowed for by managers assigning resources to projects on a part-time basis.

Formal project communication tends to follow the cycle of project meetings. For example:

- Weekly or monthly project meetings will be held with the Project Manager and the individual team leaders
- A monthly status update will be sent to the project's Executive Sponsor and possibly other key stakeholders

- Exceptions and the result of quality assurance checks are reported into Project Assurance teams, who in turn will communicate the need for corrective action as necessary.

Inside each team, communication will be more focused on completing their tasks and will generally be more frequent than the project-wide communication.

There is likely to be a high level of less formal communication inside each team and also between teams to ensure that tasks are completed on time and promised resources are available when and where they are supposed to be. Extensive communication is also required as part of the handover from one team to another as the project moves from one stage or phase to another. An important rule of thumb is to document any communication that could potentially affect the outcome or the cost of the project.

Table B.6   Communication within projects

Purpose	Project communication as multiple purposes, including:
	■ To gain support from project stakeholders – this communication will focus on the scope, cost and benefits of the project and will seek to demonstrate an overall return on the project's investment
	■ To ensure that all members of the project team understand and are aligned to the objectives of the project
	■ To assign work to individuals or teams
	■ To schedule activities and ensure that resources are ready to begin their stage of the project
	■ To check on and report the progress of the project
	■ To detect and escalate potential exceptions or delays in the project
	■ To prepare project customers and audiences for the rollout of the solution being built
Frequency	The frequency, role players and content of communication will depend on the nature of the project and the type of Project Management methodology being used

Table B.7 Communication on handover of projects

Role Players	■ Project Manager and project administrative and coordination staff ■ Project Sponsor ■ Key Project Stakeholders (e.g. customers, IT Managers, Board members, users, etc.) ■ Project teams and individual contributors ■ Vendor sales and technical staff where the purchase of services or solutions are part of the project
Content	■ Gathering requirements for the solution being built by the project ■ Project scheduling ■ Project 'Marketing' information including Return on Investment or Business Case information ■ Status updates ■ Gathering information to complete a task ■ Events that could affect the scope, cost or timely completion of the project ■ Progress reporting within teams or between teams ■ Information about the results of testing ■ Notifications to teams or individuals that the project is approaching 'their' stage or activity and that they should make the appropriate preparations ■ Reporting on the successful completion of activities ■ Review of the overall success of the project ·
Context/sources	■ Project Charter ■ Project Budget ■ Statement of requirements ■ Project Schedule ■ Project meetings ■ Team meetings ■ Status and progress reports ■ Test reports ■ Customer sign-off documentation ■ Post-Implementation Review ·

B5 COMMUNICATION RELATED TO CHANGES

Change Management is covered in detail in the ITIL Service Transition publication and includes information about change communication. However, it is necessary to stress the nature of operational communication about changes.

Table B.8 Communication about changes

Purpose	To support the Change Management process by:· ■ Assessing the potential impact of and resources required for the change ■ Ensuring that each team is aware of the nature and schedule of changes that have been assigned to them ■ Building, testing and deploying changes in their environment ■ Ensuring that each team reports that progress on each change ■ Notifying Change Management that a change is ready for deployment ■ Backing out changes that were unsuccessful and communicating the results to Change Management ■ Assisting in the assessment of changes to ensure that they have been implemented correctly
Frequency	The frequency of communication related to changes is determined by the nature of the change and the times set forth in the Change Schedule. Most teams or departments will review changes on a daily or weekly basis. Each day they will discuss and prioritize all new changes assigned to them and report on the progress of changes they are working on. After each change they will report on the success of each change and ensure that any remedial action required is initiated.
Role Players	■ Change Manager, administrators and coordinators ■ Team-leaders, Department Heads, Shift Managers or Project Managers ■ Service Operation staff involved in building, testing and deploying changes (usually Technical, Application and IT Operations Management teams or department) ■ Managers of Test Environments and teams ■ Change or Release Deployment teams
Content	■ Requests for and authorization of changes ■ Reports on the feasibility of a change ■ Reports on the resources required to build, test or deploy a change ■ Change Activity Scheduling ■ Detailed descriptions of the change and the activities required of each team or department ■ Progress and status reporting of change activity ■ Test results ■ Exception Reports, including details of the execution of Back-out Plans
Context/sources	■ RFCs ■ Change Control communication (during daily or weekly operational meetings, or by e-mail, conference call or using the Change Management tools) ■ Change Advisory Board meetings ■ Release Plans ■ Projected Service Outage reports ■ Change Reviews

B6   COMMUNICATION RELATED TO EXCEPTIONS

In this context an exception refers to any occurrence that is outside normal or expected activity or performance. The most common form of exception is an Incident (which is covered in detail in section 4.2 of this publication). There are other exceptions that do not necessarily go through Incident Management, such as a process exception (which will be handled in the context of that process or by a Quality Assurance process); a team, department or individual whose performance is not up to standard (which will be handled through HR disciplinary procedures); or an exception to a vendor's contractual performance. Although these are not all directly related to Service Management, they will add overheads to the level of communication required of staff during the Service Operation phase.

Table B.9   Communication during exceptions

Purpose	Communication during or after exceptions is aimed at: ■ Informing the appropriate people of the exception ■ Assessing the significance, severity and impact of the exception ■ Ensuring that resources with the appropriate skills and seniority are involved in resolving the exception and taking action to prevent future recurrence ■ Providing updates to stakeholders that are affected by the exception
Frequency	This type of communication is reactive and ad hoc, in that it does not occur unless there is an identified exception or the risk of an exception. The frequency is thus directly proportional to the frequency of exceptions. Once an exception is detected, the frequency and content of communication will be determined by the impact, urgency and severity of the exception.
Role Players	The exact role players will depend on the type and extent of the exception, but could include: ■ Incident Management ■ The Service Desk ■ Problem Management ■ Process owners (if the exception relates to process performance) ■ Departmental managers or team leaders ■ SLM ■ Human Resource Management ■ Technology Managers and experts ■ Vendor account management staff ■ Vendor technical experts
Content	■ Description and assessment of the exception ■ Assessment of the impact. This will typically involve communication with the stakeholders who are affected by the exception ■ Estimation and then confirmation of the cost of resolution ■ A decision on what action will be taken ■ Communication of the decision taken. This is likely to be in a number of formats. For example the communication to customers is likely to contain an apology and a high-level overview of what is being done to resolve the exception. A communication to the people who are expected to resolve the exception will be more detailed and will contain clear actions and timelines ■ Confirmation that the exception has been resolved
Context/sources	■ Process Reviews ■ Change Reviews ■ Service Level Reviews ■ Events ■ Trend Analysis of processes, devices, team performance, etc. ■ Incident, Problem and Change Records ■ Customer satisfaction surveys.

B7 COMMUNICATION RELATED TO EMERGENCIES

Although ITIL specifies how to deal with urgent, high-impact situations such as disasters (IT Service Continuity Management) and Major Incidents (Incident Management), managers in the Service Operation phase will find themselves dealing with various types and scales of emergency not covered in these processes. It is important to note that this is not a separate process, rather it is a view of several processes and situations from a communication perspective.

Communication during emergencies is similar in purpose and content to communication during exceptions. The main differences are in the level of urgency and impact of the exception.

Emergency communications are usually initiated by the Incident Manager (see paragraph 4.2.5 for a discussion on Major Incidents) or by a senior IT Manager who has been designated as the escalation point for all such emergencies.

In the case where an IT Service Continuity Plan is invoked, this will include a detailed Communication Plan to be executed by the appropriate authority.

The Incident Manager or designated manager will often form a response team, and the communication is initiated and coordinated by this team.

Table B.10 Communication during emergencies

Purpose	The purpose of communication in an emergency is to immediately investigate and confirm the impact and severity of the Incident to confirm that it is indeed an emergency situation. It should also confirm that this Incident does not represent a disaster or any contingency covered in the IT Service Continuity Plans.
	As soon as the scope of the emergency has been identified, the team responsible for managing the situation will allocate resources to create an action plan and to begin resolving the emergency and restoring service.
Frequency	This type of communication does not occur unless there is a Major Incident or emergency situation.
	Once an exception is detected, the frequency and content of communication will be determined by the impact and severity of the exception, and potentially by a Service Recovery Plan.
Role Players	■ Incident Manager
	■ Senior Managers of groups responsible for the IT staff that will be required to resolve the situation
	■ Business managers and Executives (possibly including legal staff if the organization is exposed to potential legal action as a result of the incident)
	■ Customers and users
	■ IT Service Continuity Manager and Central Coordination team
	■ Senior vendor staff and managers (depending on the extent and nature of the situation)·
	■ Technical Management staff and managers
	■ Application Management staff and managers
	■ IT Operations Management staff and managers
Content	■ The nature and extent of the emergency
	■ Assessment of the impact. This will typically involve communication with the stakeholders who are affected by the exception
	■ Estimation and then confirmation of the cost of resolution
	■ A decision on what action will be taken
	■ Communication of the decision taken. This is likely to be in a number of formats. For example the communication to customers is likely to contain an apology and a high-level overview of what is being done to resolve the exception. A communication to the people who are expected to resolve the exception will be more detailed and will contain clear actions and timelines
	■ Confirmation that the exception has been resolved ·
Context/sources	■ Incident Record for Major Incidents
	■ Events
	■ Crisis or emergency meetings called by the Incident Manager, the designated manager, or the IT Service Continuity Manager

B8   COMMUNICATION WITH USERS AND CUSTOMERS

This section appears last, not because it is the least important, but because it incorporates several of the areas discussed above. An important principle in communicating with customers is that communication should not focus on internal aspects of Service Operation. The focus is on the customer or users' requirements and what IT is doing to meet them. This should not involve technical descriptions and detailed information about internal processes.

Table B.11 Communication with users and customers

Purpose	There are a number of reasons for user and customer communication in Service Operation. These include: ■ Ensuring that services have been delivered as agreed ■ Communication around fulfilling Service Requests ■ Reporting Incidents and keeping users and customers updated on their status until resolved ■ Notifying users and customers of changes that may impact them ■ Providing access to services ■ Dealing with potential security issues ■ Scheduling activities that involve users or customers, e.g. maintenance ■ Notification of special business events that require additional support or changed priorities ■ Review of customer and user satisfaction ■ Coordination during contingency situations ·
Frequency	Communication with users and customers is ongoing. The format and content of communication will be defined by the processes that are being executed. For example, communication about an Incident will be determined by the Incident Management process. Some communication will be formal and scheduled, e.g. providing reports on the performance of a service during a review meeting. Other communication will be formal, but ad hoc, e.g. communication about the status of an Incident
Role Players	The identity of the role players and their number will depend on which process is being executed, the type of situation that has occurred and the scope of what is being communicated, e.g. providing an update about the status of a Service Request will have a very different audience than when participating in a Service Level Review meeting
Content	The content of this communication will vary depending on the context. However, it is important to gear the communication to the audience. This means using service names rather than server or application names, being professional, avoiding technical jargon, not being condescending and treating customers and users with respect
Context/sources	The context of this communication is the day-to-day executing of operational activities and the delivery and support of services. Service Operation teams should not be communicating with customers or users on planning issues, strategy, design or testing – unless they have been assigned to a project team which is dealing with one of these areas

Appendix C:
Kepner and Tregoe

Appendix C: Kepner and Tregoe

Charles Kepner and Benjamin Tregoe developed a useful method to analyse problems. In this appendix, their method is presented as an example of a Problem Analysis method.

Kepner and Tregoe state that Problem Analysis should be a systematic process of problem solving and should take maximum advantage of knowledge and experience. They distinguish the following five phases for Problem Analysis (described further below):

- Defining the problem
- Describing the problem with regard to identity, location, time and size
- Establishing possible causes
- Testing the most probable cause
- Verifying the true cause.

Depending on time and available information, these phases can be realized to a greater or lesser extent. Even in situations where only a limited amount of information is available, or time pressure is high, it is worthwhile adopting a structured approach to Problem Analysis to improve the chances of success.

C1   DEFINING THE PROBLEM

Because the investigation is based on the definition of the problem, this definition has to state precisely which deviation(s) from the agreed service levels have occurred.

Often, during the definition of a problem, the most likely problem cause is already indicated. Take care not to jump to conclusions, which can guide the investigation in the wrong direction from the beginning.

In practice, problem definition is often a difficult task because of a complicated IT Infrastructure and non-transparent agreements on service levels.

C2   DESCRIBING THE PROBLEM

The following aspects are used to describe the problem, i.e. what the problem IS:

- **Identity**. Which part does not function well? What is the problem?
- **Location**. Where does the problem occur?
- **Time**. When did the problem start to occur? How frequently has the problem occurred?

- **Size**. What is the size of the problem? How many parts are affected?

The 'IS' situation is determined by the answers to these questions. The next step is to investigate which similar parts in a similar environment are functioning properly. With this, an answer is formulated to the question 'What COULD BE but IS NOT?' (Which parts could be showing the same problem but do not?).

It is then possible to search effectively for relevant differences in both situations. Furthermore, past changes, which could be the cause of these differences, can be identified.

C3   ESTABLISHING POSSIBLE CAUSES

The list of differences and changes mentioned above most likely hold the cause of the problem so possible causes can be extracted from this list.

C4   TESTING THE MOST PROBABLE CAUSE

Each possible cause needs to be assessed to determine whether it could be the cause of all the symptoms of the problem.

C5   VERIFYING THE TRUE CAUSE

The remaining possible causes have to be verified as being the source of the problem. This can only be done by proving this in one way or another – for example by implementing a change or replacing a part. Address the possible causes that can be verified quickly and simply first.

Appendix D:
Ishikawa Diagrams

Appendix D: Ishikawa Diagrams

The Ishikawa Diagram, also known as the Fishbone, Cause-and-Effect or Tree Diagram, is a tool used for systematically identifying and presenting all the possible causes of a particular problem on a chart. The technique is named after its developer, Kaoru Ishikawa (1915-89), a leader in Japanese quality control. An example is shown below.

The main goal is represented by the spine or trunk of the diagram and primary factors are represented as branches. Secondary factors are then added as stems, and so on. Creating the diagram stimulates discussion and often leads to increased understanding of a complex problem. These diagrams are extensively used in identifying solutions to systemic problems, such as identifying the cause of productivity loss on assembly lines, or lower customer satisfaction levels in a service organization.

The basic technique of developing these diagrams, together with a very simple example, is shown here. A problem-solving team will use the Ishikawa Diagram as follows:

1 Prepare a blank diagram in a format that can be viewed by the entire group. This could be a flipchart, board, projected through a data projector from a PC, etc.
2 Define the problem that the group is trying to solve in clear and specific terms and write it in the box at the 'fish head' box of the diagram.
3 Write the cause categories into the tips of the 'fish bones'. These should be fairly broad categories as the exact causes are not yet known. An example is shown in Figure D.1 in which the group is trying to find the cause for unacceptable levels of network downtime.

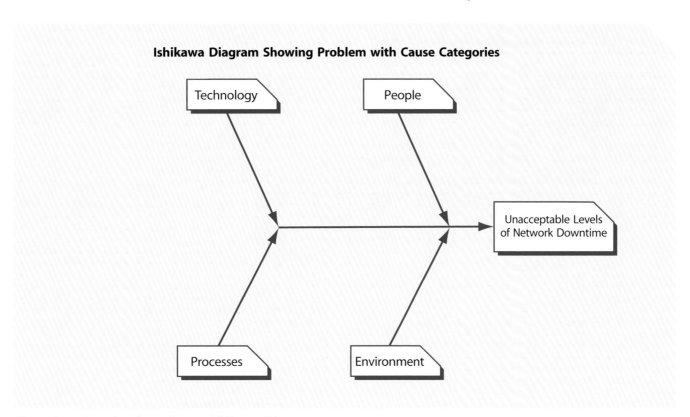

Ishikawa Diagram Showing Problem with Cause Categories

Figure D.1   Sample of starting an Ishikawa Diagram

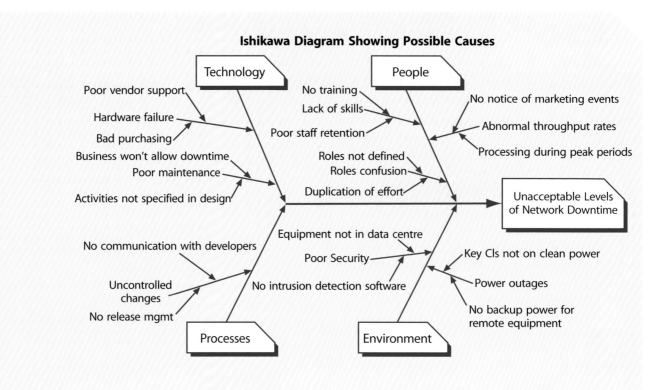

Figure D.2 Sample of a completed Ishikawa Diagram

4 Use brainstorming techniques to get participants to suggest possible causes, and note these on the relevant branch of the diagram. A simple diagram has been completed in Figure D.2.

5 Interpret the diagram. This could be done by ranking the top causes based on experience and available data. Once the top causes have been selected, each one will be investigated further according to its rank and priority

Appendix E:
Detailed description of Facilities Management

Appendix E: Detailed description of Facilities Management

The purpose of this appendix is not to provide a detailed explanation of all aspects of Facilities Management. Rather, it will highlight the most important activities to assist in positioning some of the other functions and in identifying where specific processes impact on good Facilities Management and vice versa.

Facilities Management will provide information to Configuration Management regarding the location and status of CIs, and will also be an integral part of Change Management, Capacity and Availability Planning and Service Continuity Management.

The main components of Facilities Management are as follows.

E1   BUILDING MANAGEMENT

Although many Building Management activities are outsourced or contracted to other suppliers, they are still the responsibility of Facilities Management. Typical activities include:

- **Cleaning**. This could be done by employees or by third parties. It is very important here to ensure that cleaning staff comply with all access control and confidentiality policies.
- **Waste disposal**, including separation of items for recycling, hazardous items (e.g. batteries, liquids and gases such as refrigerant for air-conditioning units), confidential documentation.
- **Installation of physical facilities**, such as cabling, power, raised floors, secure entry and exit systems, offices, furniture, etc.
- **Parking**. This should include allocation of staff and contractor parking, visitors' parking and parking for handicapped staff or visitors. Facilities management will also include documenting and enforcing any policies around who should park where.
- **Access Control and Security Monitoring**. This is covered in more detail in section E6 below and also in Appendix F.
- **Signage**, i.e. ensuring that the building can be found but is not obviously a key location worthy of attack.

E2   EQUIPMENT HOSTING

Facilities are not managed simply because they exist and are owned by an organization. They are managed so that the people and equipment they contain can be used for specific purposes. In the case of IT Facilities, such as Data Centres, this adds some very specific demands to the manager of that facility.

One of these is the hosting of IT equipment. This is not just a case of providing a room and allowing the Technical Management teams to install and manage equipment. Different types of equipment have very specific requirements of the facility in which it is housed, for example:

- Water-cooled equipment needs access to cool water – which has to be supplied by the facility
- The weight of equipment varies and has to be distributed so as not to place too much stress on the floor
- Electrical supply may vary for different types of equipment.

If equipment is simply placed in the Data Centre in the order in which it is received, it will be very difficult to find anything and staff may have to cross the floor several times to tend to similar equipment. This traffic jeopardizes the integrity and security of other equipment on the floor.

This means that Facilities Management has to own the responsibility of planning and designing the layout of the Data Centre for optimal access and security of the equipment that will be hosted there. At the same time, it should be remembered that this equipment is being used to deliver IT services, and any requirements for that service need to be taken into account in hosting the equipment. For example, Data Centre standards may have to be changed in order to accommodate a non-standard server.

In addition, most Data Centres also offer the following hosting activities:

- Receipt of new equipment
- Unpacking, configuring and installing standard equipment
- Producing and maintaining Data Centre layout diagrams

2f

■ Managing the schedule of any maintenance activity to equipment hosted in the Data Centre

■ Disposing of retired equipment.

From this list of activities, it is clear that Facilities Management should not be seen as a separate function, but very much part of the overall operation of IT in the organization.

E3   POWER MANAGEMENT

Power Management refers to managing the sourcing and utilization of power sources that are used to keep the facility functional. This definition of Power Management has a number of implications, which are discussed below.

Facilities Management's first task in managing power is to determine the power requirements for the facility. This includes defining:

■ What the power is going to be needed for – e.g. office space, equipment in the Data Centre, the cafeteria, etc.

■ When that power is going to be needed. Some operations require a consistent supply of electricity 24 hours a day. Others, such as office space, will use more electricity during the day and very little at night. Others only need electricity at a specific time

■ How much power is going to be needed

■ What type of power will be used. Although most organizations use electricity, in many locations the heating systems are dependent on natural gas.

Facilities Management will also be responsible for establishing a contract with utility companies, or in many cases the local authority or municipality that provides that service. This will include an agreed rate and a level of availability. This has become very important in locations where the electricity supply is variable due to lack of infrastructure or due to over-utilization by general consumers.

Facilities Management will be responsible for establishing standby power sources for power failures, disasters and other contingencies. This is generally in the form of Uninterruptible Power Supplies (UPSs) for key equipment, and also generators powered by an alternative energy source (usually diesel). Facilities Management is responsible not only for supplying these alternatives, but also for testing them, keeping supplies of the fuel and maintaining them.

It needs to be said that any alternative power source needs to be modelled and tested to ensure that it is able to handle the required demand and also that it will automatically be activated following a power failure.

Another key activity of Facilities Management is to manage the utilization of power. Traditionally, the role of Facilities Management was just to ensure that power was available. However, as natural resources become scarcer and expensive, more attention is being focused on techniques to manage utilization more responsibly.

One such approach is the dynamic management of power in Data Centres. The principle is that during peak processing periods, more computers will be used to do the work. As the workload reduces, the work is centralized onto fewer computers, while those that are not being utilized are powered down or placed into standby mode. This requires a significant integration between the activities of IT Operations Management, Technical Management and all the Service Design processes. This is discussed in more detail under the section about Data Centre strategies.

E4   ENVIRONMENTAL CONDITIONING AND ALERT SYSTEMS

Facilities Management ensures that physical conditions within the Data Centres or computer rooms are maintained at the correct levels for optimal IT Operations. These conditions include:

■ Temperature

■ Humidity

■ Air quality

■ Freedom from environmental risks, such as fire, flooding, etc.

Temperature is maintained through heating and cooling systems, as well as the layout of the equipment in the facility. This will require the following activities:

■ Ascertaining the heat output for CIs and their optimal operating temperature.

■ Identifying the total cooling requirement for all equipment in the facility as well as for specific items. For example, an air conditioner may be able to keep a Data Centre at a constant temperature, but there may be equipment that needs to be kept at a lower temperature.

■ Modelling the overall heating and cooling requirements as well as mapping specific areas in the facility that may be naturally warmer or cooler. This information is used to identify where the best location is for specific equipment. It is important to note that when new equipment is installed in a facility, it will change the mapping of cooler and warmer areas in the facility, hence the requirement for more sophisticated mapping and modelling techniques. These models will also need to take into account seasonal variances in temperature. For example, some facilities may need to be heated in winter and cooled in summer.

- Purchase and maintenance of air conditioning units with sufficient capacity, and maintaining these units regularly.
- Investing in backup air-conditioning units that can be used if a main unit fails, or to provide extra cooling capacity on exceptionally hot days (although this should be a rare exception – if the backup unit is used too frequently this implies that initial planning was inadequate).
- Ongoing monitoring of the temperature and adjustment of cooling settings according to changes in season and equipment layout. These monitors could be linked to the Operations Bridge, which would be able to respond to any significant deviation from normal temperatures.
- Identifying and avoiding 'obvious' errors, such as locating the heat output of a major server close to the intake of an air-conditioning unit; or preventing airflow by stacking manuals in 'free' space.

Similar steps should be taken to identify ideal humidity levels and specify whether dehumidifying equipment is required.

Smoke detection equipment is usually installed as part of the overall fire control strategy of the facility and is linked to automated fire-fighting systems. However, Facilities Management should not assume that an automated response to fire threats will be adequate. Smoke detection units should be linked to the Operations Bridge and any exceptions should be investigated.

Movement detection units should be installed in all unattended operating areas. These will ensure that unauthorized access is detected and reported to Facilities Security and possibly also the Operations Bridge. This will help to enforce proper scheduling of maintenance or installation activities.

Dust and particle detection can assist in maintaining air quality around systems that are particularly sensitive. Again, monitors should be routed to the Operations Bridge so that deviations can be investigated and corrected before any significant damage occurs.

There are also a number of other types of facilities monitoring, which are based on the location of the facility.

For example, building movement monitors installed in locations with high levels of seismic activity. These act as early warning systems to indicate that a system needs to be shut down or failed over to an alternative site before a significant earth tremor or earthquake affects sensitive equipment. Similar monitors and safeguards are also being installed in facilities where there is high electrical storm activity.

These systems are collectively referred to as Building Management Systems (BMSs), although as these tools are integrated, the term is being used to refer to a single integrated management system, rather than a loose collection of tools performing similar functions. Thought should be given to using monitoring tools that are integrated into, or at least consistent with, existing monitoring tools. (See Chapter 7 for more details on tools.)

E5 SAFETY

A major concern of Facilities Management is the safety of the people working in the building. Facilities Management is therefore responsible for understanding and enforcing compliance with relevant safety standards and legislation.

Safety is enforced in the following areas:

- Building design and construction
- Layout of the rooms and equipment in the facility
- Education of all personnel about safety standards in force in the facility
- Definition of evacuation procedures and routes and gathering points in the event of a fire or other life-threatening situation
- Posting notices and information regarding any safety information of which personnel need to be aware.

E6 PHYSICAL ACCESS CONTROL

This is a very important part of Facilities Management and has grown into a specialized field. As such, the content is summarized here for convenience, but discussed in detail in Appendix F.

The major components of Physical Access Control (as discussed in Appendix F) are:

- Assistance in defining and maintaining Physical Access Controls as part of the organization's Security Policies
- Maintenance of floor plans indicating which areas are restricted
- Installation and maintenance of physical access control devices

- Monitoring and control of access to facilities
- Security staffing
- Installation and maintenance of surveillance equipment
- Protection against social engineering.

E7 SHIPPING AND RECEIVING

Large facilities require special areas where delivery can be taken of furniture, computer equipment, racks, etc. This area needs to be secured so that delivery personnel do not gain access to the rest of the facility. There also needs to be a secure store near the receiving area where items can be stored until they can be moved to their final location.

A process needs to be in place to ensure that items to be shipped are accounted for and that only those items are removed by the delivery or dispatch contractor. Wherever possible, these items should be marshalled into the secure store in the shipping and delivery area before being dispatched. This will prevent unauthorized access to the facility.

Delivery and dispatch documentation has to be completed, inspected and signed for each consignment that is delivered or dispatched. A central log of all consignments should also be maintained as a control.

E8 INVOLVEMENT IN CONTRACT MANAGEMENT

Most facilities are supplied, managed and serviced by a number of entities. Although the actual contracts with these entities would be typically be managed by the appropriate commercial and legal departments, Facilities Management will play a key role in specifying and negotiating these contracts. Typical contracts include:

- **Management of leases for leased properties**. This is quite rare, as most organizations view their Data Centre as a key asset. Leasing such facilities would be seen as a risk because of the potential that the building is sold, the lessor goes out of business or the lessor does not fulfil the contract in terms of proper maintenance.
- **Leasing or maintenance of environmental equipment**, such as air-conditioning units, environmental monitoring and alert (e.g. smoke detection and fire-fighting or suppression equipment).
- **Building maintenance contracts**. These include servicing of elevators, flooring, plumbing and electrical supply.

- **Telecommunications facilities**. Although telecommunications is usually managed by a dedicated team or department or as part of Wide Area Networking, they are often dependent on third parties to supply and maintain telecommunication equipment located in or just outside the Data Centre. In many countries these are provided by government or para-state telecommunications organizations. Management of these types of contracts requires a special skill set.
- **Security services** for the provision of physical access control and armed response services.

A very important part of Contract Management is to ensure that all third-party staff are aware of, and comply with, the security policies of the organization. This includes physical access control, confidentiality and unauthorized use of the organization's facilities or equipment. Regular audits should be held to ensure that this is being enforced.

E9 MAINTENANCE

Facilities Management is responsible for coordinating all routine maintenance activity within the building. This refers to both building maintenance as well as to the maintenance of equipment in the Data Centre.

The reason for including equipment maintenance is simply to prevent the building being exposed to too much unusual activity at any one time. Multiple teams working in different places in the Data Centre at the same time represents a security and safety risk.

It is important to note that the actual maintenance of IT equipment is carried out by the Technical Management staff, but under the coordination of Change Management and Facilities Management.

The Facilities Manager should maintain a master schedule of all planned maintenance activity to ensure that maintenance activity is properly coordinated. This schedule forms part of the overall Change Management Change Schedule and is used to ensure that there are no conflicts between routine maintenance activity and the deployment of changes.

Appendix F:
Physical Access Control

F

Appendix F: Physical Access Control

Section 5.12 and Appendix E introduced the area of Physical Access Control as part of Facilities Management. This section provides a more detailed discussion of this area.

Information Security Management is responsible for defining and documenting all access control policies. These polices will identify all physical security measures that need to be taken and which groups of employee should have access to what type of facility. Facilities Management will ensure that these policies are properly enforced. Policies should include:

■ Which areas are restricted and to whom
■ What access controls will be put in place
■ Under what circumstances access will be allowed to specific restricted areas. For example, preventing all access to a Data Centre floor unless an authorized RFC number is typed into a keypad
■ How access control will be monitored
■ A statement of privacy policies and what information has to be known in order to permit access

■ Policies regarding the surveillance of personnel, e.g. what may be recorded, where and whether there are any exceptions.

Most organizations use multiple levels of access control, starting with access to the property, then moving to access to specific areas in the building and then to specific functions, equipment or rooms. Each level of security is enforced using different mechanisms and personnel, thus providing additional security.

All facilities should have a documented, current floor plan which indicates exactly which areas are restricted and which are not. This plan will also indicate which security measures are implemented and where. This will aid in security audits and also for the maintenance of access control equipment.

Access control devices need to be installed on all entrances and exits. The aim of these devices is to ensure that only authorized personnel have access to the restricted area. Although this appears at first glance to be a fairly straightforward subject, there are a number of items that need to be taken into account (See Table F.1).

Table F.1   Access control devices

Access control	Example	Advantages	Disadvantages
Mechanical	Lock and key	Stable and reliable Inexpensive	Requires key control Locks have to be replaced every time someone leaves the organization Can easily be compromised by anyone with knowledge of a few simple techniques
Code access	Mechanical (e.g. a pushbutton device mounted into the door) Electronic (e.g. a keypad used to arm or disarm a security alarm)	Stable Relatively inexpensive	Someone observing personnel using the device can obtain the code easily Code has to be changed every time someone leaves the organization People tend to write the code down
Electronic access	Key cards	Easy to use Can be used to track personnel's access Can be cancelled or changed centrally to suit changed requirements Can be cancelled even where staff do not return their card	Relatively expensive, although costs have decreased, and often cheaper than using human resources to physically guard each access point Dependent on power availability Can be compromised by people using specialized copying equipment

Table F.1   Access control devices *(continued)*

Access control	Example	Advantages	Disadvantages
Biometric	Retinal scanner or Voice analysis	Very reliable mechanism for identifying specific individuals Difficult to forge access More effective at countering social engineering	Dependent on the availability of power Requires more sophisticated access control systems Relatively expensive
Multiple access	Door with a key card. One person opens the door and permits access to any number of people accompanying them	Easy to move from one place to another, especially where groups are working together	Difficult to control 'Tailgating' Dependent on the security awareness of authorized personnel Extremely vulnerable to social engineering Should not be used in highly secured areas
Single access	Turnstile permits only one person to enter. The same key card can not be used to enter a second person	Easier to control access Prevents social engineering more effectively	Could become a bottleneck at peak hours Requires more intensive surveillance and staffing
Uni-directional access	Revolving door allowing only access or only exit. Typically used in airports where security personnel are only concerned about people entering the airport, but not about those exiting	Good for situations where there is no need to monitor what people take out, but where things they take in could cause significant damage	Requires more monitoring to ensure that people do not attempt to go through the wrong direction Typically uni-directional; also implies additional scanning equipment and surveillance
Bi-directional access	Access-controlled door	Good for general access to restricted areas	People exiting can provide access to unauthorized personnel moving in Could be a bottleneck (e.g. in bi-directional turnstiles people going out have to wait for people coming in)
Active	Requires action by personnel to gain access, e.g. swiping a key card or punching a code	Easier to control access More secure	Requires personnel to remember a code or to bring a key card
Passive	Passive detector unlocks an exit from inside whenever someone approaches	Provides safer exit in the event of a fire Does not require key cards for people moving to non-secure areas	Easy for unauthorized personnel to gain access simply by waiting outside the door Can be triggered from the outside by inserting something under the door and moving it within range of the sensor

As most physical access control mechanisms are not foolproof, it is important to ensure that access can be monitored and controlled. This is done by specialized security staff and by electronic surveillance equipment.

Since security is all about managing the access of people to a facility, it is fitting that people are used to enforce security measures. Larger organizations sometimes provide their own security staff, but most tend to outsource physical access control to specialized companies. This is usually for the following reasons:

- Security guards require specialized training and are usually subject to a different (almost military) disciplinary code from most company employees. This is often in conflict with the more commercial type of disciplinary code and is best managed by a different set of managers using a different management culture.
- External companies are less likely to be influenced by social engineering situations, as they have specialised training and are unlikely to understand some of the organization's internal nuances that could be used by an experienced social engineer.

Surveillance equipment is used to extend the effectiveness of both the physical access control mechanisms and the security personnel. It is important to note that no surveillance equipment can replace the presence of a trained, aware security guard, merely extend their effectiveness. Examples of commonly used surveillance equipment include:

- Video cameras to monitor key access points and also in less used access points, thus allowing a security guard to monitor several locations at once. These are usually taped and the videos stored for some time before being used again. This is to ensure that if any wrongdoing is discovered, the tapes can be used in the investigation. This means that the quality of images must be good enough to facilitate identification of people, but it also has to be in a format that makes it easy to store vast quantities of visual data.
- Access Event Logs. These typically log every entrance and exit by personnel using electronic access mechanisms.
- Passive detection units to detect the presence of personnel in an area that should not be staffed.
- Alarms that will notify security staff of unauthorized access or exit, often linked to an audible alarm.

No matter how secure the environment, it is dependent on the security awareness of the employees and contractors who work in the facility. Social engineering is still one of the most common breaches of physical security. Social engineering refers to the practice of gaining entry to a facility by using interpersonal and communication skills to convince someone to allow unauthorized access to a building, restricted area, restricted equipment and data; or to cabinets containing confidential documents.

Examples of social engineering include:

- Posing as a legitimate contractor or employee of the organization. The usual technique is to approach security personnel and state that they have forgotten their access card. An Access Log is signed and a visitor's card produced. There is often no real checking of whether the person is a legitimate employee, especially in busy reception areas.
- Posing as someone who has a reason to gain unauthorized access to the facility, e.g. a utilities worker or fire inspector.
- An ex-employee or contractor approaching people with whom they are familiar to allow them access.
- 'Tailgating', where a person simply follows an authorized employee through an entrance that they have opened.

Social engineering is best countered by enforcing strict compliance with access control procedures, continuing education programmes, regular briefings of security personnel and stringent audits.

A growing number of companies offer services to test the rigour of access control with people who specialize in using social engineering techniques.

Glossary

Acronyms list

ACD	Automatic Call Distribution		DIKW	Data–to–Information–to–Knowledge–to–Wisdom
AM	Availability Management		ELS	Early Life Support
AMIS	Availability Management Information System		eSCM–CL	eSourcing Capability Model for Client Organizations
ASP	Application Service Provider		eSCM–SP	eSourcing Capability Model for Service Providers
BCM	Business Capacity Management		FMEA	Failure Modes and Effects Analysis
BCM	Business Continuity Management		FTA	Fault Tree Analysis
BCP	Business Continuity Plan		IRR	Internal Rate of Return
BIA	Business Impact Analysis		ISG	IT Steering Group
BRM	Business Relationship Manager		ISM	Information Security Management
BSI	British Standards Institution		ISMS	Information Security Management System
BSM	Business Service Management		ISO	International Organization for Standardization
CAB	Change Advisory Board		ISP	Internet Service Provider
CAB/EC	Change Advisory Board/Emergency Committee		IT	Information Technology
CAPEX	Capital Expenditure		ITSCM	IT Service Continuity Management
CCM	Component Capacity Management		ITSM	IT Service Management
CFIA	Component Failure Impact Analysis		itSMF	IT Service Management Forum
CI	Configuration Item		IVR	Interactive Voice Response
CMDB	Configuration Management Database		KEDB	Known Error Database
CMIS	Capacity Management Information System		KPI	Key Performance Indicator
CMM	Capability Maturity Model		LOS	Line of Service
CMMI	Capability Maturity Model Integration		M_o_R	Management of Risk
CMS	Configuration Management System		MTBF	Mean Time Between Failures
COTS	Commercial off the Shelf		MTBSI	Mean Time Between Service Incidents
CSF	Critical Success Factor		MTRS	Mean Time to Restore Service
CSI	Continual Service Improvement		MTTR	Mean Time To Repair
CSP	Core Service Package		NPV	Net Present Value
CTI	Computer Telephony Integration			

OGC	Office of Government Commerce		SPOF	Single Point of Failure
OLA	Operational Level Agreement		TCO	Total Cost of Ownership
OPEX	Operational Expenditure		TCU	Total Cost of Utilization
OPSI	Office of Public Sector Information		TO	Technical Observation
PBA	Pattern of Business Activity		TOR	Terms of Reference
PFS	Prerequisite for Success		TQM	Total Quality Management
PIR	Post-Implementation Review		UC	Underpinning Contract
PSA	Projected Service Outage		UP	User Profile
QA	Quality Assurance		VBF	Vital Business Function
QMS	Quality Management System		VOI	Value on Investment
RCA	Root Cause Analysis		WIP	Work in Progress
RFC	Request for Change			
ROI	Return on Investment			
RPO	Recovery Point Objective			
RTO	Recovery Time Objective			
SAC	Service Acceptance Criteria			
SACM	Service Asset and Configuration Management			
SCD	Supplier and Contract Database			
SCM	Service Capacity Management			
SDP	Service Design Package			
SFA	Service Failure Analysis			
SIP	Service Improvement Plan			
SKMS	Service Knowledge Management System			
SLA	Service Level Agreement			
SLM	Service Level Management			
SLP	Service Level Package			
SLR	Service Level Requirement			
SMO	Service Maintenance Objective			
SoC	Separation of Concerns			
SOP	Standard Operating Procedures			
SOR	Statement of requirements			
SPI	Service Provider Interface			
SPM	Service Portfolio Management			
SPO	Service Provisioning Optimization			

Definitions list

The publication names included in parentheses after the name of a term identify where a reader can find more information about that term. This is either because the term is primarily used by that publication or because additional useful information about that term can be found there. Terms without a publication name associated with them may be used generally by several publications, or may not be defined in any greater detail than can be found in the glossary, i.e. we only point readers to somewhere they can expect to expand on their knowledge or to see a greater context. Terms with multiple publication names are expanded on in multiple publications.

Where the definition of a term includes another term, those related terms are highlighted in a second colour. This is designed to help the reader with their understanding by pointing them to additional definitions that are all part of the original term they were interested in. The form 'See also Term X, Term Y' is used at the end of a definition where an important related term is not used with the text of the definition itself.

Acceptance

Formal agreement that an IT Service, Process, Plan, or other Deliverable is complete, accurate, Reliable and meets its specified Requirements. Acceptance is usually preceded by Evaluation or Testing and is often required before proceeding to the next stage of a Project or Process.

Access Management

(Service Operation) The Process responsible for allowing Users to make use of IT Services, data, or other Assets. Access Management helps to protect the Confidentiality, Integrity and Availability of Assets by ensuring that only authorized Users are able to access or modify the Assets. Access Management is sometimes referred to as Rights Management or Identity Management.

Account Manager

(Service Strategy) A Role that is very similar to Business Relationship Manager, but includes more commercial aspects. Most commonly used when dealing with External Customers.

Accounting

(Service Strategy) The Process responsible for identifying actual Costs of delivering IT Services, comparing these with budgeted costs, and managing variance from the Budget.

Accredited

Officially authorized to carry out a Role. For example, an Accredited body may be authorized to provide training or to conduct Audits.

Active Monitoring

(Service Operation) Monitoring of a Configuration Item or an IT Service that uses automated regular checks to discover the current status. See also Passive Monitoring.

Activity

A set of actions designed to achieve a particular result. Activities are usually defined as part of Processes or Plans, and are documented in Procedures.

Agreement

A Document that describes a formal understanding between two or more parties. An Agreement is not legally binding unless it forms part of a Contract. See also Service Level Agreement, Operational Level Agreement.

Alert

(Service Operation) A warning that a threshold has been reached, something has changed, or a Failure has occurred. Alerts are often created and managed by System Management tools and are managed by the Event Management Process.

Application

Software that provides Functions that are required by an IT Service. Each Application may be part of more than one IT Service. An Application runs on one or more Servers or Clients. See also Application Management, Application Portfolio.

Application Management

(Service Design) (Service Operation) The Function responsible for managing Applications throughout their Lifecycle.

Application Portfolio

(Service Design) A database or structured Document used to manage Applications throughout their Lifecycle. The Application Portfolio contains key Attributes of all Applications. The Application Portfolio is sometimes implemented as part of the Service Portfolio, or as part of the Configuration Management System.

Application Sizing

(Service Design) The Activity responsible for understanding the Resource Requirements needed to support a new Application, or a major Change to an existing Application. Application Sizing helps to ensure that the IT Service can meet its agreed Service Level Targets for Capacity and Performance.

Architecture

(Service Design) The structure of a System or IT Service, including the Relationships of Components to each other and to the environment they are in. Architecture also includes the Standards and Guidelines that guide the design and evolution of the System.

Assessment

Inspection and analysis to check whether a Standard or set of Guidelines is being followed, that Records are accurate, or that Efficiency and Effectiveness targets are being met. *See also* Audit.

Asset

(Service Strategy) Any Resource or Capability. Assets of a Service Provider including anything that could contribute to the delivery of a Service. Assets can be one of the following types: Management, Organization, Process, Knowledge, People, Information, Applications, Infrastructure, and Financial Capital.

Asset Management

(Service Transition) Asset Management is the Process responsible for tracking and reporting the value and ownership of financial Assets throughout their Lifecycle. Asset Management is part of an overall Service Asset and Configuration Management Process. *See also* Asset Register.

Asset Register

(Service Transition) A list of Assets that includes their ownership and value. Asset Management maintains the Asset Register.

Attribute

(Service Transition) A piece of information about a Configuration Item. Examples are: name, location, Version number, and Cost. Attributes of CIs are recorded in the Configuration Management Database (CMDB). *See also* Relationship.

Audit

Formal inspection and verification to check whether a Standard or set of Guidelines is being followed, that Records are accurate, or that Efficiency and Effectiveness targets are being met. An Audit may be carried out by internal or external groups.

Automatic Call Distribution (ACD)

(Service Operation) Use of Information Technology to direct an incoming telephone call to the most appropriate person in the shortest possible time. ACD is sometimes called Automated Call Distribution.

Availability

(Service Design) Ability of a Configuration Item or IT Service to perform its agreed Function when required. Availability is determined by Reliability, Maintainability, Serviceability, Performance, and Security. Availability is usually calculated as a percentage. This calculation is often based on Agreed Service Time and Downtime. It is Best Practice to calculate Availability using measurements of the Business output of the IT Service.

Availability Management

(Service Design) The Process responsible for defining, analysing, Planning, measuring and improving all aspects of the Availability of IT services. Availability Management is responsible for ensuring that all IT Infrastructure, Processes, Tools, Roles, etc. are appropriate for the agreed Service Level Targets for Availability.

Availability Plan

(Service Design) A Plan to ensure that existing and future Availability Requirements for IT Services can be provided Cost Effectively.

Back-out

See Remediation.

Backup

(Service Design) (Service Operation) Copying data to protect against loss of Integrity or Availability of the original.

Balanced Scorecard

(Continual Service Improvement) A management tool developed by Drs Robert Kaplan (Harvard Business School) and David Norton. A Balanced Scorecard enables a Strategy to be broken down into Key Performance Indicators. Performance against the KPIs is used to demonstrate how well the Strategy is being achieved. A Balanced Scorecard has four major areas, each of which has a small number of KPIs. The same four areas are considered at different levels of detail throughout the Organization.

Baseline

(Continual Service Improvement) A Benchmark used as a reference point. For example:

- An ITSM Baseline can be used as a starting point to measure the effect of a Service Improvement Plan
- A Performance Baseline can be used to measure changes in Performance over the lifetime of an IT Service
- A Configuration Management Baseline can be used to enable the IT Infrastructure to be restored to a known Configuration if a Change or Release fails.

Benchmark

(Continual Service Improvement) The recorded state of something at a specific point in time. A Benchmark can be created for a Configuration, a Process, or any other set of data. For example, a benchmark can be used in:

- Continual Service Improvement, to establish the current state for managing improvements
- Capacity Management, to document performance characteristics during normal operations.

See also Benchmarking, Baseline.

Benchmarking

(Continual Service Improvement) Comparing a Benchmark with a Baseline or with Best Practice. The term Benchmarking is also used to mean creating a series of Benchmarks over time, and comparing the results to measure progress or improvement.

Best Practice

Proven Activities or Processes that have been successfully used by multiple Organizations. ITIL is an example of Best Practice.

Brainstorming

(Service Design) A technique that helps a team to generate ideas. Ideas are not reviewed during the Brainstorming session, but at a later stage. Brainstorming is often used by Problem Management to identify possible causes.

Budget

A list of all the money an Organization or Business Unit plans to receive, and plans to pay out, over a specified period of time. *See also* Budgeting, Planning.

Budgeting

The Activity of predicting and controlling the spending of money. Consists of a periodic negotiation cycle to set future Budgets (usually annual) and the day-to-day monitoring and adjusting of current Budgets.

Build

(Service Transition) The Activity of assembling a number of Configuration Items to create part of an IT Service. The term Build is also used to refer to a Release that is authorized for distribution. For example Server Build or laptop Build.

Business

(Service Strategy) An overall corporate entity or Organization formed of a number of Business Units. In the context of ITSM, the term Business includes public sector and not-for-profit organizations, as well as companies. An IT Service Provider provides IT Services to a Customer within a Business. The IT Service Provider may be part of the same Business as its Customer (Internal Service Provider), or part of another Business (External Service Provider).

Business Capacity Management (BCM)

(Service Design) In the context of ITSM, Business Capacity Management is the Activity responsible for understanding future Business Requirements for use in the Capacity Plan. *See also* Service Capacity Management.

Business Case

(Service Strategy) Justification for a significant item of expenditure. Includes information about Costs, benefits, options, issues, Risks, and possible problems. *See also* Cost Benefit Analysis.

Business Customer

(Service Strategy) A recipient of a product or a Service from the Business. For example, if the Business is a car manufacturer then the Business Customer is someone who buys a car.

Business Impact Analysis (BIA)

(Service Strategy) BIA is the Activity in Business Continuity Management that identifies Vital Business Functions and their dependencies. These dependencies may include Suppliers, people, other Business Processes, IT Services, etc. BIA defines the recovery requirements for IT Services. These requirements include Recovery Time Objectives, Recovery Point Objectives and minimum Service Level Targets for each IT Service.

Business Objective

(Service Strategy) The Objective of a Business Process, or of the Business as a whole. Business Objectives support the Business Vision, provide guidance for the IT Strategy, and are often supported by IT Services.

Business Operations

(Service Strategy) The day-to-day execution, monitoring and management of Business Processes.

Business Perspective

(Continual Service Improvement) An understanding of the Service Provider and IT Services from the point of view of the Business, and an understanding of the Business from the point of view of the Service Provider.

Business Process

A Process that is owned and carried out by the Business. A Business Process contributes to the delivery of a product or Service to a Business Customer. For example, a retailer may have a purchasing Process that helps to deliver Services to its Business Customers. Many Business Processes rely on IT Services.

Business Relationship Management

(Service Strategy) The Process or Function responsible for maintaining a Relationship with the Business. Business Relationship Management usually includes:

- Managing personal Relationships with Business managers
- Providing input to Service Portfolio Management
- Ensuring that the IT Service Provider is satisfying the Business needs of the Customers

This Process has strong links with Service Level Management.

Business Service

An IT Service that directly supports a Business Process, as opposed to an Infrastructure Service, which is used internally by the IT Service Provider and is not usually visible to the Business.

The term Business Service is also used to mean a Service that is delivered to Business Customers by Business Units. For example, delivery of financial services to Customers of a bank, or goods to the Customers of a retail store. Successful delivery of Business Services often depends on one or more IT Services.

Business Service Management (BSM)

(Service Strategy) (Service Design) An approach to the management of IT Services that considers the Business Processes supported and the Business value provided.

This term also means the management of Business Services delivered to Business Customers.

Business Unit

(Service Strategy) A segment of the Business that has its own Plans, Metrics, income and Costs. Each Business Unit owns Assets and uses these to create value for Customers in the form of goods and Services.

Call

(Service Operation) A telephone call to the Service Desk from a User. A Call could result in an Incident or a Service Request being logged.

Call Centre

(Service Operation) An Organization or Business Unit that handles large numbers of incoming and outgoing telephone calls. *See also* Service Desk.

Call Type

(Service Operation) A Category that is used to distinguish incoming requests to a Service Desk. Common call types are Incident, Service Request and Complaint.

Capability

(Service Strategy) The ability of an Organization, person, Process, Application, Configuration Item or IT Service to carry out an Activity. Capabilities are intangible Assets of an Organization. *See also* Resource.

Capacity

(Service Design) The maximum Throughput that a Configuration Item or IT Service can deliver whilst meeting agreed Service Level Targets. For some types of CI, Capacity may be the size or volume, for example a disk drive.

Capacity Management

(Service Design) The Process responsible for ensuring that the Capacity of IT Services and the IT Infrastructure is able to deliver agreed Service Level Targets in a Cost Effective and timely manner. Capacity Management considers all Resources required to deliver the IT Service, and plans for short-, medium- and long-term Business Requirements.

Capacity Plan

(Service Design) A Capacity Plan is used to manage the Resources required to deliver IT Services. The Plan contains scenarios for different predictions of Business demand, and costed options to deliver the agreed Service Level Targets.

Capacity Planning

(Service Design) The Activity within Capacity Management responsible for creating a Capacity Plan.

Capital Expenditure (CAPEX)

(Service Strategy) The cost of purchasing something that will become a financial Asset, for example computer equipment and buildings. The value of the Asset is Depreciated over multiple accounting periods.

Category

A named group of things that have something in common. Categories are used to group similar things together. For example, Cost Types are used to group similar types of Cost. Incident Categories are used to group similar types of Incident, CI Types are used to group similar types of Configuration Item.

Certification

Issuing a certificate to confirm Compliance to a Standard. Certification includes a formal Audit by an independent and Accredited body. The term Certification is also used to mean awarding a certificate to verify that a person has achieved a qualification.

Change

(Service Transition) The addition, modification or removal of anything that could have an effect on IT Services. The Scope should include all IT Services, Configuration Items, Processes, Documentation, etc.

Change Advisory Board (CAB)

(Service Transition) A group of people that advises the Change Manager in the Assessment, prioritization and scheduling of Changes. This board is usually made up of representatives from all areas within the IT Service Provider, representatives from the Business and Third Parties such as Suppliers.

Change Case

(Service Operation) A technique used to predict the impact of proposed Changes. Change Cases use specific scenarios to clarify the scope of proposed Changes and to help with Cost Benefit Analysis. *See also* Use Case.

Change Management

(Service Transition) The Process responsible for controlling the Lifecycle of all Changes. The primary objective of Change Management is to enable beneficial Changes to be made, with minimum disruption to IT Services.

Change Model

(Service Transition) A repeatable way of dealing with a particular Category of Change. A Change Model defines specific pre-defined steps that will be followed for a change of this Category. Change Models may be very simple, with no requirement for approval (e.g. Password Reset) or may be very complex with many steps that require approval (e.g. major software release). *See also* Standard Change, Change Advisory Board.

Change Record

(Service Transition) A Record containing the details of a Change. Each Change Record documents the Lifecycle of a single Change. A Change Record is created for every Request for Change that is received, even those that are subsequently rejected. Change Records should reference the Configuration Items that are affected by the Change. Change Records are stored in the Configuration Management System.

Change Schedule

(Service Transition) A Document that lists all approved Changes and their planned implementation dates. A Change Schedule is sometimes called a Forward Schedule of Change, even though it also contains information about Changes that have already been implemented.

Charging

(Service Strategy) Requiring payment for IT Services. Charging for IT Services is optional, and many Organizations choose to treat their IT Service Provider as a Cost Centre.

Chronological Analysis

(Service Operation) A technique used to help identify possible causes of Problems. All available data about the Problem is collected and sorted by date and time to provide a detailed timeline. This can make it possible to identify which Events may have been triggered by others.

Classification

The act of assigning a Category to something. Classification is used to ensure consistent management and reporting. CIs, Incidents, Problems, Changes, etc. are usually classified.

Client

A generic term that means a Customer, the Business or a Business Customer. For example, Client Manager may be used as a synonym for Account Manager.

The term client is also used to mean:

- A computer that is used directly by a User, for example a PC, Handheld Computer, or Workstation
- The part of a Client-Server Application that the User directly interfaces with. For example an e-mail Client.

Closed

(Service Operation) The final Status in the Lifecycle of an Incident, Problem, Change, etc. When the Status is Closed, no further action is taken.

Closure

(Service Operation) The act of changing the Status of an Incident, Problem, Change, etc. to Closed.

COBIT

(Continual Service Improvement) Control Objectives for Information and related Technology (COBIT) provides guidance and Best Practice for the management of IT Processes. COBIT is published by the IT Governance Institute. See www.isaca.org for more information.

Commercial Off-The-Shelf (COTS)

(Service Design) Application software or Middleware that can be purchased from a Third Party.

Compliance

Ensuring that a Standard or set of Guidelines is followed, or that proper, consistent accounting or other practices are being employed.

Component

A general term that is used to mean one part of something more complex. For example, a computer System may be a component of an IT Service, an Application may be a Component of a Release Unit. Components that need to be managed should be Configuration Items.

Component Capacity Management

(Service Design) (Continual Service Improvement) The Process responsible for understanding the Capacity, Utilization, and Performance of Configuration Items. Data is collected, recorded and analysed for use in the Capacity Plan. *See also* Service Capacity Management.

Component Failure Impact Analysis (CFIA)

(Service Design) A technique that helps to identify the impact of CI failure on IT Services. A matrix is created with IT Services on one edge and CIs on the other. This enables the identification of critical CIs (that could cause the failure of multiple IT Services) and of fragile IT Services (that have multiple Single Points of Failure).

Computer Telephony Integration (CTI)

(Service Operation) Computer Telephony Integration (CTI) is a general term covering any kind of integration between computers and telephone Systems. It is most commonly used to refer to Systems where an Application displays detailed screens relating to incoming or outgoing telephone calls. *See also* Automatic Call Distribution, Interactive Voice Response.

Concurrency

A measure of the number of Users engaged in the same Operation at the same time.

Confidentiality

(Service Design) A security principle that requires that data should only be accessed by authorized people.

Configuration

(Service Transition) A generic term, used to describe a group of Configuration Items that work together to deliver an IT Service, or a recognizable part of an IT Service. Configuration is also used to describe the parameter settings for one or more CIs.

Configuration Control

(Service Transition) The Activity responsible for ensuring that adding, modifying or removing a CI is properly managed, for example by submitting a Request for Change or Service Request.

Configuration Item (CI)

(Service Transition) Any Component that needs to be managed in order to deliver an IT Service. Information about each CI is recorded in a Configuration Record within the Configuration Management System and is maintained throughout its Lifecycle by Configuration Management. CIs are under the control of Change Management. CIs typically include IT Services, hardware, software, buildings, people, and formal documentation such as Process documentation and SLAs.

Configuration Management

(Service Transition) The Process responsible for maintaining information about Configuration Items required to deliver an IT Service, including their Relationships. This information is managed throughout the Lifecycle of the CI. Configuration Management is part of an overall Service Asset and Configuration Management Process.

Configuration Management Database (CMDB)

(Service Transition) A database used to store Configuration Records throughout their Lifecycle. The Configuration Management System maintains one or more CMDBs, and each CMDB stores Attributes of CIs, and Relationships with other CIs.

Configuration Management System (CMS)

(Service Transition) A set of tools and databases that are used to manage an IT Service Provider's Configuration data. The CMS also includes information about Incidents, Problems, Known Errors, Changes and Releases; and it may contain data about employees, Suppliers, locations, Business Units, Customers and Users. The CMS includes tools for collecting, storing, managing, updating, and presenting data about all Configuration Items and their Relationships. The CMS is maintained by Configuration Management and is used by all IT Service Management Processes. *See also* Configuration Management Database, Service Knowledge Management System.

Continual Service Improvement (CSI)

(Continual Service Improvement) A stage in the Lifecycle of an IT Service and the title of one of the Core ITIL publications. Continual Service Improvement is responsible for managing improvements to IT Service Management Processes and IT Services. The Performance of the IT Service Provider is continually measured and improvements are made to Processes, IT Services and IT Infrastructure in order to increase Efficiency, Effectiveness, and Cost Effectiveness. *See also* Plan–Do–Check–Act.

Contract

A legally binding Agreement between two or more parties.

Control

A means of managing a Risk, ensuring that a Business Objective is achieved, or ensuring that a Process is followed. Example Controls include Policies, Procedures, Roles, RAID, door locks, etc. A control is sometimes called a Countermeasure or safeguard. Control also means to manage the utilization or behaviour of a Configuration Item, System or IT Service.

Control Objectives for Information and related Technology (COBIT)

See COBIT.

Control perspective

(Service Strategy) An approach to the management of IT Services, Processes, Functions, Assets, etc. There can be several different Control Perspectives on the same IT Service, Process, etc., allowing different individuals or teams to focus on what is important and relevant to their specific Role. Example Control Perspectives include Reactive and Proactive management within IT Operations, or a Lifecycle view for an Application Project team.

Cost

The amount of money spent on a specific Activity, IT Service, or Business Unit. Costs consist of real cost (money), notional cost such as people's time, and Depreciation.

Cost Benefit Analysis

An Activity that analyses and compares the Costs and the benefits involved in one or more alternative courses of action. *See also* Business Case.

Cost Effectiveness

A measure of the balance between the Effectiveness and Cost of a Service, Process or activity, A Cost Effective Process is one that achieves its Objectives at minimum Cost. *See also* KPI, Value for Money.

Countermeasure

Can be used to refer to any type of Control. The term Countermeasure is most often used when referring to measures that increase Resilience, Fault Tolerance or Reliability of an IT Service.

Critical Success Factor (CSF)

Something that must happen if a Process, Project, Plan, or IT Service is to succeed. KPIs are used to measure the achievement of each CSF. For example a CSF of 'protect IT Services when making Changes' could be measured by KPIs such as 'percentage reduction of unsuccessful Changes', 'percentage reduction in Changes causing Incidents', etc.

Culture

A set of values that is shared by a group of people, including expectations about how people should behave, their ideas, beliefs, and practices. *See also* Vision.

Customer

Someone who buys goods or Services. The Customer of an IT Service Provider is the person or group that defines and agrees the Service Level Targets. The term Customers is also sometimes informally used to mean Users, for example 'this is a Customer-focused Organization'.

Dashboard

(Service Operation) A graphical representation of overall IT Service Performance and Availability. Dashboard images may be updated in real-time, and can also be included in management reports and web pages. Dashboards can be used to support Service Level Management, Event Management or Incident Diagnosis.

Definitive Media Library (DML)

(Service Transition) One or more locations in which the definitive and approved versions of all software Configuration Items are securely stored. The DML may also contain associated CIs such as licences and documentation. The DML is a single logical storage area even if there are multiple locations. All software in the DML is under the control of Change and Release Management and is recorded in the Configuration Management System. Only software from the DML is acceptable for use in a Release.

Deliverable

Something that must be provided to meet a commitment in a Service Level Agreement or a Contract. Deliverable is also used in a more informal way to mean a planned output of any Process.

Demand Management

Activities that understand and influence Customer demand for Services and the provision of Capacity to meet these demands. At a Strategic level Demand Management can involve analysis of Patterns of Business Activity and User Profiles. At a tactical level it can involve use of Differential Charging to encourage Customers to use IT Services at less busy times. *See also* Capacity Management.

Dependency

The direct or indirect reliance of one Process or Activity on another.

Deployment

(Service Transition) The Activity responsible for movement of new or changed hardware, software, documentation, Process, etc. to the Live Environment. Deployment is part of the Release and Deployment Management Process. *See also* Rollout.

Design

(Service Design) An Activity or Process that identifies Requirements and then defines a solution that is able to meet these Requirements. *See also* Service Design.

Detection

(Service Operation) A stage in the Incident Lifecycle. Detection results in the Incident becoming known to the Service Provider. Detection can be automatic, or can be the result of a user logging an Incident.

Development

(Service Design) The Process responsible for creating or modifying an IT Service or Application. Also used to mean the Role or group that carries out Development work.

Development Environment

(Service Design) An Environment used to create or modify IT Services or Applications. Development Environments are not typically subjected to the same degree of control as Test Environments or Live Environments. *See also* Development.

Diagnosis

(Service Operation) A stage in the Incident and Problem Lifecycles. The purpose of Diagnosis is to identify a Workaround for an Incident or the Root Cause of a Problem.

Diagnostic Script

(Service Operation) A structured set of questions used by Service Desk staff to ensure they ask the correct questions, and to help them Classify, Resolve and assign Incidents. Diagnostic Scripts may also be made available to Users to help them diagnose and resolve their own Incidents.

Directory Service

(Service Operation) An Application that manages information about IT Infrastructure available on a network, and corresponding User access Rights.

Document

Information in readable form. A Document may be paper or electronic. For example, a Policy statement, Service Level Agreement, Incident Record, diagram of computer room layout. *See also* Record.

Downtime

(Service Design) (Service Operation) The time when a Configuration Item or IT Service is not Available during its Agreed Service Time. The Availability of an IT Service is often calculated from Agreed Service Time and Downtime.

Driver

Something that influences Strategy, Objectives or Requirements. For example, new legislation or the actions of competitors.

Early Life Support

(Service Transition) Support provided for a new or Changed IT Service for a period of time after it is Released. During Early Life Support the IT Service Provider may review the KPIs, Service Levels and Monitoring Thresholds, and provide additional Resources for Incident and Problem Management.

Economies of scale

(Service Strategy) The reduction in average Cost that is possible from increasing the usage of an IT Service or Asset.

Effectiveness

(Continual Service Improvement) A measure of whether the Objectives of a Process, Service or Activity have been achieved. An Effective Process or activity is one that achieves its agreed Objectives. *See also* KPI.

Efficiency

(Continual Service Improvement) A measure of whether the right amount of resources has been used to deliver a Process, Service or Activity. An Efficient Process achieves its Objectives with the minimum amount of time, money, people or other resources. *See also* KPI.

Emergency Change

(Service Transition) A Change that must be introduced as soon as possible. For example, to resolve a Major Incident or implement a Security patch. The Change Management Process will normally have a specific Procedure for handling Emergency Changes. *See also* Emergency Change Advisory Board (ECAB).

Emergency Change Advisory Board (ECAB)

(Service Transition) A subset of the Change Advisory Board that makes decisions about high-impact Emergency Changes. Membership of the ECAB may be decided at the time a meeting is called, and depends on the nature of the Emergency Change.

Environment

(Service Transition) A subset of the IT Infrastructure that is used for a particular purpose. For Example: Live Environment, Test Environment, Build Environment. It is possible for multiple Environments to share a Configuration Item, for example Test and Live Environments may use different partitions on a single mainframe computer. Also used in the term Physical Environment to mean the accommodation, air conditioning, power system, etc.

Environment is also used as a generic term to mean the external conditions that influence or affect something.

Error

(Service Operation) A design flaw or malfunction that causes a Failure of one or more Configuration Items or IT Services. A mistake made by a person or a faulty Process that affects a CI or IT Service is also an Error.

Escalation

(Service Operation) An Activity that obtains additional Resources when these are needed to meet Service Level Targets or Customer expectations. Escalation may be needed within any IT Service Management Process, but is most commonly associated with Incident Management, Problem Management and the management of Customer complaints. There are two types of Escalation: Functional Escalation and Hierarchic Escalation.

eSourcing Capability Model for Service Providers (eSCM–SP)

(Service Strategy) A framework to help IT Service Providers develop their IT Service Management Capabilities from a Service Sourcing perspective. eSCM–SP was developed by Carnegie Mellon University, US.

Estimation

The use of experience to provide an approximate value for a Metric or Cost. Estimation is also used in Capacity and Availability Management as the cheapest and least accurate Modelling method.

Evaluation

(Service Transition) The Process responsible for assessing a new or Changed IT Service to ensure that Risks have been managed and to help determine whether to proceed with the Change.

Evaluation is also used to mean comparing an actual Outcome with the intended Outcome, or comparing one alternative with another.

Event

(Service Operation) A change of state that has significance for the management of a Configuration Item or IT Service.

The term Event is also used to mean an Alert or notification created by any IT Service, Configuration Item or Monitoring tool. Events typically require IT Operations personnel to take actions, and often lead to Incidents being logged.

Event Management

(Service Operation) The Process responsible for managing Events throughout their Lifecycle. Event Management is one of the main Activities of IT Operations.

Exception Report

A Document containing details of one or more KPIs or other important targets that have exceeded defined Thresholds. Examples include SLA targets being missed or about to be missed, and a Performance Metric indicating a potential Capacity problem.

External Customer

A Customer who works for a different Business to the IT Service Provider. *See also* External Service Provider.

External Metric

A Metric that is used to measure the delivery of IT Service to a Customer. External Metrics are usually defined in SLAs and reported to Customers. *See also* Internal Metric.

External Service Provider

(Service Strategy) An IT Service Provider that is part of a different Organization from its Customer. An IT Service Provider may have both Internal Customers and External Customers.

Facilities Management

(Service Operation) The Function responsible for managing the physical Environment where the IT Infrastructure is located. Facilities Management includes all aspects of managing the physical Environment, for example power and cooling, building Access Management, and environmental Monitoring.

Failure

(Service Operation) Loss of ability to Operate to Specification, or to deliver the required output. The term Failure may be used when referring to IT Services, Processes, Activities, Configuration Items, etc. A Failure often causes an Incident.

Fault

See Error.

Fault Tolerance

(Service Design) The ability of an IT Service or Configuration Item to continue to Operate correctly after Failure of a Component part. *See also* Resilience, Countermeasure.

Fault Tree Analysis (FTA)

(Service Design) (Continual Service Improvement) A technique that can be used to determine the chain of events that leads to a Problem. Fault Tree Analysis represents a chain of events using Boolean notation in a diagram.

Financial Management

(Service Strategy) The Function and Processes responsible for managing an IT Service Provider's Budgeting, Accounting and Charging Requirements.

First-line Support

(Service Operation) The first level in a hierarchy of Support Groups involved in the resolution of Incidents. Each level contains more specialist skills, or has more time or other resources. *See also* Escalation.

Fishbone Diagram

See Ishikawa Diagram.

Fit for Purpose

An informal term used to describe a Process, Configuration Item, IT Service, etc. that is capable of meeting its objectives or Service Levels. Being Fit for Purpose requires suitable design, implementation, control and maintenance.

Follow the Sun

(Service Operation) A methodology for using Service Desks and Support Groups around the world to provide seamless 24/7 Service. Calls, Incidents, Problems and Service Requests are passed between groups in different time zones.

Fulfilment

Performing Activities to meet a need or Requirement. For example, by providing a new IT Service, or meeting a Service Request.

Function

A team or group of people and the tools they use to carry out one or more Processes or Activities. For example the Service Desk.

The term Function also has two other meanings:

- An intended purpose of a Configuration Item, Person, Team, Process, or IT Service. For example one Function of an e-mail Service may be to store and forward outgoing mails, one Function of a Business Process may be to dispatch goods to Customers.
- To perform the intended purpose correctly, 'The computer is Functioning'.

Functional Escalation

(Service Operation) Transferring an Incident, Problem or Change to a technical team with a higher level of expertise to assist in an Escalation.

Governance

Ensuring that Policies and Strategy are actually implemented, and that required Processes are correctly followed. Governance includes defining Roles and responsibilities, measuring and reporting, and taking actions to resolve any issues identified.

Guideline

A Document describing Best Practice, which recommends what should be done. Compliance with a guideline is not normally enforced. *See also* Standard.

Help Desk

(Service Operation) A point of contact for Users to log Incidents. A Help Desk is usually more technically focussed than a Service Desk and does not provide a Single Point of Contact for all interaction. The term Help Desk is often used as a synonym for Service Desk.

Hierarchic Escalation

(Service Operation) Informing or involving more senior levels of management to assist in an Escalation.

High Availability

(Service Design) An approach or design that minimizes or hides the effects of Configuration Item Failure on the users of an IT Service. High Availability solutions are designed to achieve an agreed level of Availability and make use of techniques such as Fault Tolerance, Resilience and fast Recovery to reduce the number of Incidents, and the Impact of Incidents.

Identity

(Service Operation) A unique name that is used to identify a User, person or Role. The Identity is used to grant Rights to that User, person, or Roles. Example identities might be the username SmithJ or the Role 'Change manager'.

Immediate Recovery

(Service Design) A Recovery Option that is also known as Hot Standby. Provision is made to Recover the IT Service with no loss of Service. Immediate Recovery typically uses Mirroring, Load Balancing and Split Site technologies.

Impact

(Service Operation) (Service Transition) A measure of the effect of an Incident, Problem or Change on Business Processes. Impact is often based on how Service Levels will be affected. Impact and Urgency are used to assign Priority.

Incident

(Service Operation) An unplanned interruption to an IT Service or reduction in the Quality of an IT Service. Failure of a Configuration Item that has not yet affected Service is also an Incident. For example Failure of one disk from a mirror set.

Incident Management

(Service Operation) The Process responsible for managing the Lifecycle of all Incidents. The primary Objective of Incident Management is to return the IT Service to Customers as quickly as possible.

Incident Record

(Service Operation) A Record containing the details of an Incident. Each Incident record documents the Lifecycle of a single Incident.

Indirect Cost

(Service Strategy) A Cost of providing an IT Service, which cannot be allocated in full to a specific customer. For example, the Cost of providing shared Servers or software licences. Also known as Overhead.

Information Security Management (ISM)

(Service Design) The Process that ensures the Confidentiality, Integrity and Availability of an Organization's Assets, information, data and IT Services. Information Security Management usually forms part of an Organizational approach to Security Management that has a wider scope than the IT Service Provider, and includes handling of paper, building access, phone calls, etc. for the entire Organization.

Information Security Policy

(Service Design) The Policy that governs the Organization's approach to Information Security Management.

Information Technology (IT)

The use of technology for the storage, communication or processing of information. The technology typically includes computers, telecommunications, Applications and other software. The information may include Business data, voice, images, video, etc. Information Technology is often used to support Business Processes through IT Services.

Insourcing

See Internal Sourcing.

Integrity

(Service Design) A security principle that ensures data and Configuration Items are modified only by authorized personnel and Activities. Integrity considers all possible causes of modification, including software and hardware Failure, environmental Events, and human intervention.

Interactive Voice Response (IVR)

(Service Operation) A form of Automatic Call Distribution that accepts User input, such as key presses and spoken commands, to identify the correct destination for incoming Calls.

Intermediate Recovery

(Service Design) A Recovery Option that is also known as Warm Standby. Provision is made to Recover the IT Service in a period of time between 24 and 72 hours. Intermediate Recovery typically uses a shared Portable or Fixed Facility that has Computer Systems and Network Components. The hardware and software will need to be configured, and data will need to be restored, as part of the IT Service Continuity Plan.

Internal Metric

A Metric that is used within the IT Service Provider to Monitor the Efficiency, Effectiveness or Cost Effectiveness of the IT Service Provider's internal Processes. Internal Metrics are not normally reported to the Customer of the IT Service. *See also* External Metric.

Internal Service Provider

(Service Strategy) An IT Service Provider that is part of the same Organization as its Customer. An IT Service Provider may have both Internal Customers and External Customers.

Internal Sourcing

(Service Strategy) Using an Internal Service Provider to manage IT Services.

International Organization for Standardization (ISO)

The International Organization for Standardization (ISO) is the world's largest developer of Standards. ISO is a non-governmental organization that is a network of the national standards institutes of 156 countries. See www.iso.org for further information about ISO.

International Standards Organization

See International Organization for Standardization (ISO).

Internet Service Provider (ISP)

An External Service Provider that provides access to the Internet. Most ISPs also provide other IT Services such as web hosting.

Invocation

(Service Design) Initiation of the steps defined in a plan. For example initiating the IT Service Continuity Plan for one or more IT Services.

Ishikawa Diagram

(Service Operation) (Continual Service Improvement) A technique that helps a team to identify all the possible causes of a Problem. Originally devised by Kaoru Ishikawa, the output of this technique is a diagram that looks like a fishbone.

ISO 9000

A generic term that refers to a number of international Standards and Guidelines for Quality Management Systems. See www.iso.org for more information. *See also* ISO.

ISO/IEC 20000

ISO Specification and Code of Practice for IT Service Management. ISO/IEC 20000 is aligned with ITIL Best Practice.

ISO/IEC 27001

(Service Design) (Continual Service Improvement) ISO Specification for Information Security Management. The corresponding Code of Practice is ISO/IEC 17799. *See also* Standard.

IT Infrastructure

All of the hardware, software, networks, facilities, etc. that are required to develop, Test, deliver, Monitor, Control or support IT Services. The term IT Infrastructure includes all of the Information Technology but not the associated people, Processes and documentation.

IT Operations

(Service Operation) Activities carried out by IT Operations Control, including Console Management, Job Scheduling, Backup and Restore, and Print and Output Management. IT Operations is also used as a synonym for Service Operation.

IT Operations Control

(Service Operation) The Function responsible for Monitoring and Control of the IT Services and IT Infrastructure. *See also* Operations Bridge.

IT Operations Management

(Service Operation) The Function within an IT Service Provider that performs the daily Activities needed to manage IT Services and the supporting IT Infrastructure. IT Operations Management includes IT Operations Control and Facilities Management.

IT Service

A Service provided to one or more Customers by an IT Service Provider. An IT Service is based on the use of Information Technology and supports the Customer's Business Processes. An IT Service is made up from a combination of people, Processes and technology and should be defined in a Service Level Agreement.

IT Service Continuity Management (ITSCM)

(Service Design) The Process responsible for managing Risks that could seriously affect IT Services. ITSCM ensures that the IT Service Provider can always provide minimum agreed Service Levels, by reducing the Risk to an acceptable level and Planning for the Recovery of IT Services. ITSCM should be designed to support Business Continuity Management.

IT Service Continuity Plan

(Service Design) A Plan defining the steps required to Recover one or more IT Services. The Plan will also identify the triggers for Invocation, people to be involved, communications, etc. The IT Service Continuity Plan should be part of a Business Continuity Plan.

IT Service Management (ITSM)

The implementation and management of Quality IT Services that meet the needs of the Business. IT Service Management are performed by IT Service Providers through an appropriate mix of people, Process and Information Technology. *See also* Service Management.

IT Service Management Forum (itSMF)

The IT Service Management Forum is an independent Organization dedicated to promoting a professional approach to IT Service Management. The itSMF is a not-for-profit membership Organization with representation in many countries around the world (itSMF Chapters). The itSMF and its membership contribute to the development of ITIL and associated IT Service Management Standards. See www.itsmf.com for more information.

ITIL

A set of Best Practice guidance for IT Service Management. ITIL is owned by the OGC and consists of a series of publications giving guidance on the provision of Quality IT Services, and on the Processes and facilities needed to support them. See www.itil.co.uk for more information.

Job Description

A Document that defines the Roles, responsibilities, skills and knowledge required by a particular person. One Job Description can include multiple Roles, for example the Roles of Configuration Manager and Change Manager may be carried out by one person.

Job Scheduling

(Service Operation) Planning and managing the execution of software tasks that are required as part of an IT Service. Job Scheduling is carried out by IT Operations Management, and is often automated using software tools that run batch or online tasks at specific times of the day, week, month or year.

Kepner & Tregoe Analysis

(Service Operation) (Continual Service Improvement) A structured approach to Problem solving. The Problem is analysed in terms of what, where, when and extent. Possible causes are identified. The most probable cause is tested. The true cause is verified.

Key Performance Indicator (KPI)

(Service design) (Continual Service Improvement) A Metric that is used to help manage a Process, IT Service or Activity. Many Metrics may be measured, but only the most important of these are defined as KPIs and used to actively manage and report on the Process, IT Service or Activity. KPIs should be selected to ensure that Efficiency, Effectiveness, and Cost Effectiveness are all managed. *See also* Critical Success Factor.

Knowledge Base

(Service Transition) A logical database containing the data used by the Service Knowledge Management System.

Knowledge Management

(Service Transition) The Process responsible for gathering, analysing, storing and sharing knowledge and information within an Organization. The primary purpose of Knowledge Management is to improve Efficiency by reducing the need to rediscover knowledge. *See also* Service Knowledge Management System.

Known Error

(Service Operation) A Problem that has a documented Root Cause and a Workaround. Known Errors are created and managed throughout their Lifecycle by Problem Management. Known Errors may also be identified by Development or Suppliers.

Known Error Database (KEDB)

(Service Operation) A database containing all Known Error Records. This database is created by Problem Management and used by Incident and Problem Management. The Known Error Database is part of the Service Knowledge Management System.

Known Error Record

(Service Operation) A Record containing the details of a Known Error. Each Known Error Record documents the Lifecycle of a Known Error, including the Status, Root Cause and Workaround. In some implementations a Known Error is documented using additional fields in a Problem Record.

Lifecycle

The various stages in the life of an IT Service, Configuration Item, Incident, Problem, Change, etc. The Lifecycle defines the Categories for Status and the Status transitions that are permitted. For example:

- The Lifecycle of an Application includes Requirements, Design, Build, Deploy, Operate, Optimize
- The Expanded Incident Lifecycle includes Detect, Respond, Diagnose, Repair, Recover, Restore
- The Lifecycle of a Server may include: Ordered, Received, In Test, Live, Disposed, etc.

Live

(Service Transition) Refers to an IT Service or Configuration Item that is being used to deliver Service to a Customer.

Live Environment

(Service Transition) A controlled Environment containing Live Configuration Items used to deliver IT Services to Customers.

Major Incident

(Service Operation) The highest Category of Impact for an Incident. A Major Incident results in significant disruption to the Business.

Management Information

Information that is used to support decision making by managers. Management Information is often generated automatically by tools supporting the various IT Service Management Processes. Management Information often includes the values of KPIs such as 'Percentage of Changes leading to Incidents', or 'first-time fix rate'.

Management of Risk (M_o_R)

The OGC methodology for managing Risks. M_o_R includes all the Activities required to identify and Control the exposure to Risk, which may have an impact on the achievement of an Organization's Business Objectives. See www.m-o-r.org for more details.

Management System

The framework of Policy, Processes and Functions that ensures an Organization can achieve its Objectives.

Maturity

(Continual Service Improvement) A measure of the Reliability, Efficiency and Effectiveness of a Process, Function, Organization, etc. The most mature Processes and Functions are formally aligned to Business Objectives and Strategy, and are supported by a framework for continual improvement.

Mean Time Between Failures (MTBF)

(Service Design) A Metric for measuring and reporting Reliability. MTBF is the average time that a Configuration Item or IT Service can perform its agreed Function without interruption. This is measured from when the CI or IT Service starts working, until it next fails.

Mean Time To Repair (MTTR)

The average time taken to repair a Configuration Item or IT Service after a Failure. MTTR is measured from when the CI or IT Service fails until it is repaired. MTTR does not include the time required to Recover or Restore. MTTR is sometimes incorrectly used to mean Mean Time to Restore Service.

Mean Time to Restore Service (MTRS)

The average time taken to restore a Configuration Item or IT Service after a Failure. MTRS is measured from when the CI or IT Service fails until it is fully restored and delivering its normal functionality. *See also* Mean Time To Repair.

Metric

(Continual Service Improvement) Something that is measured and reported to help manage a Process, IT Service or Activity. *See also* KPI.

Middleware

(Service Design) Software that connects two or more software Components or Applications. Middleware is usually purchased from a Supplier, rather than developed within the IT Service Provider. *See also* Off the Shelf.

Model

A representation of a System, Process, IT Service, Configuration Item, etc. that is used to help understand or predict future behaviour.

Modelling

A technique that is used to predict the future behaviour of a System, Process, IT Service, Configuration Item, etc. Modelling is commonly used in Financial Management, Capacity Management and Availability Management.

Monitor Control Loop

(Service Operation) Monitoring the output of a Task, Process, IT Service or Configuration Item; comparing this output to a predefined Norm; and taking appropriate action based on this comparison.

Monitoring

(Service Operation) Repeated observation of a Configuration Item, IT Service or Process to detect Events and to ensure that the current status is known.

Objective

The defined purpose or aim of a Process, an Activity or an Organization as a whole. Objectives are usually expressed as measurable targets. The term Objective is also informally used to mean a Requirement. *See also* Outcome.

Off the Shelf

See Commercial Off the Shelf.

Office of Government Commerce (OGC)

OGC owns the ITIL brand (copyright and trademark). OGC is a UK Government department that supports the delivery of the government's procurement agenda through its work in collaborative procurement and in raising levels of procurement skills and capability with departments. It also provides support for complex public sector projects.

Off-shore

(Service Strategy) Provision of Services from a location outside the country where the Customer is based, often in a different continent. This can be the provision of an IT Service, or of supporting Functions such as Service Desk.

Operate

To perform as expected. A Process or Configuration Item is said to Operate if it is delivering the Required outputs. Operate also means to perform one or more Operations. For example, to Operate a computer is to do the day-to-day Operations needed for it to perform as expected.

Operation

(Service Operation) Day-to-day management of an IT Service, System, or other Configuration Item. Operation is also used to mean any pre-defined Activity or Transaction. For example loading a magnetic tape, accepting money at a point of sale, or reading data from a disk drive.

Operational

The lowest of three levels of Planning and delivery (Strategic, Tactical, Operational). Operational Activities include the day-to-day or short-term Planning or delivery of a Business Process or IT Service Management Process. The term Operational is also a synonym for Live.

Operational Cost

Cost resulting from running the IT Services. Often repeating payments. For example staff costs, hardware maintenance and electricity (also known as 'current expenditure' or 'revenue expenditure'). *See also* Capital Expenditure.

Operational Expenditure (OPEX)

See Operational Cost.

Operational Level Agreement (OLA)

(Service Design) (Continual Service Improvement) An Agreement between an IT Service Provider and another part of the same Organization. An OLA supports the IT Service Provider's delivery of IT Services to Customers. The OLA defines the goods or Services to be provided and the responsibilities of both parties. For example there could be an OLA:

■ Between the IT Service Provider and a procurement department to obtain hardware in agreed times
■ Between the Service Desk and a Support Group to provide Incident Resolution in agreed times.

See also Service Level Agreement.

Operations Bridge

(Service Operation) A physical location where IT Services and IT Infrastructure are monitored and managed.

Operations Control

See IT Operations Control.

Operations Management

See IT Operations Management.

Optimize

Review, Plan and request Changes, in order to obtain the maximum Efficiency and Effectiveness from a Process, Configuration Item, Application, etc.

Organization

A company, legal entity or other institution. Examples of Organizations that are not companies include International Standards Organization or itSMF. The term Organization is sometimes used to refer to any entity that has People, Resources and Budgets. For example a Project or Business Unit.

Outcome

The result of carrying out an Activity; following a Process; delivering an IT Service, etc. The term Outcome is used to refer to intended results, as well as to actual results. *See also* Objective.

Outsourcing

(Service Strategy) Using an External Service Provider to manage IT Services. *See also* Service Sourcing.

Overhead

See Indirect cost.

Pain Value Analysis

(Service Operation) A technique used to help identify the Business Impact of one or more Problems. A formula is used to calculate Pain Value based on the number of Users affected, the duration of the Downtime, the Impact on each User, and the cost to the Business (if known).

Partnership

A relationship between two Organizations that involves working closely together for common goals or mutual benefit. The IT Service Provider should have a Partnership with the Business, and with Third Parties who are critical to the delivery of IT Services. *See also* Value Network.

Passive Monitoring

(Service Operation) Monitoring of a Configuration Item, an IT Service or a Process that relies on an Alert or notification to discover the current status. *See also* Active Monitoring.

Performance

A measure of what is achieved or delivered by a System, person, team, Process, or IT Service.

Performance Management

(Continual Service Improvement) The Process responsible for day-to-day Capacity Management Activities. These include monitoring, threshold detection, Performance analysis and Tuning, and implementing changes related to Performance and Capacity.

Pilot

(Service Transition) A limited Deployment of an IT Service, a Release or a Process to the Live Environment. A pilot is used to reduce Risk and to gain User feedback and Acceptance. *See also* Test, Evaluation.

Plan

A detailed proposal that describes the Activities and Resources needed to achieve an Objective. For example a Plan to implement a new IT Service or Process. ISO/IEC 20000 requires a Plan for the management of each IT Service Management Process.

Plan–Do–Check–Act

(Continual Service Improvement) A four-stage cycle for Process management, attributed to Edward Deming. Plan–Do–Check–Act is also called the Deming Cycle.

PLAN: Design or revise Processes that support the IT Services.

DO: Implement the Plan and manage the Processes.

CHECK: Measure the Processes and IT Services, compare with Objectives and produce reports.

ACT: Plan and implement Changes to improve the Processes.

Planned Downtime

(Service Design) Agreed time when an IT Service will not be available. Planned Downtime is often used for maintenance, upgrades and testing. *See also* Downtime.

Planning

An Activity responsible for creating one or more Plans. For example, Capacity Planning.

Policy

Formally documented management expectations and intentions. Policies are used to direct decisions, and to ensure consistent and appropriate development and implementation of Processes, Standards, Roles, Activities, IT Infrastructure, etc.

Practice

A way of working, or a way in which work must be done. Practices can include Activities, Processes, Functions, Standards and Guidelines. *See also* Best Practice.

PRINCE2

The standard UK government methodology for Project management. See www.ogc.gov.uk/prince2 for more information.

Priority

(Service Transition) (Service Operation) A Category used to identify the relative importance of an Incident, Problem or Change. Priority is based on Impact and Urgency, and is used to identify required times for actions to be taken. For example the SLA may state that Priority 2 Incidents must be resolved within 12 hours.

Proactive Monitoring

(Service Operation) Monitoring that looks for patterns of Events to predict possible future Failures. *See also* Reactive Monitoring.

Proactive Problem Management

(Service Operation) Part of the Problem Management Process. The Objective of Proactive Problem Management is to identify Problems that might otherwise be missed. Proactive Problem Management analyses Incident Records, and uses data collected by other IT Service Management Processes to identify trends or significant problems.

Problem

(Service Operation) A cause of one or more Incidents. The cause is not usually known at the time a Problem Record is created, and the Problem Management Process is responsible for further investigation.

Problem Management

(Service Operation) The Process responsible for managing the Lifecycle of all Problems. The primary objectives of Problem Management are to prevent Incidents from happening, and to minimize the Impact of Incidents that cannot be prevented.

Problem Record

(Service Operation) A Record containing the details of a Problem. Each Problem Record documents the Lifecycle of a single Problem.

Procedure

A Document containing steps that specify how to achieve an Activity. Procedures are defined as part of Processes. *See also* Work Instruction.

Process

A structured set of Activities designed to accomplish a specific Objective. A Process takes one or more defined inputs and turns them into defined outputs. A Process may include any of the Roles, responsibilities, tools and management Controls required to reliably deliver the outputs. A Process may define Policies, Standards, Guidelines, Activities, and Work Instructions if they are needed.

Process Control

The Activity of planning and regulating a Process, with the Objective of performing the Process in an Effective, Efficient, and consistent manner.

Process Manager

A Role responsible for Operational management of a Process. The Process Manager's responsibilities include Planning and coordination of all Activities required to carry out, monitor and report on the Process. There may be several Process Managers for one Process, for example regional Change Managers or IT Service Continuity Managers for each data centre. The Process Manager Role is often assigned to the person who carries out the Process Owner Role, but the two Roles may be separate in larger Organizations.

Process Owner

A Role responsible for ensuring that a Process is Fit for Purpose. The Process Owner's responsibilities include sponsorship, Design, Change Management and continual improvement of the Process and its Metrics. This Role is often assigned to the same person who carries out the Process Manager Role, but the two Roles may be separate in larger Organizations.

Production Environment

See Live Environment.

Programme

A number of Projects and Activities that are planned and managed together to achieve an overall set of related Objectives and other Outcomes.

Project

A temporary Organization, with people and other Assets required to achieve an Objective or other Outcome. Each Project has a Lifecycle that typically includes initiation, Planning, execution, Closure, etc. Projects are usually managed using a formal methodology such as PRINCE2.

Qualification

(Service Transition) An Activity that ensures that IT Infrastructure is appropriate, and correctly configured, to support an Application or IT Service. *See also* Validation.

Quality

The ability of a product, Service, or Process to provide the intended value. For example, a hardware Component can be considered to be of high Quality if it performs as expected and delivers the required Reliability. Process Quality also requires an ability to monitor Effectiveness and Efficiency, and to improve them if necessary. *See also* Quality Management System.

Quality Assurance (QA)

(Service Transition) The Process responsible for ensuring that the Quality of a product, Service or Process will provide its intended Value.

Quality Management System (QMS)

(Continual Service Improvement) The set of Processes responsible for ensuring that all work carried out by an Organization is of a suitable Quality to reliably meet Business Objectives or Service Levels. *See also* ISO 9000.

Reactive Monitoring

(Service Operation) Monitoring that takes action in response to an Event. For example submitting a batch job when the previous job completes, or logging an Incident when an Error occurs. *See also* Proactive Monitoring.

Record

A Document containing the results or other output from a Process or Activity. Records are evidence of the fact that an activity took place and may be paper or electronic. For example, an Audit report, an Incident Record, or the minutes of a meeting.

Recovery

(Service Design) (Service Operation) Returning a Configuration Item or an IT Service to a working state. Recovery of an IT Service often includes recovering data to a known consistent state. After Recovery, further steps may be needed before the IT Service can be made available to the Users (Restoration).

Recovery Option

(Service Design) A Strategy for responding to an interruption to Service. Commonly used Strategies are Do Nothing, Manual Workaround, Reciprocal Arrangement, Gradual Recovery, Intermediate Recovery, Fast Recovery, Immediate Recovery. Recovery Options may make use of dedicated facilities, or Third Party facilities shared by multiple Businesses.

Recovery Point Objective (RPO)

(Service Operation) The maximum amount of data that may be lost when Service is Restored after an interruption. Recovery Point Objective is expressed as a length of time before the Failure. For example a Recovery Point Objective of one day may be supported by daily Backups, and up to 24 hours of data may be lost. Recovery Point Objectives for each IT Service should be negotiated, agreed and documented, and used as requirements for Service Design and IT Service Continuity Plans.

Recovery Time Objective (RTO)

(Service Operation) The maximum time allowed for recovery of an IT Service following an interruption. The Service Level to be provided may be less than normal Service Level Targets. Recovery Time Objectives for each IT Service should be negotiated, agreed and documented. *See also* Business Impact Analysis.

Redundancy

See Fault Tolerance.

The term Redundant also has a generic meaning of obsolete, or no longer needed.

Relationship

A connection or interaction between two people or things. In Business Relationship Management it is the interaction between the IT Service Provider and the Business. In Configuration Management it is a link between two Configuration Items that identifies a dependency or connection between them. For example Applications may be linked to the Servers they run on, IT Services have many links to all the CIs that contribute to them.

Release

(Service Transition) A collection of hardware, software, documentation, Processes or other Components required to implement one or more approved Changes to IT Services. The contents of each Release are managed, tested, and deployed as a single entity.

Release and Deployment Management

(Service Transition) The Process responsible for both Release Management and Deployment.

Release Management

(Service Transition) The Process responsible for Planning, scheduling and controlling the movement of Releases to Test and Live Environments. The primary Objective of Release Management is to ensure that the integrity of the Live Environment is protected and that the correct Components are released. Release Management is part of the Release and Deployment Management Process.

Release Process

The name used by ISO/IEC 20000 for the Process group that includes Release Management. This group does not include any other Processes.

Release Process is also used as a synonym for Release Management Process.

Release Record

(Service Transition) A Record in the CMDB that defines the content of a Release. A Release Record has Relationships with all Configuration Items that are affected by the Release.

Reliability

(Service Design) (Continual Service Improvement) A measure of how long a Configuration Item or IT Service can perform its agreed Function without interruption. Usually measured as MTBF or MTBSI. The term Reliability can also be used to state how likely it is that a Process, Function, etc. will deliver its required outputs. *See also* Availability.

Remediation

(Service Transition) Recovery to a known state after a failed Change or Release.

Repair

(Service Operation) The replacement or correction of a failed Configuration Item.

Request for Change (RFC)

(Service Transition) A formal proposal for a Change to be made. An RFC includes details of the proposed Change, and may be recorded on paper or electronically. The term RFC is often misused to mean a Change Record, or the Change itself.

Request Fulfilment

(Service Operation) The Process responsible for managing the Lifecycle of all Service Requests.

Requirement

(Service Design) A formal statement of what is needed. For example, a Service Level Requirement, a Project Requirement or the required Deliverables for a Process. *See also* Statement of Requirements.

Resilience

(Service Design) The ability of a Configuration Item or IT Service to resist Failure or to Recover quickly following a Failure. For example an armoured cable will resist failure when put under stress. *See also* Fault Tolerance.

Resolution

(Service Operation) Action taken to repair the Root Cause of an Incident or Problem, or to implement a Workaround. In ISO/IEC 20000, Resolution Processes is the Process group that includes Incident and Problem Management.

Resource

(Service Strategy) A generic term that includes IT Infrastructure, people, money or anything else that might help to deliver an IT Service. Resources are considered to be Assets of an Organization. *See also* Capability, Service Asset.

Response Time

A measure of the time taken to complete an Operation or Transaction. Used in Capacity Management as a measure of IT Infrastructure Performance, and in Incident Management as a measure of the time taken to answer the phone, or to start Diagnosis.

Responsiveness

A measurement of the time taken to respond to something. This could be Response Time of a Transaction, or the speed with which an IT Service Provider responds to an Incident or Request for Change, etc.

Restoration of Service

See Restore.

Restore

(Service Operation) Taking action to return an IT Service to the Users after Repair and Recovery from an Incident. This is the primary Objective of Incident Management.

Retire

(Service Transition) Permanent removal of an IT Service, or other Configuration Item, from the Live Environment. Retired is a stage in the Lifecycle of many Configuration Items.

Review

An evaluation of a Change, Problem, Process, Project, etc. Reviews are typically carried out at predefined points in the Lifecycle, and especially after Closure. The purpose of a Review is to ensure that all Deliverables have been provided, and to identify opportunities for improvement.

Rights

(Service Operation) Entitlements, or permissions, granted to a User or Role. For example the Right to modify particular data, or to authorize a Change.

Risk

A possible event that could cause harm or loss, or affect the ability to achieve Objectives. A Risk is measured by the probability of a Threat, the Vulnerability of the Asset to that Threat, and the Impact it would have if it occurred.

Risk Assessment

The initial steps of Risk Management. Analysing the value of Assets to the business, identifying Threats to those Assets, and evaluating how Vulnerable each Asset is to those Threats. Risk Assessment can be quantitative (based on numerical data) or qualitative.

Risk Management

The Process responsible for identifying, assessing and controlling Risks. *See also* Risk Assessment.

Role

A set of responsibilities, Activities and authorities granted to a person or team. A Role is defined in a Process. One person or team may have multiple Roles; for example, the Roles of Configuration Manager and Change Manager may be carried out by a single person.

Rollout

(Service Transition) See Deployment.

Most often used to refer to complex or phased Deployments or Deployments to multiple locations.

Root Cause

(Service Operation) The underlying or original cause of an Incident or Problem.

Root Cause Analysis (RCA)

(Service Operation) An Activity that identifies the Root Cause of an Incident or Problem. RCA typically concentrates on IT Infrastructure failures. *See also* Service Failure Analysis.

Scalability

The ability of an IT Service, Process, Configuration Item, etc. to perform its agreed Function when the Workload or Scope changes.

Scope

The boundary, or extent, to which a Process, Procedure, Certification, Contract, etc. applies. For example the Scope of Change Management may include all Live IT Services and related Configuration Items, the Scope of an ISO/IEC 20000 Certificate may include all IT Services delivered out of a named data centre.

Second-line Support

(Service Operation) The second level in a hierarchy of Support Groups involved in the resolution of Incidents and investigation of Problems. Each level contains more specialist skills, or has more time or other resources.

Security

See Information Security Management.

Security Management

See Information Security Management.

Security Policy

See Information Security Policy.

Server

(Service Operation) A computer that is connected to a network and provides software Functions that are used by other Computers.

Service

A means of delivering value to Customers by facilitating Outcomes Customers want to achieve without the ownership of specific Costs and Risks.

Service Asset

Any Capability or Resource of a Service Provider. *See also* Asset.

Service Asset and Configuration Management (SACM)

(Service Transition) The Process responsible for both Configuration Management and Asset Management.

Service Capacity Management (SCM)

(Service Design) (Continual Service Improvement) The Activity responsible for understanding the Performance and Capacity of IT Services. The Resources used by each IT Service and the pattern of usage over time are collected, recorded, and analysed for use in the Capacity Plan. *See also* Business Capacity Management, Component Capacity Management.

Service Catalogue

(Service Design) A database or structured Document with information about all Live IT Services, including those available for Deployment. The Service Catalogue is the only part of the Service Portfolio published to Customers, and is used to support the sale and delivery of IT Services. The Service Catalogue includes information about deliverables, prices, contact points, ordering and request Processes.

Service Continuity Management

See IT Service Continuity Management.

Service Culture

A Customer-oriented Culture. The major Objectives of a Service Culture are Customer satisfaction and helping Customers to achieve their Business Objectives.

Service Design

(Service Design) A stage in the Lifecycle of an IT Service. Service Design includes a number of Processes and Functions and is the title of one of the Core ITIL publications. *See also* Design.

Service Desk

(Service Operation) The Single Point of Contact between the Service Provider and the Users. A typical Service Desk manages Incidents and Service Requests, and also handles communication with the Users.

Service Failure Analysis (SFA)

(Service Design) An Activity that identifies underlying causes of one or more IT Service interruptions. SFA identifies opportunities to improve the IT Service Provider's Processes and tools, and not just the IT Infrastructure. SFA is a time-constrained, project-like activity, rather than an ongoing process of analysis. *See also* Root Cause Analysis.

Service Hours

(Service Design) (Continual Service Improvement) An agreed time period when a particular IT Service should be Available. For example, 'Monday–Friday 08:00 to 17:00 except public holidays'. Service Hours should be defined in a Service Level Agreement.

Service Improvement Plan (SIP)

(Continual Service Improvement) A formal Plan to implement improvements to a Process or IT Service.

Service Knowledge Management System (SKMS)

(Service Transition) A set of tools and databases that are used to manage knowledge and information. The SKMS includes the Configuration Management System, as well as other tools and databases. The SKMS stores, manages, updates, and presents all information that an IT Service Provider needs to manage the full Lifecycle of IT Services.

Service Level

Measured and reported achievement against one or more Service Level Targets. The term Service Level is sometimes used informally to mean Service Level Target.

Service Level Agreement (SLA)

(Service Design) (Continual Service Improvement) An Agreement between an IT Service Provider and a Customer. The SLA describes the IT Service, documents Service Level Targets, and specifies the responsibilities of the IT Service Provider and the Customer. A single SLA may cover multiple IT Services or multiple customers. See also Operational Level Agreement.

Service Level Management (SLM)

(Service Design) (Continual Service Improvement) The Process responsible for negotiating Service Level Agreements, and ensuring that these are met. SLM is responsible for ensuring that all IT Service Management Processes, Operational Level Agreements, and Underpinning Contracts, are appropriate for the agreed Service Level Targets. SLM monitors and reports on Service Levels, and holds regular Customer reviews.

Service Level Requirement (SLR)

(Service Design) (Continual Service Improvement) A Customer Requirement for an aspect of an IT Service. SLRs are based on Business Objectives and are used to negotiate agreed Service Level Targets.

Service Level Target

(Service Design) (Continual Service Improvement) A commitment that is documented in a Service Level Agreement. Service Level Targets are based on Service Level Requirements, and are needed to ensure that the IT Service design is Fit for Purpose. Service Level Targets should be SMART, and are usually based on KPIs.

Service Maintenance Objective

(Service Operation) The expected time that a Configuration Item will be unavailable due to planned maintenance Activity.

Service Management

Service Management is a set of specialized organizational capabilities for providing value to customers in the form of services.

Service Management Lifecycle

An approach to IT Service Management that emphasizes the importance of coordination and Control across the various Functions, Processes, and Systems necessary to manage the full Lifecycle of IT Services. The Service Management Lifecycle approach considers the Strategy, Design, Transition, Operation and Continuous Improvement of IT Services.

Service Manager

A manager who is responsible for managing the end-to-end Lifecycle of one or more IT Services. The term Service Manager is also used to mean any manager within the IT Service Provider. It is most commonly used to refer to a Business Relationship Manager, a Process Manager, an Account Manager or a senior manager with responsibility for IT Services overall.

Service Operation

(Service Operation) A stage in the Lifecycle of an IT Service. Service Operation includes a number of Processes and Functions and is the title of one of the Core ITIL publications. See also Operation.

Service Portfolio

(Service Strategy) The complete set of Services that are managed by a Service Provider. The Service Portfolio is used to manage the entire Lifecycle of all Services, and includes three Categories: Service Pipeline (proposed or in Development); Service Catalogue (Live or available for Deployment); and Retired Services. See also Service Portfolio Management.

Service Portfolio Management (SPM)

(Service Strategy) The Process responsible for managing the Service Portfolio. Service Portfolio Management considers Services in terms of the Business value that they provide.

Service Provider

(Service Strategy) An Organization supplying Services to one or more Internal Customers or External Customers. Service Provider is often used as an abbreviation for IT Service Provider.

Service Reporting

(Continual Service Improvement) The Process responsible for producing and delivering reports of achievement and trends against Service Levels. Service Reporting should agree the format, content and frequency of reports with Customers.

Service Request

(Service Operation) A request from a User for information, or advice, or for a Standard Change or for Access to an IT Service. For example to reset a password, or to provide standard IT Services for a new User. Service Requests are usually handled by a Service Desk, and do not require an RFC to be submitted. See also Request Fulfilment.

Service Strategy

(Service Strategy) The title of one of the Core ITIL publications. Service Strategy establishes an overall Strategy for IT Services and for IT Service Management.

Service Transition

(Service Transition) A stage in the Lifecycle of an IT Service. Service Transition includes a number of Processes and Functions and is the title of one of the Core ITIL publications. See also Transition.

Shift

(Service Operation) A group or team of people who carry out a specific Role for a fixed period of time. For example there could be four shifts of IT Operations Control personnel to support an IT Service that is used 24 hours a day.

Single Point of Contact

(Service Operation) Providing a single consistent way to communicate with an Organization or Business Unit. For example, a Single Point of Contact for an IT Service Provider is usually called a Service Desk.

Single Point of Failure (SPOF)

(Service Design) Any Configuration Item that can cause an Incident when it fails, and for which a Countermeasure has not been implemented. A SPOF may be a person, or a step in a Process or Activity, as well as a Component of the IT Infrastructure. See also Failure.

Specification

A formal definition of Requirements. A Specification may be used to define technical or Operational Requirements, and may be internal or external. Many public Standards consist of a Code of Practice and a Specification. The Specification defines the Standard against which an Organization can be Audited.

Stakeholder

All people who have an interest in an Organization, Project, IT Service, etc. Stakeholders may be interested in the Activities, targets, Resources, or Deliverables. Stakeholders may include Customers, Partners, employees, shareholders, owners, etc.

Standard

A mandatory Requirement. Examples include ISO/IEC 20000 (an international Standard), an internal security standard for Unix configuration, or a government standard for how financial Records should be maintained. The term Standard is also used to refer to a Code of Practice or Specification published by a Standards Organization such as ISO or BSI. See also Guideline.

Standard Change

(Service Transition) A pre-approved Change that is low Risk, relatively common and follows a Procedure or Work Instruction. For example, password reset or provision of standard equipment to a new employee. RFCs are not required to implement a Standard Change, and they are logged and tracked using a different mechanism, such as a Service Request. See also Change Model.

Standard Operating Procedures (SOP)

(Service Operation) Procedures used by IT Operations Management.

Standby

(Service Design) Used to refer to Resources that are not required to deliver the Live IT Services, but are available to support IT Service Continuity Plans. For example a Standby data centre may be maintained to support Hot Standby, Warm Standby or Cold Standby arrangements.

Statement of requirements (SOR)

(Service Design) A Document containing all Requirements for a product purchase, or a new or changed IT Service.

Status

The name of a required field in many types of Record. It shows the current stage in the Lifecycle of the associated Configuration Item, Incident, Problem, etc.

Storage Management

(Service Operation) The Process responsible for managing the storage and maintenance of data throughout its Lifecycle.

Strategic

(Service Strategy) The highest of three levels of Planning and delivery (Strategic, Tactical, Operational). Strategic Activities include Objective setting and long-term Planning to achieve the overall Vision.

Strategy

(Service Strategy) A Strategic Plan designed to achieve defined Objectives.

Super User

(Service Operation) A User who helps other Users, and assists in communication with the Service Desk or other parts of the IT Service Provider. Super Users typically provide support for minor Incidents and training.

Supplier

(Service Strategy) (Service Design) A Third Party responsible for supplying goods or Services that are required to deliver IT Services. Examples of suppliers include commodity hardware and software vendors, network and telecom providers, and outsourcing Organizations. *See also* Underpinning Contract, Supply Chain.

Supplier Management

(Service Design) The Process responsible for ensuring that all Contracts with Suppliers support the needs of the Business, and that all Suppliers meet their contractual commitments.

Supply Chain

(Service Strategy) The Activities in a Value Chain carried out by Suppliers. A Supply Chain typically involves multiple Suppliers, each adding value to the product or Service. *See also* Value Network.

Support Group

(Service Operation) A group of people with technical skills. Support Groups provide the Technical Support needed by all of the IT Service Management Processes. *See also* Technical Management.

System

A number of related things that work together to achieve an overall Objective. For example:

- A computer System, including hardware, software and Applications
- A management System, including multiple Processes that are planned and managed together. For example, a Quality Management System
- A Database Management System or Operating System that includes many software modules that are designed to perform a set of related Functions.

System Management

The part of IT Service Management that focuses on the management of IT Infrastructure rather than Process.

Tactical

The middle of three levels of Planning and delivery (Strategic, Tactical, Operational). Tactical Activities include the medium-term Plans required to achieve specific Objectives, typically over a period of weeks to months.

Technical Management

(Service Operation) The Function responsible for providing technical skills in support of IT Services and management of the IT Infrastructure. Technical Management defines the Roles of Support Groups, as well as the tools, Processes and Procedures required.

Technical Observation

(Continual Service Improvement) A technique used in Service Improvement, Problem investigation and Availability Management. Technical support staff meet to monitor the behaviour and Performance of an IT Service and make recommendations for improvement.

Technical Support

See Technical Management.

Test

(Service Transition) An Activity that verifies that a Configuration Item, IT Service, Process, etc. meets its Specification or agreed Requirements.

Test Environment

(Service Transition) A controlled Environment used to Test Configuration Items, Builds, IT Services, Processes, etc.

Third Party

A person, group, or Business that is not part of the Service Level Agreement for an IT Service, but is required to ensure successful delivery of that IT Service. For example, a software Supplier, a hardware maintenance company, or a facilities department. Requirements for Third Parties are typically specified in Underpinning Contracts or Operational Level Agreements.

Third-line Support

(Service Operation) The third level in a hierarchy of Support Groups involved in the resolution of Incidents and investigation of Problems. Each level contains more specialist skills, or has more time or other resources.

Threat

Anything that might exploit a Vulnerability. Any potential cause of an Incident can be considered to be a Threat. For example a fire is a Threat that could exploit the Vulnerability of flammable floor coverings. This term is commonly used in Information Security Management and IT Service Continuity Management, but also applies to other areas such as Problem and Availability Management.

Threshold

The value of a Metric that should cause an Alert to be generated, or management action to be taken. For example 'Priority 1 Incident not solved within four hours', 'more than five soft disk errors in an hour', or 'more than 10 failed changes in a month'.

Throughput

(Service Design) A measure of the number of Transactions, or other Operations, performed in a fixed time. For example, 5,000 e-mails sent per hour, or 200 disk I/Os per second.

Total Quality Management (TQM)

(Continual Service Improvement) A methodology for managing continual Improvement by using a Quality Management System. TQM establishes a Culture involving all people in the Organization in a Process of continual monitoring and improvement.

Transaction

A discrete Function performed by an IT Service. For example transferring money from one bank account to another. A single Transaction may involve numerous additions, deletions and modifications of data. Either all of these complete successfully or none of them is carried out.

Transition

(Service Transition) A change in state, corresponding to a movement of an IT Service or other Configuration Item from one Lifecycle status to the next.

Trend Analysis

(Continual Service Improvement) Analysis of data to identify time-related patterns. Trend Analysis is used in Problem Management to identify common Failures or fragile Configuration Items, and in Capacity Management as a Modelling tool to predict future behaviour. It is also used as a management tool for identifying deficiencies in IT Service Management Processes.

Tuning

The Activity responsible for Planning changes to make the most efficient use of Resources. Tuning is part of Performance Management, which also includes Performance monitoring and implementation of the required Changes.

Underpinning Contract (UC)

(Service Design) A Contract between an IT Service Provider and a Third Party. The Third Party provides goods or Services that support delivery of an IT Service to a Customer. The Underpinning Contract defines targets and responsibilities that are required to meet agreed Service Level Targets in an SLA.

Unit Cost

(Service Strategy) The Cost to the IT Service Provider of providing a single Component of an IT Service. For example the Cost of a single desktop PC, or of a single Transaction.

Urgency

(Service Transition) (Service Design) A measure of how long it will be until an Incident, Problem or Change has a significant Impact on the Business. For example a high Impact Incident may have low Urgency, if the Impact will not affect the Business until the end of the financial year. Impact and Urgency are used to assign Priority.

Usability

(Service Design) The ease with which an Application, product, or IT Service can be used. Usability Requirements are often included in a Statement of Requirements.

Use Case

(Service Design) A technique used to define required functionality and Objectives, and to design Tests. Use Cases define realistic scenarios that describe interactions between Users and an IT Service or other System. *See also* Change Case.

User

A person who uses the IT Service on a day-to-day basis. Users are distinct from Customers, as some Customers do not use the IT Service directly.

User Profile (UP)

(Service Strategy) A pattern of User demand for IT Services. Each User Profile includes one or more Patterns of Business Activity.

Utility

(Service Strategy) Functionality offered by a Product or Service to meet a particular need. Utility is often summarized as 'what it does'.

Validation

(Service Transition) An Activity that ensures a new or changed IT Service, Process, Plan, or other Deliverable meets the needs of the Business. Validation ensures that Business Requirements are met even though these may have changed since the original design. *See also* Verification, Acceptance, Qualification.

Value for Money

An informal measure of Cost Effectiveness. Value for Money is often based on a comparison with the Cost of alternatives. *See also* Cost Benefit Analysis.

Value Network

(Service Strategy) A complex set of relationships between two or more groups or Organizations. Value is generated through exchange of knowledge, information, goods or Services. *See also* Partnership.

Variance

The difference between a planned value and the actual measured value. Commonly used in Financial Management, Capacity Management and Service Level Management, but could apply in any area where Plans are in place.

Verification

(Service Transition) An Activity that ensures a new or changed IT Service, Process, Plan, or other Deliverable is complete, accurate, Reliable and matches its design specification. *See also* Validation, Acceptance.

Version

(Service Transition) A Version is used to identify a specific Baseline of a Configuration Item. Versions typically use a naming convention that enables the sequence or date of each Baseline to be identified. For example Payroll Application Version 3 contains updated functionality from Version 2.

Vision

A description of what the Organization intends to become in the future. A Vision is created by senior management and is used to help influence Culture and Strategic Planning.

Vital Business Function (VBF)

(Service Design) A Function of a Business Process that is critical to the success of the Business. Vital Business Functions are an important consideration of Business Continuity Management, IT Service Continuity Management and Availability Management.

Work in Progress (WIP)

A Status that means Activities have started but are not yet complete. It is commonly used as a Status for Incidents, Problems, Changes, etc.

Work Instruction

A Document containing detailed instructions that specify exactly what steps to follow to carry out an Activity. A Work Instruction contains much more detail than a Procedure and is only created if very detailed instructions are needed.

Workaround

(Service Operation) Reducing or eliminating the Impact of an Incident or Problem for which a full Resolution is not yet available. For example by restarting a failed Configuration Item. Workarounds for Problems are documented in Known Error Records. Workarounds for Incidents that do not have associated Problem Records are documented in the Incident Record.

Workload

The Resources required to deliver an identifiable part of an IT Service. Workloads may be Categorized by Users, groups of Users, or Functions within the IT Service. This is used to assist in analysing and managing the Capacity, Performance and Utilization of Configuration Items and IT Services. The term Workload is sometimes used as a synonym for Throughput.

Index

Index